D0181125

NEVER
GIVE UP!

Ron Heagy
with Donita Dyer

Bethel Baptist Church
P.O. BOX 167
AUMSVILLE, OR 97325

Scripture quotations are taken from the Holy Bible: New International Version®. NIV®. Copyright © 1973, 1978, 1984 by the International Bible Society. Used by permission of Zondervan Publishing House. The "NIV" and "New International Version" trademarks are registered in the United States Patent and Trademark Office by International Bible Society.

Cover by Ronald Tibbs

Many incidents in this book occurred 20 years ago and have been recreated from author's and other family members' shared memories. While dialogue and some minor details may differ from the actual events, the main facts of the story are true. Names have been changed in some cases to protect identities.

NEVER GIVE UP!
Copyright © 2002 Ron Heagy Jr. and Donita Dyer
Second Edition © 2005

ISBN 0-9754172-0-7

All rights reserved. No part of this publication may be reproduced, stored in a retrieval system, or transmitted in any form or by any means—electronic, mechanical, digital, photocopy, recording, or any other—except for brief quotations in printed reviews, without the prior permission of the publisher.

Printed in the United States of America.

This book is dedicated to the best friend I have ever had; the only person who has ever truly allowed me to be myself. She has shown me True Love…
Kelli Vonette Heagy

Contents

Thinking Twice

~

An easy look. A broad smile. A strong chin, cool blue eyes, and a shock of blond, wavy hair. I liked Ron Heagy as soon as I saw him wheel through my office door. I liked him even more when I heard him speak; his words were honest, spiced with humor, and voiced straight from the heart.

I watched him as he spoke, trying to guess his height, wondering whether he had ever walked in his scuffed cowboy boots. I glanced at the beautiful young woman who sat at his side. She leaned forward, resting her head on her fist while listening intently to every word.

"I'm so grateful for my family," Ron sighed, shaking his head. I blinked back tears, thinking of the sacrifices my parents made, the tears and prayers offered at my bedside when I was first injured. Yes, family and friends have made a big difference in Ron's life. So has God.

That's why I saw myself in Ron. We can't help but see ourselves in him. I'm not saying we want his wheelchair, but we want his attitude. Wheelchair or no, we yearn to live that nobly, speak that boldly, fight off discouragement that manfully. We long to mirror his heart and soul, recast by God's suffering-shaking power. He's a walking—I should say wheeling—visual example of 2 Corinthians 12:10: "I delight in weaknesses…in difficulties. For when I am weak, then [in Christ] I am strong."

Ron manhandles more serious dilemmas than most of us do, even than I do, a lower-level quadriplegic in a wheelchair. And if God can sustain him, then we *all* ought to be boasting in our weaknesses. When folks who face lesser conflicts—such as sow bugs in the shower—see someone gracefully handle greater conflicts, it speaks volumes.

And not just to believers in God, but also to those who don't believe. The watching world is forced to swallow its pride and drop its jaw in amazed disbelief at Ron's tenacious trust in God. Ron's life is a living proof that God works. Christianity asserts some pretty broad and sweeping claims; the stronger the claims, the stronger their substantiation must be. God eagerly invites unbelievers (and vacillating believers) to examine the foundations of Ron's faith. His witness is as bold as the claims upon which it rests, and this makes people think twice about the Lord.

Yes, the world needs more stories of inspiration. There can never be too many testimonies of how God's power shows up best in weakness. "When we are weak, He is strong," says the Bible. If I ever forget that, I can be reminded by looking at the way Ron nudges the chin control on his wheelchair and powers his way, unflinchingly, into the future.

JONI EARECKSON TADA

Acknowledgments

⁓

It takes more than desire, skillful writing, and a compelling story to produce a successful book. Of equal importance are the readers and the silent team members who work diligently behind the scenes, sometimes without praise or recognition.

I would like to thank my coauthor, Donita Dyer, who devoted many months to listening, interpreting, and turning my rambling thoughts into a concise, coherent manuscript. Little did I know when I was 18-years-old and lying in a hospital bed in Huntington Beach, California, that she was just a few miles away praying for me, a total stranger. I thank God for bringing her back into my life years later to help me write this book.

Thanks also to Joni Eareckson Tada for her kind words of encouragement. After my accident, Joni's movie, her books, her mouth paintings, and her testimony were a tremendous inspiration to me. May God bless you, Joni, for the wonderful work you and your organization are doing for disabled individuals worldwide.

Without the loving care and prayers of my family—Mom, Dad, Pennie, Mike, Grandma Heagy, and Grandma Buckmaster—I would not be here to tell my story. Thanks also to Aunt Donna for assisting and inspiring my artistic abilities.

There have been many other special people who have also generously given of themselves, their time, and their money in helping to make my dreams of a camp for disabled children a reality. My profound thanks to each and every one of them, particularly Cliff and Jeanie McCord, Don and Jane Miller, Steve and Catherine Raack, Joey and Rich LaBelle, Mark and Kathe Gouin, Susan Jones and family, and my faithful right hand man, caretaker, and friend, Daniel Webster Doe.

Cover photography and design by my friend, Ronald Tibbs (www.ronaldtibbs.com).

Foreword

~

Welcome to my story. My life has been filled with moments of soaring hope and moments of overwhelming despair, with times of great joy and times of great sorrow, and with periods full of love and periods of crushing heartbreak. I have been generous and I have been self-absorbed. This is a story of strength and weakness, and of courage and fear. It is a story of faith in God. It is the story of the fate dealt to me by "the great wheel of life."

At 17, I was a wrestler, skier, body builder and football star with a scholarship to Oregon State University waiting for me. During spring break, I dove into a large wave at a Southern California beach. As I hit an offshore sand bar hidden by the surf, I felt my head snap backwards. That was the last time I was able to move anything below my neck. I have been a quadriplegic since the day before my eighteenth birthday.

There is an Irish memoir called *Rotha Mór an tSaoil*—The Great Wheel of Life. It tells the story of Michael MacGowan (1865-1948), the oldest of twelve children from a poverty-stricken family, who was born into a three-roomed thatched cottage in Gaelic-speaking Donegal, Ireland. It describes his emigration to America, his trek across the continent from the steel mills of Pennsylvania to the mines of Montana, and his adventures in the Klondike gold rush of the 1890s. While McGowan describes the hardships he suffered as he was whirled around on the great wheel of life, he also describes the times when life was good and he was happy...the times when he was atop the great wheel of life. Yet, despite all the obstacles—known and unknown—he pursued new opportunities. Time and again he says, "had we known what was in front of us," he and his friends would not have undertaken his perilous winter journey to the Yukon in search of the prosperity that enabled him to return to his native Ireland.

Indeed, none of us knows what lies ahead. I remember a moment in time when I was atop the great wheel of life, a time when the present was perfect, the future promising. I was a senior at Central Linn High School, just three months away from graduating. A football scholarship was waiting for me at Oregon State University, and I was sure a career with an NFL team, hopefully the Dallas Cowboys, loomed in the future. I could even envision my photograph on the cover of *Sports Illustrated* some day. But for now, one of the prettiest girls in our school was beside me, her head resting against my shoulder.

The vibrant sounds of a Christian rock band pulsated through the crowded auditorium as 2,000 enthusiastic teenagers swayed back and forth with the beat. Karla, my date, smiled at me, her blue eyes sparkling as she sang along with the band. I slipped my arm around her shoulders, causing her long blonde hair to curl over the leather sleeve of my letterman's jacket. She snuggled against me contentedly, and at that moment I felt like the luckiest guy alive.

As the song ended, a wheelchair rolled down the aisle. A pale, gaunt teenage boy was seated in the chair, which was being pushed by an attractive girl. When they reached the front of the auditorium, the girl aligned his chair with the front row, then slipped into a nearby seat that had been saved for her. Just then the band started playing again, and the guy in the wheelchair turned to the girl and smiled. She smiled back, but as others cheered and grooved to the music, he sat quietly watching.

A mixture of pity and disdain kept drawing my eyes back to the guy in the wheelchair. *How sad*, I thought. *He's just an observer, not a participant. He can't play football, can't even hold his girlfriend's hand. Surely no one could be content strapped in a metal monster like that.* I pulled Karla closer, nodded toward the guy in the wheelchair, and whispered in her ear, "Man! I could never live like that. I'd rather be dead!"

Had I known my fate as I sprinted through the shallow surf on that spring day just a couple of weeks later, it would have been too much to bear. Not knowing our fate forces us to hope and to trust in God.

My life has been blessed with family, friends and partners without whom I would not have survived. They have devoted themselves selflessly to me. I have not always shown how much I have appreciated them for their constant care. I have often been preoccupied with my own goals and priorities. I have learned much as I have been whirled around on my great wheel of life. I have learned to be more sensitive to feelings and needs of others…especially those closest to me.

This book is called *Never Give Up!* because even in those times of despair, sorrow, heartbreak, weakness, and fear I have found the innerstrength that has inspired me to battle on. All of us have obstacles that stand in the way of our being able to make a difference in the world. But God has also given us the gifts we need to overcome those obstacles.

1

California Dreamin'

~

Spring break was just a few days away, and I still hadn't finalized plans for my long-anticipated vacation. One part of me—the mature, responsible side—said I should stay home in Brownsville, Oregon and help Dad work on the two-story log home we were building for our family.

His salary as a pipe fitter and millwright was modest. And, with three growing kids to feed, our parents usually stretched the budget to the limit. But they had somehow managed to purchase a beautiful piece of property on the Calapooia River as the site for our dream home. Since most of their savings had gone into buying the land, the house had proceeded slowly and in spurts, as funds became available to buy the necessary building materials.

Dad put in a full 40-hour week at the mill, sometimes more. Then, as soon as he came home and changed clothes, he headed for the log house, sometimes working until after sunset. The foundation, plumbing, and framework were finished, so the house's skeleton had begun to look like the home it would some day become. I helped whenever possible on weekends and after football practice.

Although duty called on my week off, so did pleasure. Two summers before at a Teen Mission camp in Florida, I had met Annette. After our training session had ended, she had been sent to Holland, and I had gone to Brazil, but we kept in touch by telephone. The following year, when she visited me in Oregon, my entire family had fallen in love with

1

her. Now Annette wanted me to spend spring break with her family in Southern California.

Although Mom and Dad were crazy about her, I wasn't sure how they would feel about my taking off for California when there was work to be done at home. I respected my parents and wanted their approval, especially Dad's. Excelling in sports had always been one way to achieve that approval. I had done well in wrestling, snow skiing, weightlifting, bodybuilding, pole vaulting, and motorcycle racing. Sports had actually become a passion with me, especially football. I wore jersey number 33 with pride and enjoyed being the team's starting fullback.

Cheers of the crowd, congratulatory hugs of teammates, and the compliments of teachers and other adults made my bumps and bruises seem worthwhile. But Dad's words meant the most to me. Whether our team won or lost, as we ran off the field and headed for the locker room, he invariably patted me on the back and said, "Good game, son."

Dad was proud of me. So was Mother, but she also had a growing concern about my attitude and inflated ego. She had a special knack for catching me flexing my muscles in front of the mirror while admiring my six-foot-two-inch, well-developed body.

My parents were aware that a star athlete in a small high school could easily get into trouble when it came to dating. During one of our work sessions, I had confided to Dad that the girl I was dating at the time let me know she placed no physical limitations on our relationship. My father, remembering his own youth, advised me on keeping my emotions under control, and so far I had managed to do that. But even after I broke up with the girl, those temptations remained.

So, my parents had been greatly relieved when a couple of nights earlier, at a Bible study, I had rededicated my life to the Lord. Mom and Dad hadn't always been Christians themselves, but now they were serving God and encouraging their children to do the same. We were a close family that shared our dreams, had devotions regularly, and worked together toward the same goals.

Since Annette was a Christian and we shared the same standards, I shouldn't have been surprised when Dad encouraged me to spend spring break in California. "You need a vacation, son," he said. "It would be hard for me to get off work, and you couldn't do much working alone. This summer, after you graduate, we'll finish the house."

I smiled and said, "Thanks, Dad," grateful to have such an understanding father.

Later when I went outside to work on my car and get it ready for the trip, Mike was waiting for me. "How about letting me go with you?" he pleaded.

"You've gotta be kidding!" I scoffed. "No way am I going to take my kid brother along to visit a girlfriend."

"But I'm not a kid anymore," he argued. "I'm almost 13. Please! If I promise not to get in your way?"

I rolled my eyes and shot him a look of lofty superiority. "Well… maybe. If you do my chores for the next week, I'll think about it."

That's all it took for Mike to become my willing slave. He waxed the VW, polished the chrome on my motorcycle, made both our beds, took out the trash, and became my "gofer."

On the afternoon before I planned to leave, he plopped down beside me on the couch. "Okay Ron, I've done everything you asked. Are you gonna take me with you?"

I patted his head condescendingly. "No way, little brother."

He was outraged. "Why not?" he retorted.

"You'd cramp my style."

Overhearing the conversation, Mom intervened on Mike's behalf. "That isn't fair, son," she told me.

"But Mom," I argued. "This is my last big fling before school is out for the summer. Be reasonable. Taking your kid brother along to visit your girlfriend is not cool."

Mother looked at me, her arrogant eldest son, and without batting an eyelash said, "Either Mike goes along or you're both staying home."

What more could I say?

2

Smashed in L.A.

~

ave fun, boys, but be careful," Mom cautioned as Mike and I pulled out of the driveway early in the morning, headed for Southern California.

Be careful? I silently mused as the car gained momentum. For me, taking chances was a challenge. Nothing thrilled me more than riding up the side of a mountain on my motorcycle with the throttle wide open. That's how I'd broken my leg! Pinning an opponent to the mat during a wrestling match and tackling burly football players during a game made my adrenaline flow. The bigger they were, the harder they fell.

With youthful abandonment I cruised down the freeway that morning thinking Ron Heagy Jr. was indestructible. I had everything going for me—a girlfriend back home, a job, and a modest bank account. Who could ask for more?

I glanced over at Mike, who was already asleep and softly snoring, his head resting on his chest. "Hey, you're supposed to be keeping me company," I said, poking him.

He blinked his eyes and sat up straight. "Sorry. I was too excited to sleep last night. Are you hungry?"

"No, not yet. Mike, we've hardly started."

"How long 'til we get there?"

"Don't start buggin' me with stupid questions, or I'll leave you at the next service station," I kiddingly threatened.

Mike didn't respond. He grabbed an apple out of the lunch Mom had packed for us and gobbled it up. Then he tackled a sandwich, wolfing it down as well. Before long my little brother was snoozing again.

As we neared L.A. several hours later, traffic gradually got heavier. Our hometown had two-lane streets and no traffic signals. Maneuvering the Love Bug through a growing, eight-lane river of cars, trucks, and buses in evening rush-hour traffic was a new experience for me. While glancing in the rearview mirror to check on a truck behind us, I failed to see the cars ahead of us suddenly stop.

"Watch out!" Mike yelled, bracing himself.

I shoved the brake pedal clear to the floorboard, and the tires skidded as we hurtled toward a new, silver Mercedes. Whack! The impact sent us flying into the windshield, since neither of us was wearing our seat belt.

"Mike! Mike! Are you all right?" I yelled, shaking his shoulder.

"Yeah, I'm fine," he answered in a shaky voice.

The driver of the Mercedes—a man about nine feet tall—got out rubbing his neck. Oh, man! What now? I wondered. If that guy has a whiplash and the accident was my fault, he'll sue for sure. My insurance will go up, and Dad will be furious.

"I'm so sorry, sir," I started to explain as the well-dressed gentleman walked around his car to survey the damage.

"Looks like you got the worst of it," he said, glancing at the Bug. The windshield had cracked when our heads struck it, and both fenders now rested on the wheels. The hood latch was busted, and the front hood yawned open as if the car was panting in pain. "I can't see any damage to my car, except a little scratch in the chrome above the license plate. You're from out of state?" he asked after checking our license plate.

I nodded. "Yes, sir. We live in Oregon, and this is the first time I've driven in such heavy traffic."

Glancing at the huge traffic jam that was already forming, he said, "Son, if you and the other kid are all right, let's just pretend this didn't happen, okay? I don't seem to have any damage, and I think it's pretty clear that you're at fault. So, let's just be on our way. How does that sound to you?"

"Fine! Thanks, sir. Thanks a million!" I heaved a sigh of relief as he got back into his Mercedes and drove away. Meanwhile, the truck driver behind us impatiently honked his horn and yelled for us to get going.

Mike and I pushed the mortally wounded VW, my former pride and joy, onto the shoulder.

"What are we gonna do now, Ron?" Mike asked, looking first at me and then at the Love Bug's crunched fenders.

"Let's try to pull them back into shape," I answered, grabbing a tire iron to use as a crowbar and starting to work. "C'mon, Mike, pull. Harder." Finally we pried the accordion-pleated fenders away from the tires and wobbled back into traffic. The steering wheel shimmied, and the hood, tied down with the cord from my swimming trunks, constantly bobbed up and down.

I glanced at my brother and noticed a red welt on his forehead. "Sure you're okay, Mike?"

"Yeah. How about you?"

"I've got a few bumps and bruises, but nothing serious. Wish I could say the same for my car," I lamented. "What's Annette going to think when we come in lookin' like a couple of bedraggled down-and-outers? Man! What a bummer!"

Mike wasn't nearly as concerned about making a good impression on my girlfriend as I was. "Look at the bright side, Ron," he answered with a grin. "The worst is over. We're gonna have a great time surfing and goin' to Disneyland."

3

Last Day in Paradise

~

It wasn't the entrance I had planned, but a couple of hours later—tired, stiff, and less self-confident—I rang Annette's doorbell.

"Ron!" she exclaimed and gave me a big hug. "It's good to see you." Then she spotted Mike. "Wow! What happened to your forehead?"

"Check it out for yourself," he answered, pointing to the Love Bug and giving her a quick explanation.

"Are you guys all right? That's what's important." She hooked her arms through ours. "Come in. You must be beat. Mom has a good dinner ready, and after we've eaten, you guys can both crash."

"Don't say 'crash,'" Mike protested, rubbing his forehead.

"Sorry," Annette laughingly apologized. "You can catch up on sleep tonight. Tomorrow my brother Justin and I will take you to the Magic Kingdom."

"Great!" Mike responded. "I can hardly wait."

I nodded indulgently like a protective parent. "Okay, Disneyland tomorrow morning, but will we have time to go to the beach too? I'm dying to try my hand at surfing."

"Sure. We'll come home, grab a bite to eat, change into our swimsuits, and head for the beach. Justin's a great surfer; he'll show you how it's done," she said.

The following morning we were up bright and early, ready to begin our great adventure. Disneyland proved to be all we expected and more. We went on the rides, laughed, joked, and teased each other while weaving our way through Main Street USA. We posed for pictures with Goofy, devoured expensive hamburgers, guzzled frosties, and tried on Mickey Mouse ears that were on display in gift shops. It was an awesome day—four teenagers on our own in the Magic Kingdom.

But by midafternoon, I'd had enough of Donald and Pluto. "Hey guys, I'm hot, tired, and eager to learn how to surf," I told them.

Sixteen-year-old Justin agreed. "Great! There's still time to give you a surfing lesson." He flashed me a knowing grin. "But don't expect to ride the waves on your first try."

We headed back to their house, changed into our swimsuits, grabbed Justin's surfboard from the garage, piled back into the car, and headed west.

"Here's what you do," Justin began as we wove our way through the traffic. "It's easiest to spot a good set of waves from the beach, so you wait there until you see a good surge coming up. Then you grab your board, sprint into the water, fling yourself on the board, and paddle like crazy with your arms. That's the hardest part. You've got to get beyond the breakers. Then, when a swell rolls in, go at it at an angle and try to get up and over it."

"Doesn't sound like much of a challenge to me," I told him. "Paddle the board out, ride it back in. If you can do it, so can I." *Surfing takes more muscle than brain,* I thought to myself. *Fortunately, I've got both brain and brawn, so it won't be any problem for me to stand up on my first try. Wait until they see what a pro-athlete can do.*

I was still in a cocky, self-confident frame of mind as I parked my Bug on the bluff overlooking the strand. "Make way everybody; here we come," I yelled as the four of us sprinted down the steps, two at a time. Bright sunlight shining on the swells made them look as smooth as glass—until they crested and came crashing toward shore in a frenzy of white foam, bringing with them surfers who leaned forward and gracefully rode to shore.

The breeze was brisk, the sand warm beneath our feet as we spread our beach blankets and shed our sweatshirts. Michael lazily stretched out in the sand and looked up at me with admiration and gratitude.

"Thanks for letting me come along. You said I'd cramp your style, but I haven't, huh?"

"Well…not so far, but see that you behave yourself. Okay?" I turned and flipped Justin on the thigh with my beach towel. "Okay, buddy, show us how it's done."

He flashed a cocky grin, looking toward the horizon. Suddenly, he picked up his board and ran into the water, quickly flopping down on it and paddling through the surf. Justin swam out so far we could hardly see him. Then, as the wave rolled in and the surfers were lifted up, we spotted his bright swim trunks. He expertly hopped to his feet, then slowly rose up until he was standing on the board as it streaked under the curl and carried him onto the beach.

"Ooooooo-EEEEE!" I yelled, cupping my hands around my mouth and cheering him on. "Awesome! Man, I gotta try this."

"Think you can do it?" Justin called from the water.

"Sure. No problem."

"Okay, come get the board."

I trotted through the frothy water with cool confidence. There were lots of sunbathing mermaids on the beach that afternoon, all of whom I assumed were watching me. I stuck out my chest and hoped to wow them, not only with my powerful build but with my athletic prowess. *After all, if I can dart down the football field like a fox dodging a pack of hounds, I can easily master the surfboard. I betcha there aren't any other guys on the beach today who can bench press 300 pounds or who have won as many wrestling matches as yours truly. No sweat! I'll make everyone sit up and take notice, including Annette.*

Following Justin's instructions, I laid on the board and paddled out through the surf, stopping momentarily when a breaker washed over me, filling my eyes and nose with salt water. I coughed and snorted, then started out again, noting to take the next breaker at an angle. After what seemed like half an hour, I turned back to look at the beach and was surprised to see I hadn't come far at all. I worked so hard at my paddling that I was exhausted and out of breath when I finally joined a couple of other guys who were resting on their floating boards beyond the breakers, waiting for a ride back to the beach.

"Heads up, dudes!" one of them called suddenly when a swell started toward us.

I glanced warily over one shoulder and grabbed my board with a hand on each side. *Here we go!* I told myself excitedly as the board and I began to scoot through the churning water at what seemed at least a hundred miles per hour. I pushed up with my arms and pulled my body into a crouching position, my heart pounding as hard and loud as the breakers. Standing on that slender board in the midst of turbulent, churning water, however, was quite another matter.

Okay, don't panic. You can do it, I kept telling myself. But instead of rising to my feet, I rode the board humped up with my chest against my knees, bouncing along like a turtle riding a rocket. My hands were glued to that board. No way could I turn loose! *It looked so simple when Justin did it. Why didn't I pay more attention to his instructions?*

Just then the board jerked sharply back into the wall of the wave, and the curl crashed over me. I was instantly knocked off the board and sent tumbling head-over-heels and sputtering, all the way to shore. I hauled myself up on the beach and lay there, heaving and gasping for air. *So much for making a good impression,* I thought morosely as Mike hurried to my side. By then, I was coughing and wheezing in an effort to clear the salt water from my lungs and nose.

"Wow, Ron! Was that ever a wipeout!" he shouted, laughing and alerting every good-looking girl within a hundred yards to my bedraggled presence amid the seaweed and other flotsam that had washed ashore with me.

"Shut up, Mike," I snapped while rising unsteadily to my feet. He handed me a towel to wipe my face. "I'll do it this time. Watch and see."

By now I was tired and my neck, still sore from the auto accident, throbbed from the cold water. But determined to become a surfer, I wasn't willing to give up without a fight. Jumping aboard, I paddled once more toward Indonesia. Finally in position, I waited, then again felt the swell lift my board and me high into the air. *Steady! Take it easy!* I told myself. *Don't make any false moves.*

I was back in the turtle position, a blob of hunched-up nerves and muscles clinging to a piece of fiberglass that skimmed the front of the wave like a hot knife cutting butter. Suddenly the board wheeled, and out of the corner of my eye, I could see a wall of water rising beside me. The image so disconcerted me that I turned my head to look at it.

Immediately the board plunged into the churning foam, knocking me over backward and sending me tumbling violently out of control.

"Ron, are you okay?" Mike called when I once again arrived unceremoniously at the water's edge, a beached whale barely able to pull myself onto the sand.

"Yeah," I said, "I'm fine. Man, this is harder than it looks!"

"You'll get it," Justin said encouragingly. "Just keep trying. You're doing great."

"Yeah, I'm getting better at landing on the beach," I answered sarcastically.

Refusing to quit, I went back for more punishment, but as hard as I tried, I never made it to my feet on the board. Finally, exhausted, I settled down on the beach towels with Annette, Justin, and Mike to watch the sun set on the Pacific. The waves had died down a little, but there were still a few diehards out on the water, nimbly standing upright on their boards, sailing across the face of a wave.

My eyes were red and my throat still burned from all the salt water that I had swallowed, but my girlfriend didn't seem to notice. Michael, however, was not so magnanimous. "So much for macho man," he quipped with a snide laugh.

"Shut up, Mike. That's enough out of you."

"Oops. Sorry. I promise not to tell everybody back home that you wiped out."

"Mark my words, Mike," I told my brother, my resolve and confidence returning, "I'm gonna learn to surf. I'm gonna ride that board or die trying."

4

Wipeout

~

hat a great day this is going to be! I thought as the sunshine slipped a bright finger through the blinds of the guest bedroom and pried open my eyelids. I glanced over at Mike.

"It's about time you woke up," he teased. "We're going to the beach today, or have you forgotten?"

"How could I forget? I'm gonna stand on that surfboard today."

"Yeah, you'll probably ogle the good-looking girls too."

"You know me too well, little brother. Besides, you're rapidly becoming a girl-watcher yourself."

He grinned, picked up his pillow, and swatted me with it before hopping out of bed.

"Hey you guys, have fun today," Annette called from the hall before leaving for her part-time job. "See you this evening."

"Thanks. We will, and don't you flirt with all the good-looking guys."

The weather was bright and beautiful when Justin, Mike, and I arrived at Huntington Beach—warm and balmy with just a hint of a breeze. We stood on the bluff for a few minutes, enjoying the panoramic view. From this vantage point, the blue sea and the blue sky seemed to stretch into infinity. Only the silhouette of Catalina Island interrupted the horizon.

15

"Come on, slowpokes!" I shouted over my shoulder while descending the steps to the beach two at a time. "We haven't got all day." I already had my feet in the surf by the time Justin and Mike arrived at the water's edge. The waves sloshing against me were freezing cold.

We stood there, staring at the water, which lay as smooth as glass before us except for a few small waves that rolled quietly over the sand. No wonder we were the only ones there with a surfboard. There was no surf!

"Tide's too high, and those waves aren't big enough," Justin announced with an air of authority. He spread a blanket on the sand and started dabbing lotion on his nose. "Might as well cool our jets for a while."

"Okay, but would you mind taking a picture of Mike and me first?" I handed him my camera in exchange for his surfboard, flexed my biceps, and struck what I hoped was an impressive pose.

After the shutter snapped, Justin quipped, "Cool—now you'll have a picture to show your parents."

"What do you mean?" Mike challenged. "Ron wants to parade that picture in front of his girlfriends in Brownsville."

"Shut up, Michael," I snapped, irritated that he would say such a thing in front of Annette's brother. I gave him a glaring look that said, "One more remark like that and I'll leave you stranded on the beach."

Mike just grinned.

We all stretched out on the sand, but soon the sun felt too hot on my chest. Rolling over on my stomach, I propped myself on an elbow and glanced at the vast expanse of blue. The beach scene was awesome. Cumulus clouds were lazily drifting by, and seagulls circled overhead, calling to each other as they soared past us with their sleek wings outspread. Long-legged snipes scurried back and forth, playing tag with incoming waves, and a couple of small children were gathering shells in brightly colored pails as their mother looked on. Watching the scene, I idly picked up a handful of sand and let it sift slowly through my fingers. *What a perfect way to spend spring break,* I thought.

Eventually, though, my restlessness returned. I poked my brother. "Come on, let's take a dip."

"Nah, the water's too cold. Besides, I wanna get a good tan so the kids back home will know we've been to California," Mike answered, rolling over on his stomach and stretching his arms above his head.

His body seemed thin compared with my solid 195 pounds. I tried to remember myself as a 120-pound 13-year-old like Mike with scrawny arms and undeveloped muscles and chuckled at the comparison.

"Cool your jets," Justin agreed, not even bothering to look up.

Determined not to waste any more time, I walked toward the shoreline and dipped my toes in the ocean. *Brrr! It's icy cold,* I thought. While hesitating, considering whether to take the plunge or return to the comfort of the warm sun on my beach towel, I watched a swell move toward shore, gaining momentum as it approached. I waited until the wave crested. Then, with a running start, I sprinted through the shallow surf and dived head first into the breaker that would change my life forever.

Tons of churning water rushed over me, as my dive propelled me forward toward an offshore sand bar lurking beneath the swell.

The next moment my head hit the wall of sand. I felt a crunching sensation and heard a loud crack as my head snapped backward, striking my back sharply between the shoulder blades. My body was instantly rendered numb—except for an excruciating pain that knifed upward from my neck. At the same time, a loud high-pitched ringing filled my head.

The wave swirled on, carrying me with it, tumbling and thrashing; the down surge pushed me to the sand, viciously scraping my face against the shell-strewn bottom. I needed air! Desperately wanting to force my way to the surface, I tried to kick—but my legs weren't moving. I longed to push myself off the sand with my hands and get my head above the surface, but my arms too seemed to flail lifelessly in the surging water. I felt myself being carried by the undertow away from the beach.

It all happened so quickly. One minute I was in complete control of my body, a carefree 17-year-old casually challenging the current. A split second later I was a helpless, broken child being swept out to sea.

What's happening to me? My mind frantically tried to make sense of the chaos that tossed me about in its stubborn grip. I needed air and could see sunlight on the water's surface, but I couldn't reach it. *I'm drowning!* I realized. *Please God, please God, please God! Don't let me die. Not like this. Please God! Please God! Help me!*

God *did* help me.

He reached down with two scrawny, 13-year-old arms and lifted me toward the light.

5

The Rescue

~

A fter I had trotted off toward the water, Mike had rolled over and closed his eyes. Then he raised his head again to watch me take the plunge. He saw my arms go up, my elbows next to my ears, and saw my head go under the wave, my wet back glistening in the sun. He started to lie back down, but something made him keep watching.

As he saw my body flip in a quick somersault, an uneasiness came over him. He watched the surf, waiting for my head to reappear.

Something's wrong, he realized.

No one was in the water. No swimmers, no surfers. *Wait. What was that?* Without a word to Justin, Mike was running toward the water before he even knew why.

"Ron-n-n-n!"

He had seen only a flash of color as one small wave rose, then broke—just a dot of dark blue that was quickly swallowed up by the churning water. But he ran toward it as though propelled from a mortar, locking his eyes on the spot where he'd seen my swim trunks appear briefly above the surface.

The undertow was rolling me like a barrel, bouncing my helpless body off the bottom, a flailing tangle of arms and legs being swept out to sea.

"Ron! Ron! Where are you?" Mike screamed, running through the shallows, then suddenly dropping into water over his head as the bottom fell away. He frantically treaded water, fighting the tide to stay in the spot

19

where he'd seen me pop up a moment before. Sucking in a deep breath of air, he plunged under the surface, anxiously trying to see through the froth and bubbles.

Nothing.

He popped up, struggling to see but blocked by the swell of the waves. He sucked in a quick breath and dived below the surface again.

Nothing.

He swam, not knowing which way to go but instinctively heading out, into deeper water.

"Ron-neeeeeeee!" he called again and again.

He dived once more and caught a glimpse of me, eerily tumbling in slow motion as the current pulled me away from him. With the determination of an Olympic contender, Mike plunged down again, pressing his feet to the sandy bottom as he aligned himself under me and pushed me upward.

Meanwhile, I was fighting my own battle, hoping, praying, and holding my breath while bouncing about like a bottle. Finally, my lungs feeling as though they would burst, I resigned myself to the inevitable and frantically gulped, fully expecting to suck in a mouthful of salt water. Instead, my lungs filled with fresh ocean air.

A pair of scrawny arms were tightly wrapped around me, although I couldn't feel them at the time. My little brother was struggling with all of his strength to hold my head above water, and because of my overpowering size and weight, he was having a difficult time keeping us both afloat. By now we were in deep water and in deep trouble as well. My sibling, the kid I hadn't wanted to bring with me to California, was risking his life to save me. I gulped in a great gasp of the salty air, opened my eyes, and glimpsed the sun…before my head once again slid below the surface.

I sank, my eyes desperately searching through the ascending bubbles to make sense of what was happening. A body streaked down through the water beside me, and then once again I rocketed upward, my head breaking the surface and my lungs once again drawing in the blessed air.

"Mike!" I yelled, astonished to see his head suddenly pop up beside mine. But as I sank again, a new fear took over. *He's gonna drown too! I've got to save him!*

"Mike!" I cried out a moment later when my head once again popped to the surface. "Go back, Mike!"

A swell rose up behind us and rushed over our heads, choking me and drowning out my words as I again sank below the surface.

"No, Ron!" he stubbornly shot back, his voice as waterlogged as my own and his legs frantically thrashing the water. "I can't let you drown!"

By the time he had reached me I was in 12, maybe 15, feet of water. His only chance to rescue me was to repeatedly dive to the bottom, press his feet against the sand, and push me upward and in, toward the beach.

When his head popped to the surface beside me, he tried to hold me up while treading water and catching his breath, but I was too heavy, even in the salt water. Again and again we sank back down; again and again Mike planted his feet on the bottom and *pushed*, sending me upward.

Somehow, Mike finally towed me into the shallows. I looked at my arms and legs. They seemed detached from my body, each one floating in a different direction. By now we were both exhausted, and I was having difficulty breathing.

"Prop me up. Hurry! Can't...can't breathe," I gasped. Mike held me in a sitting position against his chest, but that didn't seem to help. My head flopped from side to side, and I must have momentarily blacked out, because the last thing I remember saying was, "Mike, lay me down again. I'm... I'm..."

Justin, lying on the beach, was unaware of the life-and-death struggle unfolding just a few yards from shore. He finally looked up and saw Mike in the chest-deep water, struggling to grip me around my waist so my head was kept above the waves. His shoulders heaving with panic and exhaustion, Mike screamed over the surf, "Justin! Justin! HELP!"

Justin galloped over the shallow water. "What happened?" he shouted.

"I don't know. I don't know. But help me! Help me!" Mike was frantically babbling, totally wiped out and functioning on nothing but adrenaline.

Justin grasped one of my arms as Mike grabbed the other. They started dragging me back to the beach, but my head snapped back, the water sweeping over it as they tried to move me. Awkwardly, they grabbed my hair to keep my head up while trying to run with me across the 20 yards of water. My head bounced and bumped as they struggled to lift the dead weight of almost 200 pounds and get me to dry land. I could feel the bones grinding in my neck.

As they finally neared the shore, Mike was spent. "Go get help, Justin. Hurry!"

A lone woman was sunbathing several yards away. "Help!" Justin cried, waving his arms. "Call an ambulance! We need help! Hurry!"

The woman dropped a magazine she had been reading, jumped to her feet, and disappeared across the sand.

Mike and Justin crumpled beside me in the waves, too exhausted to drag me the last few feet to shore. As Justin knelt over me, wiping water out of my eyes, Mike stood between me and the outgoing current, shaking and sobbing while trying to prevent the tide from sweeping me back out to sea.

Repeatedly washed by waves that rocked me toward the beach then back into Mike's legs, I was having great difficulty breathing. My lungs, partially paralyzed, desperately fought for air.

"Mike...," I wanted to say thanks. I needed to tell him how much he meant to me. But instead I gasped out, "Prop me...up...Mike... quick...can't...catch...my breath."

He dropped down behind me and struggled to lift me, grunting and groaning as he pulled my limp body into a sitting position, my back pressed against his chest. I felt the crunching sensation again as my head dropped forward, my chin resting on my chest. Another jolt of lightning-sharp pain blinded me, and a renewed sense of panic chilled my heart as my air supply was cut off by the weight of my head crimping my neck.

"Down...put me...down!...I'm...choking!"

Mike quickly backed away slightly, letting my head bump down his chest and come to rest in his lap. I tried to cough to clear my throat of the salt water, but nothing happened; my lungs, bubbling with ingested water and wracked with spasms, were no longer under my control.

I looked at Mike's terrified face, bending over mine. His eyes were wide, and he was still breathing in big, heaving gulps. I heard water swishing around my head and felt sand washing into my ears.

"I'm...gonna...die...Mike," I gasped while struggling to pull oxygen into my paralyzed lungs. "Gonna...die."

"No, Ron! You can't," Mike protested between sobs.

"I…love…you…little brother…Tell…Mom…Dad…Pennie…I…love them…too." The words were jerky, but he understood my message.

"No, Ron. You are NOT going to die!" Mike held my face between his two trembling hands, my back resting on his knees. Then he turned his face upward, swallowed a sob, and closed his eyes. "Oh, God," he shouted, in a desperate plea. "Don't let my brother die! *Please* don't let Ronnie die!"

The beach was deserted. Finally, the woman Justin had sent for help reappeared and hollered, "I called 911! They're on the way!" Then she ran back to the parking area to wait for them and lead them to us.

We huddled, three desperate and terrified kids, locked in a tragic scene in the middle of a beautiful setting. "Paradise" I'd called it when we had first arrived.

The minutes ticked by. I felt as if I'd been there forever, the cold surf gently lapping my body. As I drifted in and out of consciousness, I knew I was dying.

"They're here!" Justin shouted. He waved his arms and screamed to the paramedics, "Here! Here we are!"

Three uniformed men awkwardly struggled through the loose sand, carrying heavy cases and a backboard.

"Help!" Mike screamed, on the edge of full hysteria. "Help us! We need help!"

After another long minute, a stranger's face appeared above mine. "How you doin'?" the paramedic asked.

"I hurt."

"Where?"

"Neck…head…can't breathe…no feeling…legs."

He pressed an oxygen mask to my face, forcing clean, cool air into my lungs. "That better?" he asked, but all I could do was blink my eyes in response. Then they fastened a stabilizer splint around my head and neck to hold it in place. "Hang in there, fella," he continued. "We're going to lift you onto a stretcher and take you to the hospital." He smiled. "The doc will check everything out, so don't worry. You'll get good care at HBIH. They have some of the best specialists in Orange County."

Another spike of pain pierced my neck as they pushed the gurney into the waiting ambulance.

I drew in ragged, shallow breaths, closing my eyes and drifting in and out of darkness.

The doors slammed shut and the siren wailed, but the sounds seemed far away to me. The paramedic's voice was flat and unemotional. "HBIH, we are inbound from the beach, six minutes out with a 17-year-old male..." As he rattled off medical jargon and numbers, he put a reassuring hand on my forehead.

Then there was another sound. Someone was crying. Low, hiccuping sobs were coming from somewhere in the back of the ambulance.

They were coming from me.

"Don't worry, buddy; it'll be all right." The paramedic leaned closer to my face, his mouth bent up in a confident smile. "The docs'll take good care of you."

I was ashamed of my tears. In the past, no matter what happened, I shrugged off the pain. Now the tears rolled down my face, and I couldn't even raise my hand to brush them away.

Abject misery enveloped me, and I sobbed uncontrollably under the oxygen mask. My body trembled spastically. I was slipping into shock. But before I plunged completely into the darkness, a question slowly formed in my mind.

"Mike...," I moaned. "Where's...Mike?"

6

Angel of Mercy

~

F or Mike, the events of that morning occurred alternately in fast-forward and ultra-slow motion. Pulling me to shore, holding my head out of the water, and waiting for the ambulance, he felt time pass with excruciating slowness.

But once the paramedics arrived, everything happened very quickly. In only a moment they had me strapped to the backboard with an oxygen mask tightened over my nose and mouth. Then they were hustling me back over the sand to the waiting ambulance.

Mike, blue with cold and shivering with anxiety, hurried to keep up as the medics carried me across the beach. When they reached the ambulance, the men quickly opened the doors and slid my gurney onto a rack. One of the men immediately headed for the driver's seat, and another stepped up beside me in the back. The third man turned to Mike and Justin.

"Boys, we can only take one of you," he said, talking fast. "How old are you?" he asked, looking at Mike.

"Thirteen."

"And you?"

"Sixteen," Justin replied.

"Hop in," the driver said, motioning to Justin as he spoke. "We need to get going."

In another split second the passenger door slammed shut, and the ambulance pulled out with its siren screaming. Mike, frightened and bewildered, was left standing alone on the bluff, thousands of miles from home with no money and no way to call for help.

Even now, years later, Mike has trouble describing what happened next. In fact, he doesn't even like to talk or think about it, because the memories are still too painful.

Devastated by the thought that he had lost his brother and feeling hopelessly abandoned, it took a while before he was able to move. Then all he knew to do was go back to the beach blanket we had been lying on so peacefully less than an hour earlier. Reluctantly he retraced his steps, scuffing his feet in the sand. Ron's VW key is probably in the pocket of his blue jeans, he thought. But what good will that do me? I can't drive without a license, and no way could I find Annette's house.

He glanced around the beach. It was nearly deserted. Only the sea gulls and sand snipes had remained to keep him company. Impulsively, Mike threw himself onto the blanket, buried his face in his arms, and started to sob.

"I didn't cry loud enough for anyone to hear me," he recalls. "But that cry was coming from a broken heart. I felt so lost, so alone, and I didn't know what to do. More than anything else, I wanted to be with Ronnie, but I didn't even know where they had taken him! I had no idea what to do, so I just lay there and cried. I wanted to talk to Mom and Dad. They would understand how sad and lonely I felt. They'd tell me what to do next."

Time passed slowly, but eventually Mike heard a woman's voice that caused him to look up. An older woman was standing there, wearing a big straw hat and a brightly colored sundress.

"It's okay, Mike," she said with a smile. "Everything is going to be all right. Ronnie's hurt, but he's not going to die."

It never occurred to Mike to ask how she knew his name.

"You must be worn out. Why don't you come to my house?" she asked, pointing to a beach house on the bluff. "You can have some cookies and lemonade. You'll feel better then."

Like most parents, ours had warned us kids never to talk to strangers, not to go home with anyone we didn't know, and above all not to get into cars with strangers. But Mike says, "It never occurred to me that she was a stranger. She knew our names."

Mike doesn't remember what the woman's house looked like, but he does remember climbing the steep stairs up to her deck from the beach, and he remembers sitting with her at her dining table and being served cookies and lemonade as she continued talking to him in the same comforting tone.

"Ronnie has broken his neck," she told him matter-of-factly. "He'll be paralyzed, but he's not going to die. He's going to live, and you'll see, Mike. God will be glorified in Ronnie's life."

Mike has no idea how long he sat at the woman's table. He only knows that sometime later he went back down the steps and returned to the beach blanket, feeling hopeful. A sense of peace had overcome his anxiety.

The accident had occurred sometime before noon, and Mike was there alone on the beach until late in the day, perhaps four o'clock. Then he heard someone call his name again. This time it was Annette and Justin's mother, who had come to bring him home.

We never learned who befriended Mike that day. Some people insist it must have been a dream. But Mike doesn't concern himself with their theories or the woman's identity.

He simply calls her "the angel."

7

The Nightmare

~

T he dream seemed so real. A nurse stood beside my bed, unwrapping a needle. Without speaking to me or looking toward my face, she worked quickly and seriously, connecting the needle to a coil of tubing and pulling it straight to untangle a kink. When she lowered her hands to work on a tray table, I could no longer see what she was doing.

My heart pounded. I wanted to turn my head and watch, but my head seemed to be encased in a block. Only my eyes and lips could move, and my mouth didn't seem coordinated with my brain. When I tried to speak, the words came out slurred and low, like a tape recording played at slow speed.

What was she doing?

In the past, I had prided myself about being fearless in competition, a tough guy who never showed pain. Whenever I got smashed by a vicious tackle on the football field or got slammed to the mat during a wrestling match, I jumped up with a grin and insisted it didn't hurt. But shots—that was different! Just seeing a hypodermic needle made me freak out; my heart would pound and a cold sweat would pop out all over my body.

What a baby! I often chided myself. *You get flattened by a 200-pound gorilla on the football field and shrug it off, and now you're acting like a sissy just because of a little old shot!*

As my dream continued, I heard a package being opened, then I smelled alcohol. Through my lowered eyes, I strained to see. The top of the nurse's arm jiggled as though she were swabbing something. I smelled alcohol. But I couldn't see her hands, and I couldn't feel anything, so she obviously wasn't swabbing my arm. What was she doing?

Then she held the needle up again and popped a plastic cover off it. My heart started pounding in the old, familiar way, and a trickle of sweat rolled into my eye as she bent down, again lowering the needle out of my sight. Here it comes, I thought, biting down on my lip and bracing for the sting of the needle piercing my arm.

Nothing.

The nurse held up a roll of adhesive tape and ripped off two pieces, then once again worked below my line of sight. Finally I heard paper being wadded up. At last, she glanced up at me.

"There you go. All done," she said, her lips turning upward into a quick, tight grin before she left my bedside.

"Wait!" I said. But she didn't hear me—or couldn't understand me.

This is a dream, right? A conversation began in my mind. Of course it's a dream. If it were really happening, I would have felt the alcohol being swabbed on my arm. I would have flinched when the needle went in. I would have been able to bend my neck and see what she was doing. So it was a dream. Just a dream. That's right, pal. All you have to do is wake up, and it'll be spring break again. You'll be in California visiting Annette. You and Mike will be at the beach....

Suddenly I remembered.

The beach. The sun, hot on my back. Diving headfirst into the surf. The sensation of bone grinding against bone in my neck. Churning helplessly against the sand. Struggling for air. Dying for a breath. Mike's head suddenly bobbing beside mine in the rolling swells....

A sound came from somewhere deep within me. Half cry, half groan, it filled the room and reverberated in my ears. Instantly, a woman's face appeared above mine. Another nurse appeared above me. She wore green surgical scrubs and a stethoscope looped around her neck.

"Ron," she said gently, touching my forehead and smiling into my eyes. "How are you feeling?"

"Aaahhhhggggg."

"Does your head hurt?" she asked, nodding to show she already knew my answer.

"Yes-s-s-s." The sound hissed out of me like air escaping from a balloon.

"Do you remember what happened?"

"I was swimming…hit my head."

"That's right. You dived into a sand bar. You've broken some bones in your neck, and you're in Huntington Beach Inter-Community Hospital."

She held a thermometer in front of my face, waited for me to open my mouth, then slid it under my tongue. "You are a lucky young man," she said.

I shot an angry look at her smiling face. *Lucky. Yeah, right!*

"You're *lucky* to be *alive*," she said evenly, reading my thoughts.

I became aware of the sounds around me. Soft voices a few feet away. Rubber soles squeaking on a tile floor. A voice over an intercom, paging a doctor.

As the nurse withdrew the thermometer, I had my question ready. "Why…why can't I feel anything?"

She smiled and picked up my hand, holding it up so I could see her do it. "You can't feel anything, Ron, because your body is paralyzed."

It took a minute for me to understand.

"Paralyzed?"

"Yes," she said in the same calm, even voice. "Your neck is broken between the second and third cervical vertebrae, and your spinal cord has been injured."

Paralyzed. The word ricocheted in my mind like an out-of-control bullet. "What…what does that mean?"

The nurse's voice was soft as she answered. "Medically speaking, you have something called quadriplegia. That means you're paralyzed from the neck down."

Paralyzed. I couldn't get past that word. I was paralyzed…from the neck down. There was one more awful question I had to ask, but I had to ask God to help me say the word. Please God. Please don't let it be…

"Is it permanent?"

She continued to look steadily into my face, but a shadow seemed to dim her eyes as she answered. "We'll just have to wait and see, Ron…and hope for the best."

No! No! No! Not me! This wasn't happening to ME! This was a dream, a nightmare. Oh, please, God! Please, let me wake up. Lord, wake me up! No, no, no!

"I…I…can't…no…no!" I protested. "I…who's going to drive my little brother back to Oregon? I…I gotta play football to get my scholarship. I *can't* be paralyzed." Exhausted, I stopped, too overwhelmed to continue.

"Honey," the nurse answered softly, touching her fingertips to my forehead to brush aside a strand of hair. "Your mom and dad are on their way; they'll be here soon. Your brother is okay. Don't worry about other things right now. Just concentrate on getting better. That's what's important."

I closed my eyes, giving in once more to the darkness. Then a surprising thought flickered for an instant in my mind.

"What time is it?" I asked.

"Just after midnight," the nurse replied.

"And the date? Is it March 18 now?"

"Yes, March 18, as of a few minutes ago. Why?"

For a moment I couldn't get the words out. They caught in my throat as I sank deeper into the pool of misery.

"It's my birthday," I said, staring at the ceiling. "I just turned 18."

8

Trauma and Tears

~

Mom was alone on our homesite that afternoon doing laundry when the phone rang. She closed the washer lid before stepping across the room to pick up the receiver.

"Mrs. Heagy?" a man's voice asked.

"Yes."

"This is Dr. Evans at Huntington Beach Inter-Community Hospital in California."

Instantly, a cold wave of fear swept over her. "Who?" Mom asked. She held the phone to her ear with one hand and fumbled for a chair with the other.

"Mrs. Heagy, I'm sorry. Your son has been in an accident."

"*Which* son?" she asked, her heart pounding.

"Ron," the doctor said. "He's here in the hospital."

"And Mike? Where's Mike?"

"Uh...Mike?"

"My other son, Mike—the younger one."

"Oh, I'm sorry. I...didn't know there was another son. I don't know where Mike is," the doctor said hesitantly, unprepared for the question. "Only Ron was brought in."

"How is he? What happened? Is he all right—"

The doctor interrupted. "Mrs. Heagy, I'm sorry. I have to tell you that it does look serious."

Mom sensed that the doctor was trying to break the harsh news in the gentlest way possible.

"Serious?"

"He had a surfing accident. He broke his neck."

"Oh—oh…."

"Mrs. Heagy, we need to begin treatment right away, but we're going to need your signature to do that. Could you please send us a wire, giving us permission to go ahead?"

Now it seemed as if the doctor's voice was fading, his words replaced by a roaring noise that filled Mom's head. She closed her eyes, trying to focus.

"Yes…yes, anything…of course." She had no idea how to go about sending a telegram, but that didn't matter. "Is Ronnie…is he going to be all right?"

"Mrs. Heagy, the situation is grave. We're doing all we can, and I feel fairly confident right now that he's going to make it. But there's really no way we can know…I hope you'll prepare yourself for the worst, Mrs. Heagy. There's a chance your son may not survive the night. It's touch and go right now. Could you and your husband get down here as quickly as possible? We've got him on high doses of painkillers, and we're making him as comfortable as possible, but he's still in considerable distress. He's having trouble breathing," the doctor continued.

"He…he can't breathe?" Mom gasped.

"We need to do a tracheotomy and put him on a ventilator," Dr. Evans said. "But I'd really like to wait to do that, if possible, until you get here. He, uh, well, he won't be able to talk to you once we do the trache."

"We'll be there just as soon as we can," Mom said, stifling a sob as she hung up the phone. Instantly, she picked up the receiver again and called the paper mill.

It was unusual for my dad to receive a personal call while he was at work. When he got the message to call home, he quickly stopped what he was doing and headed for the telephone, feeling a knot form in his stomach.

"Ronnie's been hurt—he's been in an accident!" Mom blurted out as soon as she heard his voice.

Dad immediately started for home, praying constantly as he drove. Back at the homesite, Mom, who was recovering from a hysterectomy a few weeks before, hurriedly looked through the garage's attic for the old suitcase, dragged it down the stairs and over to the travel trailer, and quickly filled it with clothes for her and Dad. She called my sister, Pennie, at a friend's house and made arrangements for her to stay there until she and Dad returned.

"Mom, is Ronnie going to be all right?" Pennie asked, her voice full of fear.

"I don't know, honey. I just don't know."

Until that day, the only flight Mom had been on was in a tiny single-engine plane that took her on what was supposed to be a joyride—but wasn't. Under normal circumstances, she would have been scared to death to board the big jet in Portland. But circumstances were no longer normal. The focus of her fear that night was on the broken body of her son, lying in a hospital nearly 1,000 miles away.

A friend drove them the 90 miles from Brownsville to Portland. It was dark by the time the plane taxied to the end of the runway and then soared off into the foggy night sky, heading south. The flight took a little less than two hours.

"It was indescribable, the way I felt that night," Mom later recalled. All these years later, tears still come as quickly now as they did during that terrible trip into the unknown. "I had never been to Los Angeles, never been anywhere that big," she said. "Coming from a little town of 600 people and flying into a place like LAX was overwhelming. We were both so worried, so scared of what was happening to Ronnie."

Annette's parents met Mom and Dad at the airport, and although they offered love and encouragement to these people they had never met, they had no news to give them. Guarding my privacy, the hospital had refused to release any information.

Mentally and physically exhausted, my parents arrived in the wee hours of the morning and went immediately to the intensive care unit. The room was a wheel of curtained partitions, each one outlined with blinking lights, beeping monitors, and spiraling tubes and cords. My cubicle stood out from the others because I lay in a traction device called a Stryker frame, a canvas and steel contraption that held my body in rigid traction. A 50-pound weight attached to a large, surgical-steel "halo" secured my neck in place with caliper screws embedded in my skull.

I lay either faceup or facedown on the frame's stiff canvas sling. Every two hours the nurses turned me over, a procedure that was performed 12 times a day for the next five weeks—and I dreaded it every time. First, after being careful to position my arms so they wouldn't fall through the webbing, nurses laid a second canvas frame on top of me and fastened it securely to the one I was already lying on, sandwiching me in between. Then, while one nurse held the weight that kept my neck in traction, the other flipped my bed over. Each frame had an opening for my face so that when I lay facedown I stared directly at the floor.

Fortunately, I was on my back when Mom and Dad arrived. In the dimmed lighting of the quiet room, I opened my eyes and found Mom's tear-filled eyes smiling into mine.

"Hi, Mom," I said simply.

"Oh, Ronnie!" She whispered, pressing her lips together tightly to hold back the sobs. "Oh, Ronnie!" She slipped her arms carefully along mine and rested her wet cheek against my face. It was a strange sensation, knowing she was hugging me yet feeling only her soft face brushing mine.

"Son, how are you doing?" I rolled my eyes to the other side and smiled up at Dad.

"I'm sorry, Dad! I—"

"Son, you have nothing to apologize for. You just think about getting well," my father said softly in his strong, steady voice. "You're in God's hands, Ronnie. God is here with you, with all of us. He hasn't forgotten you. He loves you, and we love you. It's going to be all right."

Dad was not one to show emotions, but his eyes were also brimming with tears. He leaned down and touched his forehead to mine, then laid his hand on my chest. He prayed in that soft, familiar voice, earnest and calm. "Lord, thank You for letting us be here with our son. Thank You for Ronnie. We love him, Lord, but we know You love him even more. Please be with him, dear Jesus. Give him courage and strength to accept whatever lies ahead. We know that when we trust You, all things work together for good. Dear Lord, we ask that You heal Ronnie's injuries, if it is Your will. And we ask this of You, the Great Physician, in Jesus' name. Amen."

Mom stroked my cheek and smiled at me again. I was so relieved to have them there. Tears filled my eyes too. "Mom...it hurts, Mom. It really hurts."

"I know it does, Ronnie. Just hang in there. It'll get better. I know it will." Mom's face, drawn and mottled by crying, creased into a loving smile. "We love you, son. We love you so much."

The doctor was summoned when my parents arrived. He called them out into the hallway and explained what needed to be done.

"Ron's diaphragm and lungs are partially paralyzed," he said. "That's why he's having so much trouble breathing. We need to do a tracheotomy—but as I told you on the phone, I can't promise anything. He's in very critical condition; we could still lose him. But if he makes it through the surgery, makes it through the night, I think his chances are pretty good."

"What exactly is a tracheotomy, Doctor?" Dad asked.

"It's an incision in his windpipe that will let us attach a machine that will help him breathe."

"A respirator?" my mother asked. "You're going to put him on a respirator? Life support?"

"Yes, Mrs. Heagy, that's what we need to do. He's having too much trouble breathing on his own; we're not sure he can keep it up. This will be like an insurance policy. It'll help him breathe and clear his lungs while we wait to see how much his body is able to heal on its own."

"How long?" Mom asked him.

The doctor hesitated a moment before he answered with one grim word: "Indefinitely."

9

When There Still Was Hope

~

Mom was massaging my shoulders eight days later when something wonderful happened.

"Mom." I only had the use of my voice as the respirator exhaled for me, so my speech came in puffs and spurts, making it often unintelligible. "Mah...I...I feeh..."

"What did you say, Ronnie? You need something?"

"I...FEE it...FEE IT!"

"You can feel this?" she asked, her hand resting on my chest, her eyes wide with excitement.

"Yes-s-s-s."

Within two more days, the tingling sensation had spread clear down to the middle of my back. I was thrilled, and Mom and Dad were ecstatic. The doctor, however, was noncommittal.

"This is a positive sign," he said, nodding as I told him I could feel him touching my torso. "As I've told you, we still have reasons to be optimistic. Your spinal cord was damaged but not severed. If it had been cut, there would be no hope that you could regain the use of your arms or legs. I have to caution you that this sensitivity may not last. And even if it does, it may not mean you'll ever walk again. We just don't know at this point."

You don't know me, Doc, I wanted to say. *This is just the beginning. I'll be walking out of here before long. I've got a life ahead of me, and quadriplegia isn't part of my plans!*

39

The next step in my treatment was fusion surgery, in which the verte-brae in my neck would be wired together to help give my head and neck some stability. But first I had to be in traction long enough for my verte-brae to realign, my lungs to clear, and my temperature to go down.

On a Friday ten days after the accident, my doctor said all signs were go. "If you're free of fever Monday morning, we'll proceed with the surgery," he told us.

I actually looked forward to having my neck fused, rationalizing that the sooner it was over, the sooner I could get on with my plans for the future. My courage lasted until just after midnight Sunday night. Unable to sleep, my thoughts ran wild.

Mom and Dad had spent their nights with Annette's parents for a week or so after they arrived in California but soon were invited to stay with George and Nancy Christian, who lived near the hospital and whose family in Oregon attended our home church in Brownsville. They were at the Christians' home that Monday morning when the phone rang at 2:00 a.m., awakening everyone in the house. They all assumed something terrible had happened to me. Mom was relieved to hear the nurse say, "Mrs. Heagy, Ron wants to talk with you."

"Talk? He's talking?" Mom stammered, not yet awake and momen-tarily confused. For nearly two weeks my speech had been almost inde-cipherable because of the respirator. What she didn't know was that I had persuaded the nurse to close off my trache opening and hold the telephone to my lips.

"Mom?"

"Ronnie, are you all right?"

"I'm fine. I just…I just wanted to tell you and Dad that I love you."

"Oh, Ronnie! You scared us to death, calling in the middle of the night. Honey, you know we love you too. We'll see you in just a few hours, and we'll be praying for you. Don't worry about the surgery. God is with you."

It had been nearly two weeks since I'd actually spoken to my parents. And in the early hours of that morning, I desperately needed to tell them one more time how much I loved and appreciated them both.

The surgery took five hours. Finally, the doctor pushed through the doors into the surgical waiting room where Mom and Dad were eagerly awaiting news. He smiled reassuringly. "Well, Mr. and Mrs. Heagy, you can relax. The surgery was successful," the doctor told them. "We were able to scrape away the crushed bone and fuse the broken vertebrae. That should make a big difference for him."

The long days continued, a seemingly endless cycle of treatments, pain, and quiet boredom broken only by the acts of thoughtfulness of visitors and staff members.

Several local pastors came to the hospital to pray with us and to encourage me after hearing about my accident. Strangers dropped in occasionally. One, a man married to a talented flutist, brought his wife to play for me. Another visitor left behind an envelope. When Dad opened it, he found $300 and a note that said simply, "To help with expenses."

One day Kathy, my favorite nurse, smuggled her daughter's hamsters into my cubicle and proudly told me one of the little critters was named after me. She also found a way to put a small television set under the Stryker frame so I could watch sports events. (Later my Uncle Dave hung a mirror over the frame so it was reflected there too.) Other times Kathy somehow found time to sit by my bed just to talk or read to me.

After stewing about it for weeks, I screwed up my courage one morning and asked her the question that had plagued my thoughts since I'd arrived in ICU. It took a while for her to understand what I was trying to say. When she finally understood, Kathy smiled kindly and said, "Don't worry, Ron. You haven't lost your virility, if that's what you mean. You are still quite capable of having sex and fathering children. Most quadriplegics are." She patted my shoulder in a reassuring way. "You won't be impotent. You can still produce sperm."

I closed my eyes in blessed relief. I could still dream....

Buoyed by these acts of kindness and hopeful after the neck-fusing surgery, we expected to see spectacular results right away. Instead, my condition deteriorated. I was too nauseous to eat, so I was fed intravenously and was sedated most of the time. My weight dropped, and my temperature rose. Pressure sores formed on my heels, and the sores became infected. Several times the medical staff tried to wean me off the respirator, but they finally gave up. I could not breathe on my own.

Mom and Dad did everything they could think of to keep my spirits up. They printed encouraging Bible verses in bold black letters and stuck some on the ceiling above my Stryker frame and taped others on the floor so I could read and memorize them while lying on my stomach.

At first, one of the verses made me scoff indignantly. It was Hebrews 13:5-6: "God has said, 'Never will I leave you; never will I forsake you.' So we say with confidence, 'The Lord is my helper; I will not be afraid. What can man do to me?'"

Right, I thought sarcastically. *Where was God when I broke my neck? He deserted me! When I needed Him, He wasn't there.*

Then I thought of Mike and how he had charged into the surf to save me, and I realized God was there.

Still, I couldn't help but question whether life was worth living. I certainly didn't want to live like this! I hadn't expected my recovery to take so long or to be so painful. Every morning when my parents stepped into the room, they seemed a little older, a little more exhausted than the day before. Despite their cheery greetings and fervent prayers, behind their smiles and optimism, I knew they were suffering as much as I was.

On April 2, Mom wrote in her journal:

> I hurt so much for my son. Why, Lord, does he have to suffer such pain? I only wish it could be me instead of him.... This has been a hard day for Ronnie. When they tightened the screws that hold his halo in place, he lay there, so still, with big tears rolling down his face. The nurse says he will eventually get used to the pressure the headgear causes, but I sometimes wonder how much more he can take....
>
> Seeing Ronnie like this makes me think of how much Jesus suffered when they embedded that crown of thorns on his head. The pain had to be terrible. And poor Mary suffered too; I certainly know that! I know how helpless she must have felt when they nailed her son on the cross between two thieves. Her son died. Thank God, mine is still alive....
>
> Jesus promised to come back someday and take us to be with him. I wish it could be today....

The next day Mother's journal entry sounded more optimistic:

> Last night Ronnie's legs moved. The doctor said it is probably reflex motion, but we still think it is a hopeful sign. Today when I tickled his feet, one toe moved. I could have shouted for joy! Whoever would have thought I'd get so excited over seeing my son move his big toe?
>
> Thank You, Lord, for another day.

10

Torment and Tears

~

Annette had come to visit. Undaunted by finding that I was turned facedown in the Stryker frame, she dropped to the floor and lay on her back, scooting over until her face was almost directly under mine.

"Hi, Ron!" she greeted me with her beautiful, crinkly-eyed smile. "How are you doing?"

My heart did a somersault. I was so happy to see her, so glad she had come. It was easy for me to feel abandoned by my friends even when I *knew* better. Obviously there was no way my Oregon friends could get there, although Karla had called and asked my mom if she should come down. I'd told Mom to say no; I just couldn't bear for Karla to see me in this condition. *If she comes here and sees me like this, I thought, she'll make a U-turn in the doorway and never look back!*

Although I didn't see many kids my age, I had frequent visits from adults, despite the ICU's posted rules that limited visits to five minutes every hour. Dottie, the charge nurse, was good about looking the other way whenever someone came to see me. As long as they didn't stay too long, she was very tolerant of my visitors, understanding how devastating it was for me to be so terribly injured and so far from home.

Nancy and George Christian, my parents' hosts, came regularly, as did Annette's parents. But Annette and her brother were in school and holding down part-time jobs, so they weren't able to come very often. I also sensed that it was hard for Annette to see me lying there so helplessly

43

with the screws in my head and the respirator connected to my throat, breathing for me.

That's why I was so eager for Annette to talk with me that day. I was feeling lonely and wanted her to know how happy her visits made me. Annette's cheery monologue always lifted my spirits as she rattled off funny anecdotes about her latest adventures and activities, things she'd seen at the beach, or jokes she'd heard at school.

One day she reminded me about the time we had hidden behind a bus at the mission training camp in Florida. Since it was our last night together at the camp, I had kissed her. We laughed—or at least she laughed and I smiled as the respirator wheezed—remembering how our harmless little escapade ended when a faculty member caught us and shooed us back to our cabins.

As Annette had reminisced about our first kiss, I had watched her lips and wondered if I would ever again be able to kiss a girl or hold her hand as I once had held Annette's.

This morning, as she visited with me, I wanted so much for her to laugh again and tell me funny stories. Mom and Dad had excused themselves and headed for the hospital coffee shop "to let you two talk," Mom had said, walking out the door. As I was lying facedown toward the floor and Annette was lying on the floor looking up at me, I realized that drool was beginning to escape from my lips and drip onto the floor. Although I was embarrassed, Annette grabbed a paper towel, mopped it up, and kept right on talking.

"Ron, I'm so sorry this has happened to you," she said, reaching up and touching my cheek. "I'm so sorry." There was a pause, then she said, "Well, gotta go."

Wait! You just got here! I wanted to shout after her. *Don't leave yet. Stay and talk. But she was gone.*

After Annette left, I lay there, alone in the room, tears dropping to the floor onto the stack of damp paper towels. I was trapped, a prisoner in a concrete cell, unable to wipe my tears, scratch an itch, blow my nose, or push the hair out of my eyes. I felt helpless and frustrated, wondering how—and if—this nightmare would ever end.

Each day brought some new form of torment. I had always been modest, so much so that my school friends had teased me about it. When we had to weigh before a wrestling match, my buddies thought nothing of stripping down to the skin, but not me. I always left my underwear on. Only once had I taken off my briefs, and that was when I exceeded the weight limit for my wrestling class by half a pound and was trying to shed a few quick ounces.

In the hospital, modesty was a thing of the past, a characteristic of "normal" people. Here, I was at the mercy of the medical staff—mostly women, a lot of them attractive *young* women—who bathed me, changed my hospital gown, replaced my condom catheter, massaged my powerless muscles, and cleaned me up after embarrassing accidents. Each experience left me feeling hurt and humiliated. Even though I couldn't feel or see what they were doing, I *knew*. And even though I felt better after each change or treatment, I dreaded them for hours in advance when I knew they were coming.

The worst embarrassment occurred when a nursing instructor, looking for a way to give her young students hands-on experience, chose me for the male model they would use as they learned to insert a urinary catheter.

Mom and Dad had left for lunch when the group filed into my ICU cubicle and encircled the Stryker frame. Seeing me roll my eyes around the group, trying to figure out why they were there, the instructor stepped up to my bedside and introduced herself loudly, as if I had lost my hearing. "Mr. Heagy, these are nursing students," she explained cheerfully. "I'd like to acquaint them with your case. Would that be okay?"

I thought she meant they would simply go over my history; and even if I had wanted to protest, I couldn't say anything with the respirator hissing away. My eyes opened wide in shock then squeezed shut as she pulled the sheet away from my body, lifted my hospital gown, and proceeded to give the class a detailed tour of my paralyzed body. My face burned with embarrassment as I heard her explaining the way the catheter functioned. Then she checked my chart and said, "It looks like it's time for a change. I'll just get a new cath and be right back; this will be a good learning experience for you."

I lay there, fully exposed before the student nurses, squeezing my eyes closed tight to keep the tears of humiliation from brimming over my eyelids as the respirator made my chest lift and fall at the same, steady rate. Finally the instructor came back in and supervised a couple of the students as they struggled to remove the catheter and replace it with a fresh one.

The experience was more than I could take. I wanted more than anything to get up and run or at least to shout for the insensitive instructor to stop, but all I could do was lie there, silently staring at the ceiling and wishing I could vanish.

When Dad returned an hour or so later, I was still red-faced and fuming. It took a while for him to figure out what I was trying to tell him, and if Kathy, one of my favorite nurses, hadn't come in and helped translate, it would have been hopeless. Finally, when he understood what had happened, he was as angry as I had been. He quickly left the room and tracked down the instructor. He told her in no uncertain terms that such thoughtlessness was not to be repeated. Evidently she got the message; I never saw her or her students again.

As much as I suffered from all the humiliating treatments, the pain was even more unbearable. Each time the halo screws had to be tightened, the pressure from the attached weights on my head caused excruciating pain. To compensate for the pressure and relieve the agony, I clamped my jaws together and kept them clinched so long they locked. A doctor finally had to pry them apart.

I was also having piercing earaches. It took several days for the doctors to figure out that the wave that had driven me into the sand bar had also forced sand into my ear canals, allowing the buildup of wax and moisture. The blockage had impaired my hearing and was causing intense pain. Even after a specialist was called in to clean my ear canals, pain in my jaws and shoulders persisted.

Another problem was the noise in ICU. Sometimes it was eerily quiet except for the beeping of monitors and the incessant *whoosh, whoosh, whoosh* of respirators. Other times, suffering patients moaned and even screamed out in misery. One night a drunk man was brought into the unit, yelling and screaming in pain after he had walked in front of a truck. He had suffered multiple fractures, the nurses told me, and later that evening he went into the DTs—delirium tremens. I wanted to smash my hands over my ears and scream along with the poor, suffering man, but all I could do was lie in the darkness and listen.

It was frustrating to be completely dependent upon others. One morning as the nurses flipped my Stryker frame, something went wrong. Somehow the monitor wires got caught in the hinges, preventing the top canvas from being fastened securely to the bottom frame before they flipped me. As they started to turn the frame, the two canvas platforms came apart, and I slid to one edge.

It was such a helpless feeling—to be falling and be completely unable to reach out or hang on to something, anything, to break the fall. All I could do was send up a hurried SOS: *Please, Lord! Help me!* Instantly the nurses spotted the problem and kept me from slipping out and cracking my head on the floor. After that traumatic experience, I felt anxious each time my bed was flipped.

Another chronic worry began during a fierce windstorm when the electricity kept flickering off and on. Each time the power blinked off, my respirator stopped for a moment, beeping, until the hospital's emergency generator kicked in and powered up everything again. The nurses assured me that the generator would *always* come on if the power failed, but it was impossible not to panic each time the respirator paused and beeped for a second or two. A couple of times some other malfunction caused it to stop for a moment. Unable to speak, let alone yell that I needed help, I immediately broke out in a cold sweat, my heart pounding as if I'd just run a mile—until the nurses, hearing the beeping alarm, came running to get it started again.

What Kathy told me made sense: "When you get scared, your heart beats faster and your body needs more air," she said. "If you can just stay calm, it will keep your heart rate down and eliminate lots of problems. Trust us, Ron. We'll be here. We won't let you down."

Mom had even better advice. "Ron, when the respirator pauses, don't panic. Don't worry about the nurses coming. Just focus on God. Soothe yourself with His Word. Instead of trying to raise your head to see if the nurses are on their way, close your eyes and imagine *Jesus* coming to help you, bringing the nurses with Him! Be filled with His peace; think of the psalm that says, 'Be still, and know that I am God.'"

You're right, Mom. I've thought it over and decided to heed your advice, I thought, smiling. *I'll try my best to lie here and "be still"—as if I could do anything else even if I wanted to!*

Just when I seemed to be conquering some of my fears and learning to handle the pain, I suffered a serious setback one morning when I suddenly became violently ill. The nurses had just turned me onto my back, and Dad wasn't there to interpret for me, so I couldn't make them understand that I was severely nauseous. I gulped and gagged. *Why can't they see that I am about to erupt like Mt. St. Helens!*

As the nurse turned to leave, I started vomiting. She quickly called for help, got me turned over, and then summoned a doctor.

"You're right," I heard the doctor tell her quietly after examining me. "It's blood. We'd better have a gastroenterologist check this out."

Thirty minutes later, the specialist was threading a tube through my nostrils and down my throat. "Swallow, Ron. Come on. You can do it," the doctor said encouragingly as I alternately swallowed and gagged. The tube he was forcing down my throat wasn't even as wide as a drinking straw, but it felt as big as a garden hose. As though reading my thoughts, he held the free end up for my inspection. "See, Ron? It's only a small tube. Keep trying. This will help us determine if the problem is a stress ulcer. Swallow harder. You can do it."

As I did my best to get the tube down, the doctor continued. "Ron, you've lost a lot of blood, and you need a transfusion," he said. "But the hospital is out of your blood type right now. We've ordered a supply from a blood bank in San Francisco, but it's gonna take a while. Hang in there!"

Next, they pumped my stomach—another painful procedure—and cauterized the ulcer with saline solution.

"Keep your fingers crossed," the doctor said after the agonizing treatment was finished. "If this is effective, we won't need to do surgery." Only one word registered in my brain. *Surgery? Oh, no! Not again! I can't take another surgery!*

The naso-gastric tube remained in place for several days, eventually causing sores in my nose and throat. *Now my misery is complete,* I thought late one night. *I couldn't possibly be in more agony. I can't move, can't speak. I'm not sure how much longer I can stand the pain in my nose and throat. Please, Lord! Please help me!*

How I yearned to yank that tube out of my stomach and throw it on the floor! It was just another item on the growing list of things I longed to do—but couldn't. It was during that time that Mom wrote in her journal:

> When we arrived at the hospital this morning, Ronnie was in serious condition. He needed more blood, and thank God it was available. After they gave him two transfusions, he seemed to rally, and the crisis passed. Poor darling. He's getting so thin. I often wonder what's running through his mind

as he stares alternately at the ceiling and the floor. If only he could talk and tell us how he feels.

Whenever another crisis came, the drugs I was given sent me plunging into a drug-induced world of horrible hallucinations that seemed terrifyingly real: Someone was chasing me. I saw spiders and other vile creatures crawling over my head, and I was desperate to bat them away. But my immobile arms refused to move. I was running up an almost endless staircase, trying to escape some unknown horror. At the top, I could see a bright light and an open door. Below was only darkness. I struggled to go up, to reach that open door, but the shadowy figure kept dragging me down...down...down into the darkness. The same hallucinations came back to haunt me over and over again.

During one nightmare I was back on the Teen Mission trip to Brazil, sleeping in a hammock again. One of my buddies yelled, "Hey, Ron. Grab the flashlight. It's your turn to kill the cockroaches tonight." Still in my hammock, I fumbled around in the darkness, found my flashlight, and turned it on. Then, directly over my head, I saw the biggest, most sinister-looking tarantula I had ever seen; it was staring at me with harsh, black eyes. I struggled to get out of the swaying hammock, but my legs wouldn't move! I tried to cover my face with one arm. My arm wouldn't move either! My heart was pumping fast. *I can't get away! I can't move!*

The drug-induced hallucinations faded away as the dosages were decreased and my ulcer healed. Finally the day came when the doctors said I could begin eating again rather than being fed through the naso-gastric tube. I immediately envisioned a huge platter of T-bone steak and french fries, but when Kathy came with my tray at lunchtime, all I saw was a cup of watery broth and a mound of wobbly green gelatin. My appetite disappeared immediately.

"Sorry, Ron. No steak and potatoes today. You've got to start out with something easy to digest. Your stomach can't handle solid food yet."

She spooned a few sips of the unappetizing broth into my mouth. I forced myself to swallow, thinking as I did that it tasted as bad as it smelled. The slippery green gelatin slid down my throat a little easier. Kathy gave me a pat of encouragement as she picked up the tray to leave.

"I know this stuff isn't very appetizing, but it's important to begin slowly. Just hang in there, and pretty soon you'll be chowing down the good stuff," she said.

Twenty minutes later I felt a familiar queasiness in the pit of my stomach. *Swallow, Ron*, I kept telling myself. *Don't throw up or they'll shove that tube down your throat again.*

Suddenly, up it came! The doctor walked into my cubicle a short while later, the dreaded tube coiled in his hands.

"Sorry, Ron. We've gotta take a look. It'll be easier this time; you'll see."

It wasn't easier. The tube seemed just as huge as they threaded it down my throat and once again pumped my stomach. What they found was even more discouraging: The ulcer hadn't healed. The hemorrhaging began again, even worse this time. The transfusions continued, with additional blood being repeatedly shipped in from San Francisco, until finally things seemed to be under control.

Although my parents tried not to show it, I knew they were becoming discouraged. I could see the fatigue in my dad's sagging shoulders and sense the worry hidden behind Mom's red-rimmed eyes. She devoted herself completely to caring for me, bathing me, talking and reading to me, and even learning to suction my trache tube. I knew she felt every piercing pain that wracked my body; she shared my frustration and despair. For that reason I tried to hide my pain and discouragement from her and turned instead to Dad when I needed to vent my feelings.

I knew Dad needed to get back home, but I dreaded the thought of him leaving me. Mom and I both needed him there in the hospital, but we knew if he jeopardized his job at the paper mill, we could lose the insurance that was paying my medical bills. It seemed like a no-win situation.

A few days later, Annette was lying on the floor under the Stryker frame, reading to me, when she paused and looked up into my face. "Is something wrong?" she asked, sensing a problem.

Sometimes in the past I had asked her to take off her glasses. Annette had beautiful eyes, and I liked to look at them. Thinking it might cheer me up, she took off her glasses. Then she reached up and put her hand on my cheek. It felt warm and soft. "You're a great guy, Ron."

Before she could say anything else, my eyes dilated and rolled back into my head. Terrified, Annette scrambled out from under the frame, called the nurses, then ran to the visitors' waiting room to summon my parents.

As Mom and Dad pushed through the doors into the intensive care unit, the PA system announced, "Code blue, ICU. Code blue, ICU." Cushioned footsteps thudded down the hall behind them as the emergency team rushed to my curtained cubicle, where the nurses were already administering CPR. A doctor quickly cut an opening into my jugular vein to start a transfusion, and then I was rushed to the OR, my parents trotting behind the gurney as staffers pushed it hurriedly down the hall.

During the surgery my heart stopped, and once again the medical team pulled me back from the brink. When I awoke later, I remembered a powerful dream—or was it something more? I had found myself drifting through a beautiful place, a spirit without a body but somehow equipped with eyes, a mouth, and a conscious mind. I became aware that, for the first time since the accident, I felt no pain. I moved in a euphoric state of contentment and heard familiar voices in the distance, excitedly thinking one of the voices was my grandfather Heagy, who had died several years earlier.

I awoke then, slowly realizing that the familiar voices belonged to my parents. Dad was standing beside my bed reading the Bible; I still remember the first verse I heard as I slowly emerged from the darkness: "Consider it pure joy, my brothers, whenever you face trials of many kinds."

As my stay in the ICU rolled into its fifth week, I could sense the pressure continuing to build on my parents. They were already having to borrow money to cope with the crisis. Dad had to return to work if he was to keep his job, and Mom didn't want to stay in California alone.

Finally, the doctors told them they could transport me by air ambulance to the rehabilitation unit at Good Samaritan Hospital in Portland. We were all happy to be heading back to Oregon, but there were still problems to overcome. For starters, the charter plane was going to cost more than five thousand dollars. I saw the lines in my dad's face deepen as the social worker who was helping us make the arrangements outlined the fees.

Then something wonderful happened—a patient from Portland needed to be moved down to L.A. We could share the cost of the jet! And then something even more wonderful occurred. Contributions began to come in. By the time we left, more than $3,000 had been contributed by friends and strangers to a fund that had been set up in my name.

On the day before we were to leave, Mom shampooed my hair and gave me a close shave. I smiled ruefully, thinking that I used to take two showers a day, and now I hadn't had a shower in five weeks.

Mother smiled as she combed my hair. "You look downright handsome," she said. "Here, see for yourself."

When she held the mirror in front of my face, the skinny guy who stared back at me looked only vaguely familiar. My skin was pasty white, my cheeks were hollow, and my eyes had a sad dullness that remained even when I smiled. I had lost more than 50 pounds—and along with it, the zest for life that had sparked my spirit.

When Annette came to say good-bye that day, I longed for her to kiss me, but she didn't. Patting me on the shoulder, she smiled her brightest smile and said simply, "Have a safe trip, Ron. And after school is out, I'll come see you in Oregon, okay?"

I searched her face for a sign of something more than friendship. I wanted to say so much to her, to thank her for sticking by me through this horrible nightmare, and to tell her I'd be back on my feet by the time she came to Oregon. But with the respirator's noisy competition, I could only manage one word. "Promise?" I asked, just a little too desperately.

Annette squeezed my shoulder and smiled. "Don't flirt with those pretty nurses at Good Sam," she teased as she moved toward the door.

Dad also said good-bye—but just for a day or two. At 3:30 a.m. on the day before our plane left Los Angeles, he climbed into the little red Love Bug, its fenders still dented, its hood still tied down with a cord, and headed home to Oregon.

Staff members also stopped by to say good-bye. Mom and Dad had given Bibles to many of them during our stay there, and most had responded enthusiastically. Inspired by Mom and Dad's powerful example of faith and trust even in the harshest adversity, many had become new Christians or had renewed their Christian commitment. As eager as we were to leave, there were plenty of tears that day as we thanked these people whose lives had become so entwined in ours.

As we said our good-byes, I told myself I'd be back to visit these friends someday. I pictured myself pushing through the familiar swinging doors of the ICU with two good arms and stepping inside on two strong legs, whole again.

11

A Voice in the Darkness

~

One of the first things I learned at Good Samaritan Hospital in Portland was that a circular bed is even worse than a Stryker frame. While the Stryker frame allows a patient to be turned sideways, the circular bed revolves like a wheel so the patient is rotated into a vertical position, as though standing, before eventually coming to rest faceup or facedown. Because of all the weeks I had been in bed, my heart had grown accustomed to my body always being in a prone position. Now, as soon as the circular bed elevated my head, blood pooled in the lower part of my body and I blacked out. Invariably, when I came to, I had a pounding headache.

Another problem was that the circular bed was obviously designed for people shorter than six feet, two inches. Each time the bed revolved, my big feet dragged the floor, causing the motor to overheat—along with the nurse's patience.

Dad had gone back to work in Brownsville, 90 miles away, but Mom stayed with me ten or twelve hours a day, massaging my muscles, soothing my fevers with cool compresses, reading to me, and just being there to keep me company. At night she slept a few hours at the home of her brother, who lived there in Portland.

On weekends, Dad, Mike, and Pennie drove up from Brownsville to give Mom a hand. Dad tried to hide his worries about the mounting medical bills, but I knew things were getting bad. I told myself, *Someday, after I'm well and playing professional football, I'll make it up to them!*

Now that I was closer to home, I looked forward to visits from my friends. Sure enough, Brian, a favorite cousin who lived in Portland, was there several times a week. But for others, the awkwardness—and to them, the hopelessness—of the situation was too much. My best friend—a guy who had been my constant companion for several years—came only once. I was eager for him to visit and had a long list of things I wanted him to tell me—everything that had happened at school since spring break. But the minute his face appeared, I could see rejection in his eyes. He kept looking away, ill at ease and never again making eye contact.

When I asked questions about school and our mutual friends, it took a long time before he could understand me, and then his answers were curt and forced. When he walked out of my room that day, he walked out of my life.

Karla, on the other hand, was so glad to see me she hugged me and cried with joy. "Oh, Ron! I've been so worried about you. All the kids at school and church have been praying. We miss you so much."

I wanted to take Karla's hand and assure her that soon things would be just like they were before. I longed to run my fingers through her long, blonde hair again and feel her standing close to me, swaying together to loud music at a concert. *Someday*, I promised myself.

The next step in my determined crawl toward recovery was getting rid of the respirator so I could be transferred to the rehab unit. But that seemed impossible. When the technician cut my assisted breath rate to three per minute, I nearly suffocated. Each breath required a conscious effort, a fight to pull air into my lungs then push it out. I was afraid to fall asleep, fearful that I would die simply because I forgot to breathe! Because of the stress, my temperature rose to 103 degrees.

When I again admitted defeat, the pulmonary specialist stood silently over my bed for a moment. Then he said, as gently as he could, "It's not your fault, Ron. I know you're trying. It's just that your lungs are partially paralyzed. You can't take in enough air on your own to inflate the lower lobes; consequently your blood doesn't get adequate oxygen. You need that respirator."

"What are you telling us?" Dad asked, his face hard and solemn.

"He needs the respirator, Mr. Heagy. I'm not sure it's a good idea to try to wean him off it."

"Are you saying he'll be dependent upon a machine for the rest of his life?" Dad asked.

The doctor wet his lips quickly and answered in a low voice, "I'm afraid so."

The room was silent, except for the *whooshing* noise of the vital—and yet hated—respirator. Dad swallowed hard. Tears rolled down Mom's face.

"I know this is not what you wanted to hear," the doctor continued. "But there are portable ventilators available now that are lightweight and quite efficient. They can even be mounted on a wheelchair."

I caught the doctor's eye and mouthed a response. "Sir...Iwoll...wiketo...rye."

Dad squeezed my shoulder and smiled at me before turning to the doctor to interpret. "Ron isn't ready to quit yet, Doc. He'd like to try one more time."

"Ron, your lungs are *paralyzed*. It's not a matter of just *wanting* to do this. Your body isn't *able* to do it. Without help you could have some serious problems." He stopped a moment and made sure I was listening carefully. "You might even die, Ron."

Dad looked at me intently. "Son, do you understand?"

I closed my eyes and nodded my head ever so slightly, my movements severely limited by the halo.

"Mr. Heagy, you understand, don't you, that the hospital can't assume responsibility for what happens?"

"We understand. I'll sign whatever papers are necessary."

Mother smiled and patted my hand. "Don't worry, Ronnie. I'll be with you during the day, and we'll turn the respirator back on at night until your lungs are stronger and can function on their own."

And that's exactly what we did—one breath at a time, until the respirator was wheeled away and the hole in my throat had healed.

It was wonderful to be able to talk again! After two months of unintelligible mumbling, I could finally express all the pent-up thoughts that had piled up in my mind. The weekend after the respirator was removed forever, Pennie, Mike, and I had a long-delayed gabfest, laughing, joking, and talking for hours.

As they started to leave Sunday night, Pennie put her arms around me. "I'd give anything for you to be well again, Ron," she said. "Mike and I miss you so much. We want you to come home."

"Hey, that may be sooner than you think. Getting off the respirator was just the first miracle. God's going to heal the rest of me too. Just you wait and see."

Pennie looked at me and smiled.

"Will you come see me play football when I'm drafted into the NFL?" I asked.

Her face brightened. "Silly," she said, shaking her head.

"No, I mean it, Pennie. I'm not going to stay in this stupid contraption forever. As soon as they take me to rehab and I can work out again, my muscles will start to come back. It'll happen. I'm gonna be all right."

"Well then, of course I'll come see you play football, Ron."

"Me too!" Mike chimed in.

"Hey! I've got something else to say to you, young man," I barked at Mike sternly.

"Yeah? What is it?" he asked warily.

I smiled at him. "Thanks, buddy. Thanks for saving my life."

Mike grinned shyly. "Ah, I didn't do it, Ron. It was God. I just helped Him out."

"I know that, Mike. I'm really starting to understand that God has been with me all the time." I paused, then smiled at him again. "I'm just glad you were there when He needed you!"

The next accomplishment was moving to a real bed. That happened when the day finally came for my halo—along with the pressure-producing calipers—to be removed. It was like being released from prison. Even though they sandbagged my head to keep it from moving, I could wiggle it just a little, and that was a real joy.

That same afternoon, a psychologist came in to interview me so he could determine whether I was mentally prepared to enter the first phase of rehabilitation. "How are you doing, Ron?" he asked.

"Much better, thank you."

"Good. I'm glad to hear that. Are you depressed?"

"No. Should I be?"

He gave me a quizzical look. "Most patients are…" The doctor cleared his throat and reframed his question. "After all you've been through, I thought you might be a bit discouraged."

He wasn't prepared for my answer. "Of course it hasn't been fun. No way! But I'm a Christian, Doctor, and I believe God is in control of my life. Without His help, I would still be on life support. He's helping me through this. He'll be with me all the way."

Mother looked at me. She winked, and I could read her thoughts: *Good answer!*

The next morning they transferred me to the sixth floor, and my therapy began in earnest. Progress was slow. After months of inactivity, the muscles and tendons in my neck were too weak to support the weight of my head. Rebuilding them was to be a slow, painstaking process. Each day my therapist massaged my neck before gently moving my head from side to side. "We need to massage the kinks out of your muscles first," she explained.

"Don't worry about hurting me," I told her. "I can take rough treatment. Used to be a wrestler, you know." I didn't want her to think that my muscles had always been flabby and my arms as skinny as pipe cleaners.

She laughed. "Be patient, Ron. We don't want to damage your fusion. These muscles and tendons need to be stretched and built back gradually."

"How long before I get to sit in a wheelchair?" I asked as though I hadn't heard her.

She kept on manipulating my neck and didn't answer right away. "I can see that you're an impatient and determined young man!" she said with a patient chuckle.

"You bet I am. I've got a football scholarship to Oregon State. I'm gonna do whatever it takes to get back on the football field again."

She stopped rubbing my shoulders and looked me straight in the eye. "Ron…that may never happen."

"Don't say that! It *will* happen, whether or not you believe it will. After all, the doctor said I'd always need a respirator, too, and look at me—" I took a deep breath and exhaled slowly to prove the point. "He was wrong."

She lifted my arm and while supporting it with one hand under my elbow asked, "Can you feel this?"

"No, not yet. But the feeling will come back. I've had pinched nerves before. It just takes time for them to heal." It was the old motormouth syndrome, returning with a vengeance.

She shook her head and looked me square in the face. "I don't think you realize how extensive your injuries are, Ron. This isn't just a pinched nerve. Your spinal cord was partially severed in the accident."

"So? My neck was broken too, but the fusion has healed it."

She raised my right leg and bent it at the knee several times before starting in on the left side. I saw what she was doing but could feel nothing, and my earlier optimism began to fade despite my bravado.

"Ron, do you understand what it means when a spinal cord is severed?"

"Not exactly. Besides, it wasn't completely severed. Only 70 percent."

"Muscles and tendons can be rejuvenated," she explained. "And bones can be fused and mended. But a severed nerve is a different story, and the spinal cord is a big bundle of nerves. It's like a banana. When it's twisted or broken, it can't be put back together."

Her words bothered me, but I still didn't accept what she was saying. *Okay, so doctors can't repair a severed spinal cord—but God can! He's already helped me defy the odds with the respirator; He'll help me walk again too. And then I'll travel the world, telling the story of what He did for me.*

If people remember May 18, 1980 as a momentous day, they probably associate it with Mt. St. Helens' eruption, an explosion that sent a plume of ashes hundreds of feet into the air and created a mudflow that destroyed everything in its path. But that was nothing compared with the accomplishment I celebrated that May morning when Dad helped the nurses lift me into a reclining wheelchair for the first time. I couldn't wait to be mobile, eagerly planning my maiden voyage down the hospital corridors.

But my enthusiasm diminished when they lifted me into the new wheelchair and I immediately tilted sideways like the Leaning Tower of Pisa. If one of the nurses hadn't caught me, I would have toppled out, flat on the floor.

Automatically, I gave myself the usual pep talk as the nurses propped me up and secured me in the chair. *No big deal, pal. So you're weak. Wouldn't anyone be after two months in bed? Once you get your strength back, you'll be able to sit up straight, and they won't have to strap you into this thing like a convict strapped in the electric chair. Keep your chin up. You'll do it!*

After all the straps were tightened and the nurses had checked that I was securely fastened in the chair, one of them adjusted the footrest to accommodate my long legs. "Are you comfortable?" she asked.

I nodded.

She patted my shoulder. "Okay, then enjoy your trial run, young man, but try not to exceed the hospital speed limit!"

Mom laughed—*What a wonderful sound,* I thought—and she asked, "Where do you want to go, Ronnie? You name it, and I'll take you there."

"First I'd like to find a full-length mirror and take a peek at myself in this fancy Rolls Royce."

"Okay. There's a mirror in the exercise room at the far end of this hall."

In high school I had often been complimented that I had the best "bod" on campus. I had also prided myself on being a sharp dresser. BMOC—that's how I had thought of myself.

Now one quick glance in the mirror shattered all my former illusions. Staring back at me was a frail, bony weakling wearing sagging socks, too-short sweatpants, and padded monster boots; his gaunt face had dark, sunken eyes, and his body reminded me of the pictures of concentration camp victims. *This can't be me! I'm looking at a 90-year-old cancer patient, slumped down into a pitiful heap in a wheelchair. His legs are like toothpicks, and his arms look like matchsticks. Where's the 18-year-old football star with the broad, muscular neck and bulging biceps? Where's Ron Heagy Jr.? And who is this bag of bones?*

My emotions, so high just a moment before, plunged to sub-zero. *I used to be somebody,* I thought morosely. *Now I'm a nobody, an 18-year-old cripple, strapped in a wheelchair, staring a hopeless future in the face.*

"Mom…maybe she was right," I said quietly.

"Who was right? Right about what?" she asked.

"My therapist. She said I might not get any better."

"But you are better, Ronnie! You're a little stronger every day."

"Will I ever walk again, Mom?"

It wasn't like Mom to dodge an issue, but she wasn't about to give up on me. "That is something only the Lord knows. Let's leave it in His hands and thank Him for this wheelchair."

On Memorial Day I was moved from a private room to a semiprivate room. For the first time since I'd been hospitalized, I had a roommate—eight-year-old Jimmy, who had been struck by an automobile while riding his bicycle. The medical team had thought the poor little guy was brain-dead, but eventually they decided his injuries weren't quite that severe, although he remained comatose. He hadn't spoken since the accident.

At first I'd been indignant to be forced to room with a little kid. *Come on!* I'd thought with disdain. *Just because I'm disabled you don't have to treat me like a pediatric case!* But since Jimmy never spoke, never made any noise, I forgot he was there most of the time.

My days were filled with intensive physical therapy designed to restore mobility to my arms. The therapists hoped to eventually make it possible for me to feed myself.

I was ecstatic when I heard the goal, but Dad was a realist. "If you regain the use of your arms, that will be wonderful, son. But don't build your hopes too high. Let's just wait and see what happens."

Then Mom dropped another bombshell. "Honey, now that you're going to be so busy with this intensive therapy, your doctors think it would be best for me not to stay in Portland any longer."

"What do you mean?" Stunned, my voice almost broke as I asked the question.

"It's been months since I've been with your dad and the kids. They've missed me, and I'm looking forward to being with them again. We'll still come for visits on the weekends and bring Karla. Besides, one of these days you'll be coming home, and I need to get everything ready. We've ordered a special telephone installed by your bed so you can call us whenever you feel like it. Okay, Ronnie? Can you handle that?"

My heart was saying, *No, Mom! Don't leave me! I CAN'T handle it!* Instead, I told her, "Sure, Mom. I understand. I'll miss you, but I'll be fine."

The occupational and physical therapy sessions stretched from morning until evening, with a break for lunch, so I didn't have a chance to feel lonely until after dinner at night. Then I could use the new telephone to stay in touch with my family and friends. My parents also bought a page turner for me, so I could read the Bible and turn the pages myself.

The atmosphere of the therapy unit was warm and relaxed. The nurses were friendly, and a special camaraderie existed among the wheel-chair patients. Some of the older ones had a knack for sensing whenever a newer patient was having a hard time. One of them, Al, assured me, "You'll get accustomed to being in a wheelchair after a while, Ron."

I smiled but shook my head. "I doubt it. I've got a scholarship to Oregon State to play football. I wanna play in the pros. Now look at me. I can't even lift a finger, much less a football."

Al chuckled. "Hey, you can still play. I do."

"From a wheelchair?"

"I play all kinds of computer games. And it's quite a challenge." He grinned. "The best part is you don't get any bumps and bruises. Just mental exercise."

"You use a computer? How?"

"By holding a pointer in my mouth. There are all kinds of things you can do with a pointer. They'll teach you in OT."

Al obviously hadn't lost his zest for life. "How long has it been for you?"

"You mean, how long have I been in a wheelchair?"

"Yes."

"Eleven years."

I looked at his serene expression and thought, *Eleven years? I would rather die than be in a wheelchair that long.*

"I know what you're thinking, Ron. You're saying, 'No way could I spend the rest of my life in a wheelchair.' But really, it isn't that bad... once you get adjusted."

"I hate being pushed around in this thing and having everyone stare at me," I whined.

"Yeah, I know what you mean. I felt the same way at first. But wait until you get your electric chair. No one will have to push you then. You can come and go as you please. And if someone stares, you can take off and leave them in the dust."

"Does it bug you when people yell, like they think you're deaf as well as paralyzed?"

Al laughed. "At first it did, but not anymore. Now I answer them in a voice barely above a whisper, and they get the message real quick."

Another patient, Bill, had broken his neck at age 16. "At the time," Bill told me, "I thought it was the end of everything. But actually my accident was only a new beginning."

I nodded grimly. *Right, pal. The beginning of hell on earth.*

Sunday, June 1, my parents came to visit, bringing along my high school diploma and my graduation mortarboard. I had missed the ceremonies back in Brownsville, but thanks to several friends and tutors, I'd completed the work needed to graduate. My parents adjusted the cap on my head and snapped a few pictures while I tried to smile and keep from thinking about how much I had missed.

The next afternoon in occupational therapy, I argued with the therapist that it just wasn't necessary for me to learn how to write with a pen held in my mouth.

"Wouldn't it be more practical to retrain the muscles in my shoulders and arms so I can use my hands again? You know, like Joni Eareckson Tada did. Then I could feed myself too," I insisted.

My therapist was a jovial and positive lady who tried to inspire her students to rise above their disabilities. "Father's Day is coming up, and I just thought you might like to make a card for your dad."

"Well…sure. Okay."

Learning to write with a pen in my mouth was a real challenge, and my first efforts were extremely crude. But when Dad read the card I had made for him, it didn't seem to matter. As he read the words I'd written so laboriously, he blinked rapidly and pressed his lips together tightly, then reached for a handkerchief to blow his nose before looking at me with twinkling eyes. "Thank you, Ronnie," he said. Seeing how moved he was by my efforts gave me the same sense of exhilaration I had always felt when he had slapped my shoulder after a football game and told me, "Good game, son. I'm proud of you."

Learning how to write with my mouth was one thing; learning how to drive with my chin was another matter completely! I was excited to learn that the Social Services Department ordered a new chin-guided chair for me, and while waiting for it to arrive, I struggled through "drivers' ed" lessons in a hospital loaner chair. In the beginning, I bumped into everything and everybody unfortunate enough to be in my way. Those who watched from a safe distance must have been thoroughly entertained, seeing me play bumper cars in the OT room.

It took a while, but I finally mastered the knack of steering it before any pedestrians were killed or maimed. After that, my chair became my most prized possession. It represented freedom. Now, all I needed was a lift into the seat, then I could scoot all over the place unassisted. Hallelujah!

I was so busy enjoying my new mobility that for several days I didn't stop to realize what the $9,000 wheelchair that had been ordered for me really meant. Finally, it dawned on me: The insurance company would not have made such an investment if there were any hope that I would regain the use of my legs. At the same time this discouraging thought wedged itself in my mind, I noticed that some of the patients in physical therapy who had come in after I did were already using walkers or crutches. Yet, I had seen virtually no improvement in my own sensory perception since therapy first began.

I finally challenged one of the therapists. "Hey man, what are all these exercises accomplishing? My arms and legs are still as numb as they were on day one. Shouldn't I be having some kind of sensation in my hands and feet by now?"

The therapist avoided eye contact. "Ron, that's the kind of question you should ask your doctor. He knows more about that than I do."

A few days later the doctor scheduled a staff conference with my parents. Although I attended the conference and it was my condition being discussed, I was pretty much excluded from the conversation.

"Mr. and Mrs. Heagy, we have tried to help your son regain at least partial mobility. At first we thought the feeling might return to his arms, but it hasn't." The doctor paused. "I think our consensus is now that there is nothing more we can do for him."

Dad was the first to recover from shock. "You mean…this is it? There's nothing more you can do?"

The doctor nodded. "I'm sorry, Mr. Heagy. We've tried everything."

"Maybe *you* have given up, Doctor, but we haven't," Dad told him.

Mother was just as emphatic. "There has to be something we haven't tried yet."

"Mrs. Heagy, please believe me. I know how you feel," the doctor continued. "But your son's injuries are permanent. Too many nerves were severed during the accident. They can't be regained. If Ron were my son, I would take him home and help him adjust." He paused. "Or you might consider a full-care facility."

Dad stood to his feet. "That isn't an option, sir. Our son won't be put in a home for the disabled as long as I am alive."

Too stunned to speak, I sat dumbly in my wheelchair as the medical staff members filed solemnly out of the room. Mom and Dad were also silent, but Mom reached across the arm of her chair and grasped my hand. "We're not giving up, Ronnie," she whispered.

Before they left that night, my parents put me in bed. Mom tucked the blankets under my chin just as she had when I was a child. "Don't worry, Ronnie. I know God has a wonderful plan for your future, and I can hardly wait to have you home with us again and find out where He'll lead us."

Dad prayed for me and asked the Lord to give me a good night's rest, then they left for home. I managed to hold back my tears until I could no longer hear their footsteps retreating down the hall. Then the dam broke. I wept uncontrollably, sobbing and crying out to God. "Lord, I don't want to live like this," I sobbed. "Please let me die. I can't take care of myself, can't dig a ditch, can't play football, can't hug my girl or hold her hand. What kind of a man is that? I'll only be a burden to my family, Lord. Please…please just let me die."

In the darkness of my room, a small, faltering voice whispered my name. "R-o-nnnn."

I held my breath and listened. Had someone come into the room unnoticed? I tried to control my gasping sobs so I could hear the voice again.

"R-o-n…"

It was Jimmy.

He hadn't spoken a word for weeks, not since he'd arrived at the hospital. I had resented being put in the same room with the tiny juvenile, considering such a pipsqueak unworthy company for me, the cool, mature, football-playing would-be surfer. I had ignored him, treated him like a vegetable, and now, in the darkness, frail little Jimmy was reaching across the sea of hopelessness, tossing a lifeline to the sobbing man in the other bed.

"Ron…," the little voice whispered again. "I…I love you."

12

Signs and Sirens

~

I never heard Jimmy speak again except in my memory, where his words have inspired and encouraged me for two decades. That night, hearing his voice as I lay crying, I felt ashamed of myself, realizing the little guy was in much worse shape than I was, but I had never heard *him* sobbing in the darkness.

Jimmy's words changed me. Oh sure, I was still paralyzed; nothing could change *that*. But I had a good mind, and I could communicate. I could reach out to others who were hurting, the way Jimmy had reached out to me.

"God, forgive me for my selfish attitude," I prayed. "Please help me remember that I am created in Your image and committed to doing Your work here on earth. Help me to be Your ambassador, Lord. Show me how to be an encourager to people who are hurting. Show me how to be like Jimmy."

Karla noticed the subtle change in my attitude, and looking back on it, I realize now that it may have given her the wrong message.

"You're one great gal, Karla. Thanks for sticking by me," I told her a few days after Jimmy had spoken.

"Don't worry, Ron. The only way you'll get rid of me is to say, 'Karla, it's over between us. Get lost! I don't ever want to see you again.'"

Karla was quiet for a few seconds, then she picked up my hand and held it to her cheek. "I can see the change in you, Ron. At first, you seemed…I don't know. It almost seemed like you were angry with God."

"I suppose I was," I answered honestly. "I felt ripped off, and in the beginning I couldn't understand why He had let this happen. Sometimes I wanted to die, but now I'm learning to live one day at a time and to let God take care of tomorrow."

Karla and I had always been able to discuss our spiritual feelings; it was a habit we'd developed in the Bible study we both attended. The first time I met her I'd been attracted by her sweet spirit as well as her good looks.

She visited me regularly, and we filled every minute with lighthearted chitchat as well as heartfelt feelings. Karla always brought me up to date on what was happening at school and with all our friends in Brownsville. As she left one day, she kissed me good-bye and promised to come back soon, then turned and disappeared down the corridor, her blonde hair bouncing as she walked.

Ten minutes later she was back. I looked up, surprised, when she quietly reappeared. "I forgot to tell you something," she said.

"You did? What?"

"I love you, Ron. You're a wonderful guy."

One Sunday when my family and Karla came to visit, Dad suggested we go for pizza at an Italian restaurant within walking distance of Good Sam. It was my first excursion away from the hospital, and I was ecstatically happy—until a stranger stopped us as Dad wheeled me back to the hospital after we'd eaten. The man glanced at me briefly, then asked Dad, "What happened to him?"

Instantly, the euphoria I'd enjoyed being out of the hospital vanished. I wanted to say, "Hey, buddy, just because I'm paralyzed doesn't mean I'm deaf too. If you want to know what happened, why don't you ask me?"

Instead, Dad said it for me, calmly answering, "My son can speak for himself, sir."

"I…I'm sorry," the stranger stammered. "I didn't mean to offend."

"I was in a diving accident and broke my neck," I told him.

"Oh…I'm sorry to hear that." The stranger walked away, and I wondered if the incident would haunt his memory as I knew it would haunt mine.

Karla and my family came back to Portland a few weekends later for the annual Festival of Roses. They spent the morning with me, then headed off for the festival. I wanted to see the parade in the worst way, but since no one had a van or other vehicle large enough to accommodate my wheelchair, it was impossible for me to go with them. Karla volunteered to stay at the hospital with me, but that didn't seem fair. "I don't want you to miss the fun because of me, Karla," I told her when the others were ready to leave. "Why don't you go with them?"

"I wouldn't enjoy it without you."

"Of course you would. After all, it will only be for a couple of hours. And I can watch the parade on television."

She shook her head and gave me a quick hug. "I'd much rather stay here, Ron. We can go places and do things together after you're better. Until then, I'm not leaving you alone. Okay?"

"Okay, if you insist—and thanks."

We had a good afternoon, just the two of us, talking and watching the festival on television. Karla's attentiveness never ceased to amaze me, but being with her also made me realize how little I had to offer her in return.

After she left that night, I lay awake thinking. *Did she realize how uncertain my future was likely to be? Would she still be faithful to me if I remained a quadriplegic? What if…?*

For most of my life, I had focused upon external qualities, measuring success in terms of personal achievements. I had been a Big Man on Campus when Karla and I had started dating. Now I was a nobody, and it didn't seem logical to me that a beautiful, popular girl like Karla could look beneath the surface and love me for the person I was inside. I knew I wouldn't have been able to do that before I became disabled myself.

Being a naive and confused young man, I asked God for an outward sign of some sort. "Lord, whatever You've got planned for me, I'll accept. I love You, Lord, and I want to do Your will. But right now I need a little reassurance. If you could give me some sign that Karla is sincere and doesn't merely feel sorry for me, it would mean a lot. I know it's silly, Lord, but if…if the fire alarm goes off tonight, I'll know it's true."

At midnight an earsplitting siren echoed through the hospital halls. The fire alarm was blaring.

Was this God's sign to me? Or was a raging inferno about to sweep through the hospital, incinerating all of us helpless patients?

It was a minute or two before a nurse appeared in the doorway. "Sorry about that. Just go back to sleep; it was a false alarm."

After she left, I lay awake, too keyed up to relax. "Lord," I whispered, "I hate to ask it, but if this really *was* a sign from You, would You please, well…would You please do it again?"

At 2:00 a.m., another false alarm rang through the building.

13

Something to Live For

~

As Uncle Bruce's station wagon rolled to a stop in front of our unfinished log cabin, my mind swirled with a dozen emotions. I was overjoyed to be coming home on a weekend furlough, a trial run to see if my family could handle my care on their own. But at the same time, the weathered framework of the log house, an abandoned skeleton silhouetted against the cloudless sky, sent me plunging into a bottomless pit of "if onlys." *If only I had stayed home during spring break and helped Dad work on our house,* I reminded myself, *it would be finished by now and I wouldn't be trapped in a wheelchair.* Instead, work on the house had all but stopped due to a lack of money and manpower.

Then I saw my crippled little car, the Bug that had carried Mike and me off on what was supposed to have been a fabulous week of fun. I had worked hard to pay for that little car. What a thrill it had been to sit behind the wheel, drive onto the school parking lot, and show off in front of the girls! Next to it was my motorcycle. *Oh, man! I can hardly wait to ride it again!* The thought popped into my mind before I could stop it.

Another emotion—*fear*—also rattled around my head. *How will Mom and Dad cope with this? Will they have the strength and endurance to handle my helplessness?*

"Welcome home, Ron," Mom said in her warm, reassuring way as she turned her head to smile at me from the front seat. She must have known what I was thinking. "There were times when we wondered if we'd ever see this day, but here you are, another prayer answered. We're so glad to have you back home with us."

"Your mom is right, Ron," Karla said, leaning over and putting an arm around my shoulders. "We've all prayed that God would bring you back to us, and He has."

Mike and Pennie came bounding out the front door. "Hi, Ron!" Mike said with a wide grin. "I was so glad you were coming home, I washed and waxed your car for you—for free. Even polished your motorcycle. How do they look?"

"Great! Thanks, Mike! But don't get any wrong ideas just because I can't drive them right now."

"Scrooge!" he taunted. "Just wait 'til I get my license. You'll want me to be your chauffeur then, but I'll make you beg."

We made it through the weekend without any serious problems, and I hated having to return to the hospital in Portland on Sunday night. But knowing I'd be back home for good in just a few days made it easier.

The following Friday, Mom pushed me in a hospital wheelchair down the corridors of Good Sam and out to my family's Volkswagen "bus." Leaving took quite a while because we had several stops to make, saying good-bye to all my caregivers. With each good-bye, I felt a little pang of worry. Leaving the hospital meant leaving behind the professional support I had relied on so totally. It also meant giving up some of my newfound mobility, because my own electric, chin-guided chair wouldn't arrive until November, and although Dad had been shopping for a van with a wheelchair lift, he hadn't been able to find one in our price range.

The drive back to Brownsville took 90 minutes, and as we pulled into the driveway again, I thought, *Well, here goes the rest of your life, Ron. It's not exactly what you had planned, but it's all you've got.*

Karla came over to spend the afternoon. It was a beautiful summer day, still warm and balmy but with a hint of the July heat that was just around the corner. We sat outside while she brought me up to date on the latest news about our friends and their activities. Many were already away at college, enrolled in the summer session; others had left to work at summer jobs. Several had gone camping at the beach over the weekend, and one couple planned to go horseback riding after church.

Karla picked up my paralyzed hand and held it to her cheek. "Someday, when you're better Ron, we'll go horseback riding too. And I can hardly wait!"

I hesitated a moment, wondering what to say. "Karla, you must get awfully bored sitting on the sidelines with me while everyone else is out having fun."

"Of course not, Ron! Why would you say such a thing?"

She held my hand in both of hers before answering. "You've got to get over being so sensitive. I'm here because I want to be. You are a special guy, Ronald Heagy, and I enjoy spending time with you. We've gone over that before. Right?"

"But…what if I *don't* get any better, Karla?" I searched her pretty face for an answer as she pondered my question.

"Of course you're going to get better! It just takes time, Ron. We've got to be patient and pray for a miracle."

After she left, I told Mom about our conversation. "Karla still thinks someday we'll be able to do the things we used to do, Mom."

"Karla could be right, Ron. Someday you may be riding horses again. Miracles do happen, you know," she answered. Mother was still pleading with God in daily prayers to give me back the use of my arms and hands so I wouldn't be totally helpless, and like Karla, she was confident her prayers would be answered.

But I no longer shared their confidence.

Our little garage-house was filled with visitors the rest of that summer as relatives took turns visiting us. Having so much company was hard on Mom while she was also attending to all my needs, but she managed everything in her usual good humor.

Never once did she or Dad complain or imply in any way that I was a burden to them. But in my overly sensitive state, the thought constantly lurked in the back of my mind that taking care of me on a 24-hour basis was becoming too much of a burden. Someone always had to be there to feed me, give me a bath, put me to bed at night, and get me up and dressed in the morning. It was a never-ending cycle!

I still needed someone to roll me over at night, and even with regular changes in position, pressure sores developed on my back and hips that required weeks to heal. Family members took turns sleeping close by my bed so they could help, but I dreaded having to disturb them—and sometimes didn't.

My sister, Pennie, and I were just as close as Mike and I had always been. Whenever she felt discouraged during our younger years, I could usually make her laugh. More than once Pennie cried on my shoulder after she'd had a disagreement with Mom and Dad or a fight with someone at school. Now our roles were reversed.

One night when I called her for help, I heard Pennie heave a sigh of exasperation as she came into my room. I didn't blame her for being annoyed. After all, she had been out late on a date, and I had awakened her from a sound sleep. But her sigh made me feel like a worm. I lay awake, crying and miserably condemning myself after she had gone back to bed.

Pennie heard me sniffling and came in again. "Ron, is something wrong?"

"No. No…I'm fine."

Pennie didn't budge. "No, you aren't fine. You're crying, for heaven's sake. Tell me what's wrong."

"It makes me feel terrible to wake you up at night, Pennie. I hate being such a burden to everyone—you, Mike, Mom, and Dad. Sometimes I wish I could die."

That's all it took to make Pennie cry too. She encircled me with both arms and put her cheek close to mine. "Oh, Ronnie. I'm so sorry. Please forgive me if I sounded impatient. You aren't a burden, and none of us mind getting up. Honest. We love you." She stroked my forehead. "If there's anything I can do to make your life easier, just tell me."

"Well…there is one thing," I said, sniffling again.

"What's that?"

"Would you please blow my nose!"

We both laughed as she took a tissue out of the box on my bedside table, held it to my nose, and dried my tears. Then she gave me a goodnight kiss before going back to bed. Pennie had Mom's tender touch.

Mike, on the other hand, had good intentions, but lacked somewhat in his execution. Like many teenagers, he was a very sound sleeper, and it was hard for me to wake him up. Each time I finally managed to awaken him, he would stagger into my dark room like a zombie, literally bouncing off the walls and asking, "Where are you?"

"Right here, Mike. I haven't moved an inch since you came in last time."

Grumbling as he groped in the darkness, he would finally stumble into the bed. "I just turned you over, man. Why do you keep bugging me?"

"Mike, that was three hours ago."

"Oh."

While still in a sleepwalking trance, he would roll me over and stumble back to bed, quickly returning to a deep sleep. The next morning he usually couldn't remember one thing that had happened during the night.

At first, everyone seemed to tiptoe around me, treating me with extra courtesy and patience, as one does a beloved grandparent who's come for a visit. Quite soon, however, the normal family patterns reemerged, including occasional bickering.

Occasionally Dad and I had an argument, usually over petty issues like the way I wanted to wear my clothes or have my hair combed. Each time we did clash, my depression increased. These confrontations made me feel I had completely lost control of my life.

Sometimes, when Dad was preoccupied, he became impatient. One morning as he dressed me, one of my hands got caught in the sleeve of my jacket, and Dad hurriedly yanked it to force my arm through. Neither of us realized that something unusual had happened until blood trickled onto my pants' leg. Only then did we discover that my little fingernail had been partially ripped off.

The mishap wasn't Dad's fault; it could have happened to anyone. But Dad felt terrible about it. "I'm sorry, Ronnie," he said, his face awash with anguish. "I didn't mean to hurt you."

"It's nothing. Don't worry, Dad," I told him. "I can't feel a thing!"

Lost in self-pity, I began interpreting everything Dad did as a gesture of frustration and impatience. I began to think again that my life was no longer worth living and wracked my mind for a way I could make a permanent exit.

It's impossible to take a drug overdose or slash my wrists without help, I thought, going down the list of possibilities. There was no place I could get to without help where I could throw myself off a cliff. Hanging was out of the question; who would I get to tie the noose? Then it came to me. *Maybe I can drown myself. Yes! That's it! The first time Dad leaves me in the shower alone, I'll put an end to everybody's misery.*

On weekends, Dad usually got me bathed and dressed in the morning so Mom could sleep a little later. I looked forward to the following Saturday, planning my suicide.

When Dad rolled me into the shower Saturday morning, I was committed. He turned on the warm water, adjusted the showerhead, and asked if I was all set.

"Sure am!" I said with the cheeriest voice I could muster.

When he left, I tilted my head back, inhaled deeply, and repeatedly sucked water into my lungs. Thinking about it now, I guess it was a pretty silly way to try to kill myself, but at the time I was seriously looking for a way out.

When Dad returned a few minutes later, he found me coughing, choking, and gasping for air. He raised my arms and pounded me on the back, asking frantically, "Ron, what happened? Are you okay?"

At first I wasn't going to tell him, but when I finally could breathe normally again, I broke down. Like a dam bursting, all my frustrations poured out in a flood of hot tears and choking accusations.

Poor Dad! He hadn't realized all these feelings had been festering inside my mind. Wrapping me in his strong arms, he apologized for being impatient and assured me that my status as his beloved son would never change. And he established a new family rule. After that, whenever anyone's feelings were hurt, we got them out in the open with a family conference. Everyone sat around the kitchen table, and we discussed our differences and found a way to solve the problem, whatever it was.

Never again did I consider suicide a viable option. Instead, I focused on my grandmother Buckmaster's philosophy. On one of her visits, I asked, "Grandma, how did you raise nine children with so little money and without losing your sanity?"

She looked at me with a twinkle in her eyes. "I did it one day at a time, Ronnie. One day at a time. And that's what you've got to do now. Don't look back. Don't worry about tomorrow. Just take it one day at a time."

Following her advice, I suffered fewer emotional upsets after that, but physical problems continued to plague me. Bladder infections were the worst. One infection followed another until it seemed I was constantly taking antibiotics.

Suspecting kidney stones, the doctor put me back in the hospital to run tests. One of the tests nearly proved fatal. When iodine dye was injected into my veins, I immediately began having breathing problems, then lost consciousness and went into cardiac arrest. Once again an expert medical team restarted my heart and brought me back from the brink.

Eventually I had to undergo more surgery to correct the problem. Although the doctors said the operation was successful, the infections have continued.

The other chronic problems I had to endure seemed minor compared with "the biggie"—incontinence. That was the hardest thing to accept, not only because it infringed on my most personal privacy but also because it was a very distasteful job for others. If my family considered me a burden, however, they did a masterful job of concealing it.

Although Dad helped with my care on the weekends, during the week most of the work fell on Mom, who lovingly showered, shaved, shampooed, dressed, and fed me every morning. She rarely finished before noon, and even though she never once complained, I knew she was enduring severe migraine headaches, and I worried that they were caused by all the stress she was under.

One day when Mom seemed especially stressed, I watched her scurrying around the house, wiping the table, putting away the dishes, and folding laundry. "I'm sorry," I said softly.

She stopped folding a towel and laid it on a stack of freshly laundered sheets before looking up at me. "What are you sorry for, son?"

"That I cause you so much extra work. I'm really sorry."

Mother walked across the room and gave me a hug. "I love you, Ronnie. You're my son. Taking care of you is a privilege, not a chore. I do get tired, but God always gives me the strength that's needed. So don't you worry about it anymore."

"I know you've having migraines…"

"I've had them for years."

"Living like this doesn't make life any easier for you. If I hadn't gone to California on that wild goose chase, the house would be finished by now, and we wouldn't be hopelessly in debt."

"God will meet our needs, Ronnie. He always has in the past, and He will in the future."

"Neither you nor Dad deserve this. You're worn out most of the time, and he works 12-hour shifts just to make ends meet. It isn't fair."

"Maybe not. But life isn't always fair, and there are some things we have no control over. This is one of them." Suddenly her expression brightened. "Besides, there's always tomorrow. Things are bound to get better."

I resolved to follow Mom's positive example and heed Grandma Buck-master's wise advice. Instead of slipping back into cesspools of remorse, I concentrated on all the things I could still do and took one day at a time.

One of the new things I tried was painting. With Mom's prodding, I read Joni Eareckson Tada's books detailing her struggle to cope with disabilities similar to mine. Inspired by Joni, later that year I enrolled in a beginning art class at Linn Benton Community College.

It was amusing to see the expression of surprise and disbelief on the instructor's face when a friend pushed me into the classroom that first morning. The other students looked at me, then at my wheelchair, and no doubt wondered if I was in the wrong room. For the first couple of weeks, I wondered the same thing as I drew crude squiggles, lopsided spheres, and unrecognizable still-life sketches with a charcoal pencil clenched between my teeth.

My first efforts were pathetic, and many times I was tempted to quit, but persistence finally paid off. By the end of that semester, I could control a pencil or pen with some degree of dexterity, and the teacher gave me a final grade of C, along with some encouraging words of praise.

Then came one of those "fork-in-the-road" experiences that would eventually give meaning and purpose to the rest of my life. Toward the middle of July, I went with Mom, Dad, and Mike to visit Pennie at Cannon Beach Conference Grounds. It literally dumbfounded me when the staff asked if I would give my testimony during one of the conference assemblies. My first reaction was to say no. I hated being stared at, and I imagined myself getting tongue-tied in front of an audience. But I knew how much it would mean to Mom and Dad to have me do it, so I reluctantly agreed.

My heart was pounding when I was rolled onto the platform and turned to face the large audience. I swallowed hard, drew in a breath, and began. Suddenly my fear and misgivings vanished. Telling my story wasn't difficult at all.

Then came the best part. The assembled teenagers responded with gratifying warmth and courtesy. Several of them even wanted to talk with me afterward.

For the first time since March 17, I felt there was something worth-while I could still do. *Maybe God can use me after all,* I thought. *Maybe this is His way of showing me how I can encourage others—like little Jimmy encouraged me.*

14

Sad and Happy Endings

〜

I n late August, most of my friends were busy working or getting ready to leave for college, but Karla—despite the fact that she was now studying to become an X-ray technician—came regularly to take me for walks or for a ride through the countryside.

As much as I enjoyed being with Karla, our relationship also had a negative side. She had not accepted my disability as irreversible, and her unchanging attitude bothered me more and more as summer came to an end. I cringed when she said things like, "When you get better, we'll go skiing."

One day as we sat by the river, she said, "Someday when you get well, we'll ride over these trails again on your motorcycle."

"Karla…," I wanted to stop her, to take her by the shoulders and make her face reality. Instead I said simply, "I think you'd better take me back home."

She looked at me with a startled expression. "Why, Ron? Did I say something that hurt your feelings?"

"No. I'm just tired. Let's go home."

As soon as Karla had disappeared down the driveway, I poured out my heart to Mom. "I love Karla, Mom. I want to marry her and have a family. I want to work and take care of her. It tortures me to know that I may never be able to do that. But even worse, I don't think she accepts the fact that I'll *never* get better."

Mom was quiet a moment, maybe thinking I was voicing my frustration with *her* unchanging hope for my future as well as Karla's. Then she said slowly, "Karla is one in a million, Ron, a girl any man could be proud to have for his wife. But if she can't face the fact that things between you may never be like they were, and if your relationship is causing you this much pain, maybe you should stop seeing each other."

"I agree, Mom. But it kills me even to think about it."

The next time Karla and I were together she seemed to sense that something was different. She squeezed my hand, held it against her cheek, and asked, "Ron, can you feel this?"

"No, Karla, my hand is numb," I answered flatly.

She squeezed it harder. "Can you feel this?"

I looked at her familiar features, at the way wisps of blonde hair curled around the nape of her neck, and I wanted to cry. "Karla, I can't feel anything—and maybe I never will. I may *never* get better, Karla; that's the reality here. I...I don't think you can deal with that fact. My disability is *permanent.*"

Shaking her head, she raised a finger to my lips as if to stop me, but I was determined to get the words out.

"Maybe...maybe we should stop seeing each other—at least for a while, until you've had time to think things through and understand what all this means."

I watched the expression change on her face from resistance to hurt. "But I love you, Ron. I always will. Can't we wait a while? Things could change. You *could* get better. Miracles happen; you know they do."

I forced myself to continue. "No, Karla. We can't live our lives waiting for a miracle. You deserve a man who can hold you in his arms and take care of you. I wish I could be that man..." My voice was trembling; it was all I could do to hold back the tears. "I wish I could, Karla—but I can't!"

She silently dropped her head and pressed her fingers hard against her lips, then raised her blue eyes to focus on mine. Finally she understood. Our future together had died in March on a California beach.

Breaking up with Karla pitched me headlong into another pit of gloom, but other things were happening that lifted my spirits. One day Dad came home from work bursting with excitement. "You'll never guess what happened," he said. "When I mentioned to my friends at the mill how hard it is to manipulate Ron's wheelchair on our gravel driveway, several men volunteered to help me pour a cement slab!"

That evening he and Mike started digging trenches and laying the forms while I watched and wished I could help. After the thoughtful friends poured the cement and completed the slab, Dad began working on the house again. On September 10, he completed the roof, nailing the last shingle in place. Now all we needed was a loan so we could hire a contractor to finish the exterior walls and install the cabinets. Our dream of a two-story, log home was about to become a reality.

A few months later, the loan was approved and the final construction began. Watching the carpenters fit in place the fragrant pine logs we'd ordered from Montana, I remembered what a bonding experience it had been for Dad and me to work on the house together. Twice we had narrowly survived accidents that could have had serious consequences. Once the extension ladder I was standing on slipped sideways, and I lost my balance. I dropped ten feet before frantically grabbing a ceiling beam and breaking my fall. Now, we both laughed as we remembered how I had clung to the beam, dangling like a monkey, until Dad propped the ladder back in place. I was lucky to escape that calamity with only some splinters and scratches—and a denuded armpit.

Laughing after I was back on the ground, Dad had said, "Better to scrape your arm than to break your neck, right?"

A few days later, the scaffolding Dad was standing on shifted under his weight, and he tumbled from the second floor to the concrete below. Scrambling to climb down from my own scaffolding to help him, I was certain he was badly hurt, but before I could get to him, he was back on his feet, brushing the dirt off his shirt and pants.

It was my turn to laugh. "Wow! That was a close call. We're pretty lucky, huh Dad?"

"No, son; I don't believe in luck. The good Lord was protecting us," he responded as he picked up his hammer. "Maybe He's warning us to be more careful."

Now, with professionals doing the work, our beautiful log cabin home was finished in record time, and we finally moved in, absorbing the pine's sweet-smelling fragrance that permeated the entire house. I don't know who was more thrilled, Mom or me. She was ecstatic to have a large, convenient kitchen, a spacious living room with a wood-burning fireplace, and a real bedroom instead of a bed in a travel trailer! And as far as I was concerned, having my own room seemed close to heaven. It became my sanctuary, a place where I could have privacy and feel in control. The bathroom was equipped with a roll-in shower, and Dad installed a telephone, my stereo system, and the television in my bedroom so I could use a mouth stick to push buttons on the remote control. Now I could watch TV or listen to music from my bed and not disturb anyone else. I also enjoyed talking to my friends on the telephone without being overheard by the entire family.

About that time, another good thing happened. Some incredibly generous people gave us a gift that brought our transportation problems to an end. Dad hadn't found a lift-equipped van we could afford, so anytime I went somewhere, my wheelchair, with me in it, had to be lifted into the side of our old VW bus—a heavy job that took two strong men. A couple of times, the chair had slipped as I was lifted in, and I fell onto the pavement. Once inside, I couldn't sit up straight because of the low roof, and traveling any distance in that cramped position was very uncomfortable. Faced with this nearly impossible challenge every time I needed to leave the house, we all had been praying for God to help us locate a van we could afford.

Our prayers were answered one day when a wonderful local couple, John and Bessie Miller, quietly presented Dad with the keys to a brand-new green Ford van, complete with wheelchair lift! I felt like Cinderella seeing her beautiful coach for the first time. But this was no fairy tale; the Millers had given us the title as well as the keys. The van was ours, a gift from two very kind people—and God.

I immediately christened it the Green Bean and from then on have traveled in comfort wherever the Lord has led.

The next summer I was delighted to receive a phone call from Annette. I had heard from her only once or twice since returning home and assumed she wasn't interested in continuing our relationship. That's why her call came as a surprise.

"I thought I might come up your way for a few days," she said. "That is, if you want me to."

"Super! We've moved into the log cabin, and I'd love for you to see it. You could share Pennie's room," I said. I didn't want her to have any misconceptions; she had to know what to expect. "The last time you saw me I was strapped on that horrible Stryker frame. Remember?"

"I sure do! So what's going on now?"

"Well, I'm in a wheelchair, and I get around pretty well. But, uh, the doctors have told me I'll never walk again."

There was the briefest silence on the other end of the line. Then she said, "I'm sorry to hear that, Ron. I thought maybe—"

"Yeah, I know. We all did, but every story doesn't have a happy ending."

After we hung up, I thought, *Well, I told her. If she wants to reconsider and not come to see me, there's still time for her to back out gracefully.*

I was overjoyed a few days later when Annette called to let me know when her plane would arrive. As my cousin Brad drove me to the airport in the Green Bean, I was as jittery as a teenager on his first date.

As Annette walked down the ramp and waved to us, I exclaimed to Brad under my breath, "Man! She's even more beautiful than I remembered."

"Cool it, dude," he answered with a grin. "Never let a pretty girl throw you for a loop."

Annette greeted us both warmly, and that familiar flirtatious spark flashed in her blue eyes when they met mine. For a second I was tempted to tell her how beautiful she looked, then I remembered Brad's warning and swallowed my words.

My family was happy to see Annette too. But, sensing that we wanted to be alone, after dinner they discreetly disappeared and left us alone in the living room. I smiled warmly, thinking how nice it was to have Annette with me. But her words were not the ones I'd hoped to hear.

"Ron, there is something I think you should know," she began, getting right to the point. "You're a great guy, and I admire you very much. But…"

I couldn't speak. When she had agreed to come to Oregon even after hearing that my disabilities were permanent, I'd assumed we could pick up our relationship where we had left off. Instead, her tone was sending a completely different message.

"I don't know how to say this without hurting you. I wish things could be different. I've tried to accept…really I have. But I simply can't cope…"

How ironic, I thought. *Just a few months ago, I was looking into Karla's big blue eyes and saying good-bye, and now here I am, lost in another pair of sparkly blue eyes, and saying good-bye again. This is the way it's going to be...I know it, I feel it. No woman will ever want to get involved with a quadriplegic.*

When she fumbled for words, stopping in the middle of the sentence, I finished it for her. "You can't cope with my disability? That's what you're saying, isn't it?"

"Forgive me, Ron. I didn't mean to hurt you."

"It's okay, Annette. I understand, and I appreciate your being honest with me, not leading me on and making me think you have feelings for me when you don't."

"I do have feelings for you, Ron," she said sincerely. "But they're feelings of friendship."

She stayed for eight days. Good old Brad chauffeured us to the coast one day and to the mountains the next. The more time we spent together, the more determined I became to prove to Annette—as well as to myself—that a disability didn't prevent me from being good company and a worthwhile individual. I felt sure Annette was enjoying herself, and that gave me encouragement.

Several times when we were riding together in the Green Bean and Brad turned a sharp corner, I purposely leaned against her shoulder. She didn't pull away. She even reached over, picked up my hand, and held it in hers.

The night before she left, we talked again about our feelings for each other. I couldn't help but hope that the time we'd spent together had made a difference, but her words set me straight. "Ron, I've enjoyed being with you again," she said. "You mean more to me than I realized. But—"

"Don't say it, Annette. I already know. But I'm glad we can still be friends."

"I'm glad you understand, Ron. Believe me, you'll always have a special place in my heart."

"Mine too, Annette. Thanks for coming. I just wonder...would you mind...? You know, you were the first girl I ever kissed, and I was hoping..."

"What?"

"Would you kiss me again, for old time's sake?"

Annette came over to my wheelchair, eased onto my lap, slid both arms around my neck, and gave me a lingering good-bye kiss.

As her lips pressed against mine, I wondered if this was the last kiss I'd ever know.

15

Quacks and Cackles

~

I had accepted my disability—almost. An entry in Mom's diary proved that we were both praying on the same wavelength. She wrote:

Dear Lord, I ask you—no, I am begging you, Lord—to give Ronnie back the use of his arms. He doesn't want to live like this and be dependent upon others for the rest of his life. You know how helpless he feels, Lord. Please, please show us what we can do, where we can go for help. We are asking You for a miracle, Lord, and I am thanking You for your answer in advance.

Friends, relatives, and chance acquaintances joined us in researching spinal cord injuries, and the assortment of discovered cures ranged from weird to outlandish. But Mom and I were willing to try almost anything. Mom put me on a megavitamin and mineral program, hoping it would help heal my damaged nerves. I gained some weight, but nothing else happened.

Next we tried various massage techniques with the same negative results.

Then came the DSMO episode. Some well-meaning soul told Mom about a brand of liniment used to heal lame horses. We were desperate enough—maybe *gullible* would be a more accurate term—to purchase an ample supply and start rubbing it on my shoulders and neck. The stuff smelled like oysters and was every bit as slimy. Not only did it have an obnoxious odor, but the nasty stuff was absorbed into my system, causing everything I ate to taste like fish. I was one grateful guy when we finally gave up on that remedy.

As a last resort, we contacted a "naturopathic doctor" in Idaho who, according to a couple of reports, had been having phenomenal results healing spinal cord injuries. When we wrote to ask for information, he sent us a complimentary video showing a formerly paralyzed young man walking without even a cane. The accompanying literature attributed the doctor's success to vitamin therapy, electrical stimulus, and something called "colonic cleansing."

It sounded impressive. Watching the video, my enthusiasm soared. *Maybe this is the miracle we've been praying for.*

On a bleak winter morning, Mom, Mike, Mom's friend Wanda, and I headed for Idaho in the Green Bean. The beautiful scenery inspired us, building our hopes and sending our imaginations running ahead to a happy future. We were driving through a winter wonderland with snowflakes floating in the air and icicles dripping from the tree branches. Despite the beautiful landscape—not to mention the icy road conditions—we were so eager to reach our destination that Mom stopped only for necessities: food, restrooms, and gasoline.

When we arrived in the Idaho city where the doctor worked, we quickly dropped our luggage at a small motel and hurried to the clinic. As she parked the van out front, I caught a glimpse of Mom's face in the rearview mirror. Her expression told me she was disappointed in the run-down condition of the neighborhood and the shabby building that housed the clinic. Inside, the doctor's office was dark, dingy, cluttered, and unappealing.

I leaned toward Mom and whispered, "Doesn't look promising, does it? Maybe we should leave while we still can."

Mom, the eternal optimist, whispered back, "Let's just wait and see."

The doctor finally came in and immediately began boasting about the success he'd had with injuries such as mine. His speech was pretty convincing, and I soon overcame my reluctance and let him lift me onto a table. He attached rubber pads to the atrophied muscles of my arms and legs. The pads were connected to a mysterious-looking machine with blinking lights and gauges. It was pretty scary, but at least he wasn't using needles, so I didn't protest.

When the doctor pulled a switch, electrical current surged through the pads, zapping my arms and legs and making them jerk uncontrollably.

"Can you feel anything, Mr. Heagy?" he asked once, pausing between jolts.

"No…not yet."

The doctor's mechanical smile broadened as he turned a dial to increase the voltage. "Sometimes it takes a little time," he assured me.

I couldn't feel my arms and legs moving, but I was pleased to see them jerk and jump. As soon as he turned off the current, however, the action stopped, and my limbs were as lifeless as ever.

I lay there wondering what would happen next.

"Your body is filled with toxins, Mr. Heagy. You'll feel better after I give you a colonic irrigation."

"A what?"

"A colonic irrigation. Your intestines need to be detoxified," he explained while unrolling a long coil of tubing that resembled a garden hose.

My eyes widened as he turned me onto my side and I realized he was about to give me an enema. With all my heart, I wanted to jump off that table and bolt out of there like a streak of lightning, but all I could do was grit my teeth and close my eyes as the treatment proceeded.

Slumping morosely in my wheelchair as we left the doctor's office, I felt disillusioned and discouraged. I wanted nothing more than to head home, but Mom and Wanda were ready to see the sights.

The ski slopes depressed me. I longed to be a participant again, to strap on skis and blast off down the mountainside. Eventually I asked Mom if we could please go home.

"Sure, honey, tomorrow," she responded. "Wanda and I want to visit the mall first."

We had left my electric wheelchair at home because it was too heavy. So while Mom and Wanda shopped, Mike pushed me aimlessly from one store to another, killing time. When the boredom eventually became too much for him, he decided to have some fun at my expense. We were cruising down the center aisle of a busy department store when the heartless little prankster turned suddenly and pushed me into the lingerie section. We were surrounded by life-size mannequins dressed in scanty

T-backs and low-cut bras, while women shoppers sorted through tables of panties on either side of us.

"Hey, Mike, what are you thinking? Let's get out of here, buddy! C'mon, let's go!" I hissed at him.

He leaned over my head and flashed a sinister grin. I recognized the gleam of vengeance in his eyes. "Remember all the times you pretended I was your punching bag when we were growing up?" he taunted.

"Oh come on, Mike. That was just kid stuff."

"Yeah, I know. Great sport! So was the time you rode me on the handlebars of your bike down to the river and jumped off so I went crashing into the water, remember?"

"That was an accident, and you know it."

"Maybe. But how about the day you took me out in that go-cart and launched me like a catapult headfirst into the mud? Was that an accident, huh? And what about the time you coaxed me to crawl into the snow cave that collapsed? I almost suffocated, and I've had claustrophobia ever since."

I started to laugh good-naturedly. "You've got too good a memory, Mike. Besides, it was all in fun."

"Yeah, I know. So is this." Mike grinned at me, turned to a rack of bras, grabbed a lacy one with cups the size of footballs, and gleefully hung it over my chest, tucking the ends behind my shoulders and back. Then he pushed me out into the main aisle, crowded with shoppers, and left me sitting there alone.

Some fun!

16

Starting Over

~

Attending college in a wheelchair hadn't been part of my plan. But after the disappointing trip to Idaho in search of a cure, I finally accepted the fact that it would be necessary to use my brain instead of brawn to earn a living. "Mind over muscle" became my motto.

Encouraged by my "fan club"—Mom, Dad, Aunt Donna, and my vocational counselor—I registered at Linn Benton Community College for the fall semester. Arleta, the pretty wife of my cousin Brad, volunteered to be my chauffeur, and we ordered a typewriter I could use with my mouth stick. Finally, after hiring students to take notes and assist me to classes, I was all set to start.

I took only two classes—speech and intermediate math—but for me that was a full load. I enjoyed both subjects and, as a result, did pretty well. In high school my grades were mediocre. I had depended on athletic achievements to get me through. So I was elated and amazed to receive an A on my first algebra test.

Each day I went to classes with a smile on my face, eager to learn, excited about the possibilities that now lay before me. And, as an added bonus, because my attitude changed from negative to positive, I made lots of new friends.

When my electric wheelchair arrived, I imagined myself scooting around campus on my own, just another college kid enjoying my freedom. But learning to manipulate the new hot rod with its chin control was much harder than I had expected. The first thing I did was crash into a table and knock off one of Mom's prized lamps. It hurtled to the floor and shattered into smithereens—and there were several more accidents after that one. Next, the power recliner malfunctioned, spilling me backward onto the floor, where I sprawled until Mom rescued me.

I quickly became disgusted and disillusioned with my new chair and determined not to use it ever again. It was easier and safer, I reasoned, to be taken to my first class each day in a conventional wheelchair than chance humiliating myself with the new metal monster that made me feel like a robot. When class was over, I would ask a classmate to push me to my next scheduled stop. It was hard, at first, asking for and accepting help. But I soon learned that having other students assist me was a good way to get acquainted, and I met lots of pretty girls! Meanwhile, my new chair sat in a corner of the garage with a blanket draped over it!

I was happy again, and it wasn't just my status as a college student that helped me make a new start with a strong, positive attitude. Earlier that year, the *Albany Democrat Herald* had published a story about my accident, including pictures of me as a wrestler and later as a quadriplegic. After the story appeared, several readers called or wrote letters to commend my Christian testimony and my positive attitude.

Two of those readers—attractive teenage girls—appeared at our house one day when I was sitting outside, bare chested in the sunshine. The pastor of a local church had driven them to our house, and when the three of them got out of the car and started walking toward the house I yelled for Mom to bring me a shirt. Unfortunately, she failed to hear my frantic SOS, so there I sat, trapped in my wheelchair with a bare chest, bare feet, and a face turning red from embarrassment as the pastor introduced himself and the girls.

Mortified, I could barely look at them as the pastor explained that the girls had read the newspaper article and wanted to meet me. They were from eastern Oregon, he said, but they were working in our area on a mission project.

When Mom finally appeared and helped me put on a shirt, I relaxed and, for the first time, allowed myself to take a good look at the girls. Both of them were attractive, but one of them was especially attractive. I loved her warm and friendly chitchat and the way she looked me in the eye as we talked. It made me wonder—could it be possible? Could she…no. *No, Ron, don't even start that stuff again,* I fumed at myself. *You've already been hurt twice, thinking pretty girls could be attracted to you the way you are. Just forget it, man!*

They stayed a half hour or so, comparing notes on their mission project in western Oregon and my trip to Brazil with Teen Missions. After they left, I blurted out, "Mom, that girl's awesome. If I were normal right now, I'd ask her for a date."

"What do you mean, if you were *normal?*" Mom snapped at me. "Just because your arms and legs don't work doesn't mean you're an inferior person. If you want to ask her out, do it!"

My fear of rejection was still as strong as ever, but Mom's words encouraged me. *What do you have to lose?* I told myself. *You'll never know for sure unless you try.*

My heart in my throat, I called Tammy.

"Hi, it's Ron—Ron Heagy."

"Oh! Hi!"

"I, uh, I enjoyed your visit yesterday. It was nice of you to drop by. Sorry I was so tongue-tied when you first got here. I needed a shirt, and that's all I could think of."

"Oh, that's okay. We should have called first. It was nice of you to let us drop in on you like that."

"I was wondering…I mean, would you like to…, well, you wanna go see a movie?"

There was the slightest of pauses before she said, "Oh! Well, sure. I'd love to."

I told her how much it irked me that I couldn't do the driving. "Don't worry about it, Ron. I'll drive. It'll be fun."

We had a good time together that night and continued dating until Tammy's mission project ended and she returned to eastern Oregon. Even then, we corresponded regularly and visited each other occasionally.

My relationship with Tammy helped me realize it *was* possible for members of the opposite sex to enjoy my company and not find the wheelchair or my disability intimidating. Tammy taught me that as long as I maintained a positive attitude about myself, others would see me in the same light.

We became good friends, and I trusted her with feelings I couldn't share with anyone else. One evening as we sat on the riverbank watching a sensational sunset, I confided to her how much I had once looked forward to someday getting married and having a family. "Now I'm afraid that will never happen."

"Well, what do the doctors say?" she asked.

"They say, 'Go for it!'" I answered with a rueful grin. "They've told me it's physically possible, but will I ever find anyone who can deal with my disabilities?"

"Ron, why not leave the future in God's hands? If it's His will," she assured me with a confident smile, "you'll marry and have children of your own. He knows what's best—for you and for me."

Ron, age 10
Pennie, age 8
Mike, age 6

Ron, age 13
Pennie, age 11
Mike, age 10

I loved to go fishing with my dad,
especially when I caught the
bigger fish.

I used to love to chop wood.

You can see the garage of our log cabin in the background.

Easter Sunday when I was 16

Mike and I as "surfer dudes" about 10 minutes before the accident.

What a difference a few moments can make.

In
those first days,
monitors tracked
my vital signs as
I hung on by a
thread and a
prayer.

One of my favorite
nurses checked that my
legs were wrapped
properly so the blood
wouldn't pool away
from my heart.

After six hours
of surgery, the
broken
bones in my neck
were fused.

Even though she was tired, Mom was always there to encourage me.

"Dad, be careful. I'm not used to someone shaving me."

I didn't make my high school graduation ceremony, but I wore the hat.

"I'm 19, and everybody loves me."

Being in a wheelchair doesn't stop me from riding over the sand dunes of Oregon.

Daniel Webster Doe has been not only a great caregiver but a good friend.

Thanks to the talent of Aunt Donna and the inspiration of Joni Eareckson Tada, I learned to paint using my mouth.

When I received my master's from San Diego State University, my smile said it all: "I told you I could do it!"

"Run Your Race," a commissioned painting for Nike World Masters Games.

My
good friend and
co-conspirator
Dave Woods

as we leave to
pick up Ann
in a limo.

My nephew Jacob helps me pull a wheelie.

After
Ray Charles
"looked" at me with
his fingers,

I autographed
a small painting
for him.

Bethel Baptist Church
P.O. BOX 167
AUMSVILLE, OR 97325

With the
King family at
Camp Attitude

Taking to the slopes
1997

Roni
2001

Mouth paintings available online. A great gift idea…

Kelli and I the day I asked my soulmate to become my wife.

The day I married my best friend. Our new family: Ron, Kelli, Jessie (10), Mattie (5), and Roni (3 1/2)

17

Julie

~

As I waited for my algebra class to start one day, an attractive girl stopped beside my wheelchair. She was carrying a tennis racket as well as her books and wore a sweatshirt tied around her slim waist. "Is this seat taken?"

I cocked my head to one side, offered what I hoped was a dazzling smile, and replied in my best cool-guy tone, "Yes, as a matter of fact. I was saving it for you. Go ahead. Sit down."

Her name was Julie, and by the time the algebra class ended, we were friends. She offered to push me to my next class.

"I'm taking psychology too," she said with a bright smile.

"Sure you don't mind?"

"Of course not. I'm familiar with wheelchairs. My oldest brother, Jim, was in a motorcycle accident, and he uses one too."

Over the next few weeks, our friendship grew, and we talked about everything under the sun. Julie was four years older than I was, and wasn't the least bit intimidated by my disability. Watching her pretty face glow with animation one day as she shared a funny story, the old idea crept back into my mind. I began wondering...*No, forget it, Ron. Just be happy that you're friends, and don't think about romance. You've been through that, remember, and you got hurt—not once, but twice! Get real, guy!*

Any remaining thoughts about being something more than a friend to Julie were zapped the day she noticed the fish emblem on the jacket I was wearing.

"Does that mean you're a Christian?" she asked.

"Yes, it does."

"Really? So am I. My fiancé is a Christian too."

"Your *fiancé?*" I repeated, caught totally off guard. "You're engaged?"

"Yes. In fact, it was my fiancé who led me to the Lord."

"That's…uh, that's wonderful, Julie." Wanting desperately to act casual and not let my disappointment show, I quickly added, "I teach a Bible study in our home once a week. We sit in front of the fireplace, have some refreshments, and just talk. You're more than welcome to join us."

"Thanks. I'd like that," she said. "Would you mind if I brought my roommate? Her name is Connie."

"That'd be great."

When Julie showed up at our house the following Wednesday evening, Connie was with her. A cute coed about my age, Connie was lots of fun to be around. She soon had all of us laughing and joking. As they were leaving, Connie leaned down to my wheelchair and said quietly, "I'd love to get together sometime, Ron. Do you like to go to movies?"

"Sure. You wanna go?"

"I'd love to."

We made a date for Friday evening at seven o'clock. I hadn't realized that anyone overheard our conversation, until Julie spotted me the next day on campus and came hurrying over. "Ron, I need to talk to you about something important."

"Is something wrong?" I was surprised by the urgency in her voice.

"Well…yes, I guess you could say something is wrong."

"What?"

"I understand you asked Connie for a date."

"Well, yeah, sort of. We're going to see a movie. Why is that wrong?" My first thought was that Julie didn't approve of her roommate becoming involved with a quadriplegic. When she didn't answer immediately, I repeated the question. "Is there a problem?"

She averted her eyes and looked at the floor. "Ron…I'm afraid…"

"Afraid? What are you afraid of? Is something going on that I don't know about? What is it?"

"Ron…I'm afraid…that…" She stopped as if to regroup. Then the words tumbled out in one quick breath. "I'm falling in love with you."

My mouth fell open. *Is this some sort of cruel joke?* I wondered. "But...I mean...I thought...you said you're engaged. I thought we were just friends."

She looked at me with a wounded expression in her eyes. "Is that all you want us to be—friends? I thought you might...well...I thought you might care for me as something more than a friend."

"B–but, Julie..." I stuttered. "Your fiancé..."

"I'm starting to think I'm making a mistake, Ron," she said, her voice rising a couple of notes as though she might burst into a sob.

"Julie, I...well, if you're sure about this..."

Almost before either of us realized what was happening, I had canceled my date with Connie, Julie had broken her engagement, and we were seeing each other regularly.

Julie was special. Beautiful and vivacious, she seemed to cast a glow that warmed me and always sent my spirits soaring. She ignored my physical limitations and made me feel like a king. As a new Christian, she seemed to appreciate my spiritual strength, and we enjoyed some long and heartfelt discussions about what being a Christian really meant. For the first time since my accident, I actually felt *needed*—and by someone very special.

I knew very little about Julie's family except that she had a brother who was a paraplegic. Then she invited Connie and me to go home with her during the Easter holidays. "I want you to meet my brothers and parents, Ron. You and Jim will get along great."

"But what about your mom and dad? How will they feel about their daughter dating a man in a wheelchair?"

"They'll love you just as much as I do, Ron," she said earnestly, meeting my steady gaze.

"But what if they don't?" I had to be sure.

"Don't worry, Ron. My parents will understand. After all, they have a disabled son."

Julie's hometown was a two-hour drive from Brownsville, and all the way there I wondered what kind of a reception I'd get. After what seemed an eternity, we rode through the town and turned onto a county road. "Almost there," Julie said. As the road forked, I expected her to turn right, pulling into the driveway of a modest bungalow surrounded by trees and flowers. Instead she turned left, gliding onto a long, curving driveway that passed through an impressive entrance gate. Continuing down the drive, we passed a small plane sitting on a private landing strip.

"Wow! What a setup. Wonder who that baby belongs to?" I mused.

"It's my dad's," Julie answered nonchalantly.

"Your father owns an airplane? Why didn't you tell me?"

She turned my way with a mischievous smile. "Because you didn't ask. That's why."

Connie laughed at my bewilderment. "Ron, you mean Julie didn't tell you that her father is a millionaire? He owns all this land and much more."

My eyes bulged, and my mouth popped open in amazement. "You're kidding!"

"No, I'm not," Connie continued. "Just wait until you see the rest of their estate. Mr. Richards is an important man in this part of the state. I'm surprised that Julie didn't mention it."

Mouth still hanging open, eyebrows raised, I shot Julie a surprised look.

She just smiled and shrugged.

We passed stands of virgin timber as well as a fruit orchard where the trees were just beginning to bud. A stream meandered alongside the winding, picturesque drive as we crossed a small meadow. Then we rolled onto beautifully landscaped grounds surrounding a sparkling, jewel-tone lake. Above the lake, built into the side of a hill, was Julie's home—a 5,400-square-foot mansion that made the Heagy home look like a dollhouse. "The tennis court is behind the house," Connie gushed, "and the racquetball court and the Jacuzzi. They're all enclosed so you can use them all year long."

My eyes moved over the estate as a million questions swirled through my head. *How could a girl from an affluent family be interested in a disabled guy with such humble roots as mine?*

At least one reassuring thought popped into my mind as I surveyed the lavish surroundings Julie called home: She certainly wasn't attracted to me because of my physical prowess or my money! Indeed, all I had to offer her was love and companionship. I hoped with all my heart that would be enough.

Julie's mother greeted us warmly. A gracious, hospitable hostess, she made me feel welcome from the very start. Like her daughter, she was unpretentious and easy to talk to, and I felt drawn to her immediately.

Julie's dad, on the other hand, was a man of few words. The child of an alcoholic father, he had left home at age 14 and, through a lifetime of hard labor, had started a business and built it into an empire.

Mr. Richards greeted me with a tight, guarded smile as his eyes took in my wheelchair and its paralyzed occupant. His careful scrutiny made me feel uneasy as I tried to guess what he was thinking. Despite Julie's reassurance, I suspected he wasn't all that happy about his daughter dating a quadriplegic.

Julie's three brothers and their families lived in homes on the estate and worked for their father. Jack was the master mechanic. He took care of the heavy equipment they used for cutting timber, hauling it to the mill, and later to market. Tom was the buyer and supervisor. He traveled around the countryside bidding on timber and then supervised the workmen who cut it. Jim was the oldest. He acted as office manager, taking care of all the company paperwork from his wheelchair.

Mrs. Richards prepared a delicious Easter feast for us that day and served it in their spacious dining room. Without my asking her, Julie willingly cut my food into bites and fed me in such an easy, unobtrusive way that it didn't seem awkward at all. I sat there, enjoying the meal and the company, still amazed to find myself in such opulent surroundings as the guest of a very fine young lady who had special feelings for me.

After dinner, Jim took me for a ride around the estate in a little tracked vehicle that splashed through marshes, eased between trees, climbed up a mountainside, and sped over the most rugged terrain imaginable as though it were a freeway.

Jim and I hit it off immediately. I admired the way he refused to let his physical impairment slow him down or diminish his joy for life. He found a way to continue enjoying many of the sports he had enjoyed before he lost the use of his legs. He snow skied in a contraption he called a ski-sit chair, and when the snow melted, he played racquetball or went whitewater rafting. Being with him was inspiring.

Late in the day, Julie drove Connie and me back to Brownsville. While Connie and I chatted easily about all the fun we'd had, Julie, her hands on the steering wheel, her eyes focused straight ahead, seemed quiet and a little withdrawn.

"Is anything wrong?" I asked after she had dropped Connie off and was taking me home. "No, Ron. Nothing's wrong. I was just thinking about how nice it was today to have you with my family. But, to be honest, I was also thinking how nice it would be to have you all to myself!"

The trip we made with Connie to Julie's home was our last as a three-some. From then on, Julie and I were strictly a couple.

One day she invited me to join her for a drive to the coast in her little Honda. "Sounds like fun," I answered. "But how will you get me into your car? Maybe we'd better take the Green Bean."

"No need to do that. I can lift you—no problem," she insisted confidently. But it *was* a problem; I was too heavy for her. After a lot of huffing, puffing, and straining, she did manage to hoist me out of my chair, but then as she tried to turn me I fell forward, face first, onto the car seat.

"Aaaaarrrgh! You've smashed my nose," I yelled, teasing her. By the time she finally got me into an upright position and strapped my shoulders against the seat, we were both laughing so hard we could barely talk. Finally, when I had caught my breath, I looked at Julie and asked, "Are you *sure* you still want to take your car instead of the van?"

"Yes, I'm sure," she snapped. "I've got to learn how to take care of you sometime, so why not now?"

Her words seemed to hang silently in the air a moment, the assumption of a lifetime commitment there.

We had a wonderful ride along the spectacular coastline. As we headed for home, however, dark clouds gradually gathered on the horizon, and it was pouring rain when we finally pulled into our driveway. Getting me *out* of the car was even more difficult than getting me in it, because my wheelchair was considerably higher than the Honda's seat. After she struggled for a couple of minutes, I suggested that Julie go in the house and ask my folks for help.

"Forget it!" she retorted hotly. "I got you in, and I can get you out!" By that time we were both soaking wet, but she wasn't giving up. She wrapped her arms under mine, braced one foot on the door frame, and lifted me up and out of the Honda seat.

"There!" she said, grunting with the effort as she pulled me upright.

Suddenly I started to slip out of her rain-soaked hands, Julie's shuffling feet tangled with my lifeless ones, and before either of us realized what was happening, we landed in the mud at the edge of the driveway, Julie sprawled on top of me.

"Oh! Ron! Oh, I'm so sorry!" she exclaimed, quickly scrambling to her knees and wiping the mud from my eyes.

"Just go get Dad," I muttered.

With a sigh of surrender, she hurried inside. I watched as lights popped on in the windows. Dad had been in bed asleep. As I waited for them in the driveway, shivering from the cold and with rain pouring onto my face, I thought, *Well, this ought to do it—force Julie to realize just how helpless I really am. I wouldn't blame her if she decides she's not ready for this kind of commitment.*

I was relieved—and only a little surprised—to realize as time went on that our shared mud-bath experience seemed to draw Julie and me closer together rather than scare her away. Perhaps it was Julie's strong maternal and nurturing instincts that led her to love me; or maybe it was just the reward of feeling needed. Whatever the reason, she spent more and more time at our place, and with each passing day, our future seemed more firmly defined as a thing we would share.

Julie and I appreciated simple pleasures, like Oregon sunsets that turned the summer sky into various shades of pink and purple before the sun slipped behind the mountains. One memorable moment we sat in the middle of a wheat field watching shooting stars streak across the sky.

Julie's love empowered me. With her encouragement prodding me to try new things, I found the courage to venture out beyond the boundaries I had imagined for myself. One of the biggest steps I took was telling Mom I wanted to move into a place of my own. I expected her to oppose the idea—and she did.

"Ronnie, I'm not sure this is a wise thing to do," Mom said. "Since your accident you've always had someone with you. Think of all the times you've needed help, and all you've had to do was yell and one of us was there. Honey, your father and I will worry about you if you move out."

"You shouldn't, Mom," I assured her with forced optimism in my voice. Although this was something I really wanted, I knew it was a risk.

But I had to know. I had to see if I could survive on my own. "I'm 21 years old, Mom. It's time to cut the umbilical cord. Why, some of my high school friends are already married."

"Yes, but it's different for you, Ronnie. You have special needs."

"That's true. But I can't depend on you and Dad forever. It's time for me to start taking care of myself," I argued.

Despite my parents' worries, I used my disability allowance from Social Security to rent half of a duplex in Lebanon, Oregon, 17 miles away from my family. I hired a full-time caregiver and moved out on faith.

My new home was in a low-rent housing project, but my affluent girlfriend didn't seem to mind. Apparently, she had decided to stick by me, no matter where I lived. Life was good, and we looked forward to the future.

Then, without warning, illness struck again.

18

Painful Decisions

❧

One day Julie and I were enjoying a leisurely afternoon at my cozy new home, and the next I was back in the hospital with a 105-degree fever.

The doctor's face was grim when he brought the test results to my room. "You have a kidney stone the size of a dime, Ron."

"And...?"

"And you need surgery. Right away."

"Oh no," I groaned, seeing the happy future I'd been dreaming about just a few hours ago quickly fade from view. During previous surgeries I'd gone into cardiac arrest twice; now the phrase "Three strikes, you're out!" kept invading my psyche.

Sensing my despair, the doctor quickly launched into a recital of the choices available to me. "The stone can be removed through conventional surgery. But there are also some newer treatments that are being used. One is laser surgery; it seems to be the coming thing. Ultrasound is also a possibility. And there's a new procedure called the basket retrieval technique. But," he continued, "we aren't equipped to do *any* of the newer procedures here."

"Who is?"

"I understand there is a hospital in San Francisco that is doing all three."

Julie drove me down to San Francisco. We went straight to the hospital and followed a trail of blood from the parking lot into the emergency room. The place was a madhouse. The victim of a drive-by shooting had just arrived, along with a gang member who had been stabbed in a street fight minutes before. A hysterical woman stood over the gang member, screaming and sobbing at the top of her lungs.

Stunned by the chaotic scene, Julie and I were tempted to turn around and head for home without even checking in. Looking back on what happened, I wish we had heeded those instincts.

Instead, Julie filled out the paperwork and positioned it for me to sign with a pen held in my mouth, then an orderly pushed me to my assigned bed in a surgical ward. The sight of the large room was only slightly less terrifying than the emergency room had been. It was over-crowded, with several beds lining the walls and leaving only a narrow aisle down the middle of the floor. Even worse, it had a foul odor, and it certainly didn't look clean.

I glanced at Julie, sharing a thought: *Let's get out of here!*

But just then a stern-looking nurse spotted us and hurried over. Her tone was so brusque and her words spoken so harshly that we found ourselves following her commands without even a murmur of dissent.

"Wait over there," she barked at Julie. Then she immediately planted her feet, sucked in a breath, pulled me out of the chair, dumped me onto the bed, and began undressing me without even bothering to close the privacy curtains. Without a word, she roughly stripped off all my clothes, tied a hospital gown around me, then abruptly turned and left, jerking her chin up as she passed Julie to signal that she could come back in.

But that treatment was nothing compared with the painful ordeal that awaited me the next morning. I expected to be wheeled off to the operating room, but instead I was taken to a treatment room where the resident physician explained matter-of-factly, "This is really very simple. I'm going to insert a catheter into your kidney and fill it with a solution that should dissolve the stone within a couple of days."

"Without a general anesthetic?" I asked, my voice ratcheting up an octave as his words registered.

"Oh yes. You'll only need a local."

I gulped. "And you said this *should* dissolve the stone. What if it doesn't?"

"Then we'll try something else."

The "simple" procedure turned out to be a painful experience. Back in my room, I confessed to Julie, "My kidney feels like it's on fire! Julie…I'm afraid to be in this place alone. Please don't leave me!"

"I'll be right here," she said. "I'm not leaving." Throughout my stay in that hospital, Julie rarely left my room except for occasional trips to the restroom or the cafeteria, even spending the nights in a chair beside my bed.

Six days later the stone still hadn't dissolved, but the skin and flesh in my groin area was badly burned from the medication, and the wounds had become infected. The bad feelings I had about this hospital were getting stronger. When the doctor came in, I told him emphatically, "Forget it! Pull the tubes. I'm getting out of here."

"It's your decision, Mr. Heagy, but I think you are being hasty," he replied calmly. "We had hoped to dissolve your kidney stone with medication, and that hasn't worked. But I'm confident we can retrieve the stone without surgery if you will let us try."

"How does the retrieval thing work?" I asked, still skeptical.

"We'll make a small incision in your side and insert a tube directly into your kidney. A surgical camera will locate the stone, and a little basket apparatus will retrieve it. The entire operation should take only 45 minutes, an hour at the most. It's really quite simple."

I thought, *Yeah, that's what you said before!* But when Julie nodded and gave me the go-ahead signal, I decided to give these guys one more try. "Okay, but if you don't have that kidney stone in your hand by tonight, I'm out of here."

Again, I received only a local anesthetic. This time I watched the procedure on a television screen above my head. At first I was fascinated by the surgeon's attempt to retrieve the stone, but 45 minutes became an hour, and one hour became two. By that time the pain was so intense I started to sweat, and my head felt like it had been hit by a sledgehammer.

The doctors' casual conversation certainly didn't inspire confidence; they seemed to be making a sport out of the whole thing. One said, "I think we've got it. Okay, tilt the basket upward. That's it. Oops…it got away. Let's try again. A little to the left, now to the right…"

Finally, after more attempts than I could count, they snared the stone and cheered like a basketball team scoring a three-pointer.

But the ordeal wasn't over. A couple of days later, my urologist suggested that I consider taking an additional step to ward off future kidney stones. The choice, he said, was "one of those good-news, bad-news scenarios."

"Let's have the glad tidings first," I suggested.

"If we cut your sphincter muscle, you probably won't develop any more kidney stones," he said, getting right to the point.

"And the bad news?" I asked.

"If we cut your sphincter muscle, you'll probably be impotent."

19

Dreams and Promises

~

T he doctor's words took me by surprise. I stared at him as if I hadn't heard correctly, then finally muttered, "You mean...I won't be able to have sexual relations?"

"Exactly."

"Oh." The word hissed out of me like pressurized air, escaping from a tire.

"You needn't make the decision right away. Take some time to think about it," the doctor said, abruptly turning toward the door.

I felt cheated. *This is great—this is the reward I get.* My mind blazed with the anguished thoughts. *So many of my buddies in high school played around, but not me. No, I did what I was supposed to do. I waited. And now look at the choice I get. Sometimes it seems like I have so little left, Lord. Then, just as something good happens to me—just as a beautiful girl comes into my life and we're thinking about a future together—then it all slips away again. How much more do I have to give up? I just don't understand, God! Why? Why me?*

"Ron...," Julie stood next to me, lifted my hand to her cheek. "Ron, it's okay. I know this is hard for you, but the important thing is your health, your *life,*" she said kissing my knuckles one by one.

The doctor performed the surgery the next morning. A few days later, feeling defeated and sad, I was lifted into Julie's little Honda for the trip home. Drowning in self-pity, mourning the loss of another dream, I

113

rode in silence, bracing myself for the moment when Julie would begin to say good-bye.

The moment came sooner than I expected. We were hardly out of the hospital parking lot when she reached over the console and patted my thigh.

"Ron, I love you," she said quietly.

I didn't answer, just tried to set my face into a mask of acceptance. Whatever she said next, I told myself, *I won't argue, I won't try to talk her out of leaving me. She's a wonderful gal. She deserves a husband who can take care of her and love her and give her children.*

"Ron...I...I hope we can spend our lives together."

It took a moment for her words to sink in.

"You mean...you're thinking...we...you would...you'll still *marry* me?" I asked, hoping with all my heart that I'd understood her correctly.

"Of course I will, silly!" she almost shouted, her face erupting into a huge smile.

On a Sunday afternoon we drove out to her parents' estate. I had rehearsed my lines in advance, but as we passed through the elegant gates, nervousness completely wiped out all my plans and preparations. When the moment finally came and I faced Julie's parents, I had hoped to lay out a beautifully poetic description of my love for their daughter, saying how much she meant to me, how happy we were when we were together. I was going to commend them for the fine job they'd done as parents and say how much my mom and dad cared for their daughter.

Instead, I completely forgot my planned speech and blurted out the first words that came to my mind: "I'm in love with your daughter." Julie's father fixed a cold, laserlike stare on me with no sign of a smile, no hint of encouragement. "We want to get married, but...but we'd like to have your blessing first."

The way I daydreamed this little scene, Julie's father would say, "Wonderful! Welcome to the family, son." Instead, he asked coldly, "How will you support my daughter?"

I have to admit, it was a logical question, one that needed to be addressed. And afterward, I thought of a dozen logical, reassuring ways I could have answered him. But with his stern gaze boring a hole straight through me, all I managed to say was, "Don't worry, sir. I'll take good care of Julie. She will never lack for anything if I can help it."

After a silence that seemed an eternity, Mr. Richards turned to Julie and asked, "Are you sure this is really what you want?"

He probably hoped she would say no. Instead, she slipped her hand under my elbow and said, "Yes, Dad. I love Ron. He's a wonderful man, and we want to be married."

"Have you really thought this thing through, Julie? Do you realize what's involved?"

"We love each other, Dad, and that's what really matters."

He finally gave his consent; I wouldn't really call it a blessing. "Okay. If that's what will make you happy, go ahead," he said gruffly. "I won't stand in your way."

Julie considered her father's acquiescence a victory, but for me it was a bittersweet experience—joy mixed with crushing humiliation. I didn't want to cry and have him think that I was a weakling, but my efforts to hold back the tears were futile. I had wanted so badly to have a good rapport with my future father-in-law, but that seemed hopeless now. Mr. Richards obviously had wanted his daughter to marry an able-bodied man—someone who would fit in and could contribute to the family business. Ron Heagy the quadriplegic fell short of his expectations. Realizing he probably thought I was marrying his daughter for her money, I vowed to myself right then and there never to ask him for help or to accept a penny of his money.

In contrast to her husband's response, Mrs. Richards' reaction was positive. She gave us both a warm hug and asked, "Have you set a date?"

"We were thinking about April," Julie said. I could hear the relief in her voice as she redirected her attention from her father's somber tones to her mother's bubbling enthusiasm. "Around the middle of the month, when the plum trees are in blossom. We'd like to have a garden wedding down by the lake."

"How romantic!" Mrs. Richards was as excited as her daughter. "We'll have Tom and Jack build a platform and an archway for you to be married under."

"Do you suppose we could find a pair of white turtledoves for the best man to release after the ceremony? That would be neat," Julie said, eager now to share all her ideas with her mother.

"I don't know why not. Oh Julie, April will be here before we know it, and that doesn't give us much time. We'll need to start shopping for a wedding gown and bridesmaids' dresses, plan the reception, and get the invitations out." Suddenly she turned to me. "Ron, dear, please have your mother make out a guest list…" Her spirited plans helped us move on from Julie's father's reluctance.

During the coming weeks, while Julie and her mother busied themselves with details for the wedding, I began exploring the possibility of transferring to a four-year college to pursue a career in counseling and psychology. It was a dream that had begun that heartrending night four years earlier when little Jimmy had called out to me in the darkness to encourage me. The desire he had instilled in me to encourage others was just as strong as ever; I believed this was the way I could best serve God.

And after my encounter with Mr. Richards, I had another reason for wanting to proceed with my career plans. I was determined to prove to him that I could support his daughter. Maybe it wouldn't be in the same lavish style that she had been accustomed to, but I wanted to give her everything that would make her happy.

I was regularly looking at college catalogs and asking God to guide me to the right school when a group of student singers from Christian Heritage College in Southern California came to our church for a Sunday service. Each singer gave a glowing description of the college and told the congregation what a blessing the school had been to him or her. As soon as I saw the list of degrees the college offered, I was convinced the singers had been sent in answer to my prayers. As Julie and I planned our honeymoon, we added a stop in El Cajon, California, to visit the campus.

The wedding was spectacular. No expense had been spared by the bride's family, and the event had the air of a storybook fantasy. In front of more than 350 guests, we repeated our vows under a beautiful lattice-work arch trimmed with flowers beside the lake that seemed to sparkle with diamonds in the sunlight. As Julie had planned, the air on that April afternoon in 1984 was laden with the intoxicating fragrance of plum blossoms. The white doves circled overhead in perfect spirals, and my heart was filled with the greatest joy I had ever known.

20

Against the Odds

~

I t came as a joyous surprise to Julie and me to discover that only half of the urologist's prediction came true. The surgery did stop the kidney stones; I've never had a recurrence. But the impotence he warned us about didn't happen. Our honeymoon was perfect in every detail, and our visit to the campus of Christian Heritage College was a pleasant preview of the four years we would spend there as busy, happy newlyweds.

The classes were challenging and stimulating, and some of my professors became supportive mentors who continue to touch my life even today. We developed many friendships and enjoyed being part of the bustling college community.

Not that there weren't setbacks. Money was tight, a problem Julie wasn't accustomed to. But she didn't complain, and just when we thought we had hit a wall and were at a dead end at finding housing we could afford, a friend told us that a professional basketball player was looking for a dependable Christian couple to house-sit and care for his dogs while he and his wife were in Italy. The arrangement was another answer to prayer.

Our happiness was complete. We loved each other; we lived in a large, comfortable home; we worked *together* toward my degree, with Julie selflessly driving me to campus and tending to all my needs; and we dreamed of a productive, love-filled future.

It wasn't easy. While my classmates effortlessly read and turned the pages of books, took notes during lectures, and wrote or typed their papers in the usual way, I depended on Julie to help me at night and used a mechanical page turner to read during the day. Later I completed my written assignments with a pen held in my mouth or a stick gripped between my teeth, often working late into the night to laboriously finish each page.

Still, the effort was rewarding, and several of my instructors were very insightful about motivating me. For example, Professor Ed Gray made it a point each semester to discover his students' God-given gifts. That's how Matt and I ended up alone in Dr. Gray's office taking a test together one day.

Matt had been blind since birth; when he wanted to "see" what people looked like, he felt their faces. His books had to be transcribed into Braille, and he took notes with a stylus. In contrast, the tasks Matt completed by touch and sound, I completed by sight and sound. Both of us found the normal means of test-taking in a quiet room full of concentrating classmates impossible. Usually we both needed to speak our answers aloud.

As Dr. Gray was handing out exams one day he said to Matt and me, "Since it's difficult for you two men to take tests with the class, why don't you go down to my office where it's quiet and tackle this one together?"

"You mean, just the two of us?" I asked, startled.

"That's right. You and Matt."

"Are you serious?"

He fastened two copies of the test to a clipboard and laid it on the tray of my wheelchair. Then, with a confident smile, he looked at me and said, "Try it."

Matt was already tapping his way toward the door. "Got any ideas?" I asked him as Dr. Gray pushed my chair up to him.

"Nope, not one," he said, deadpan. "But you lead the way, and I'll follow."

"Okay. Grab the handles of my wheelchair. Got 'em? Here we go."

As Matt pushed, I guided him with a running monologue. "A little to the left, now to the right. Great! Now straight. Keep going, keep going. Turn left again, take five steps and make a right. Oops! Back one step. Okay, here we go. We're almost there."

We finally made it to Dr. Gray's office without gouging too much plaster out of the hallway walls. By then we were both laughing, and the students we passed were watching us with amusement. I guess they had never seen a blind man pushing a wheelchair before.

"I'll tell you what, Matt," I said as we got down to work. "I can read the questions and write our answers, but you'll have to put the pen in my mouth."

"Where is it?"

"Here on my tray."

"No, not the pen, your mouth. Where's your mouth?"

"Well, it's right here below my nose…"

He ran his fingertips over my face. "Wow! You've sure got a big mouth."

I laughed. "Thanks a lot, buddy. Now, stand behind me, put your elbows on my shoulders, and hold the clipboard in front of my face."

"Like this?"

"Wrong side up." He flipped it over. "That's better. Now hold it still. I'll mark my answers first. That way no one can accuse me of cheating. Then I'll read the questions aloud, and you can tell me what to write for you. How does that sound?"

Most of the questions were multiple choice or true and false, so it didn't take us long. We finished the exam and returned to the classroom before most of the other students were finished.

"Well done!" the professor raved. Then he added softly, "With man this is impossible, but with God all things are possible."

By the time the basketball player and his wife had returned from Italy, we had saved enough money to rent a little apartment in a middle-class neighborhood filled with dogs and kids who were fascinated by my electric wheelchair. I sometimes invited them to sit on my lap and go for rides.

Julie loved hearing about the challenges and high jinks I experienced on campus. Every night she laughed and cheered as I recounted the day's activities and misadventures. As the weeks passed and our lives became more completely entwined, I marveled at the joy that now filled my life and thanked God for this beautiful, caring woman.

As the wife of a struggling college student, Julie's standard of living had been downscaled considerably, yet she seemed happy. I kept telling her that once I got my degree and began my career, our financial status would improve. In the meantime, I tried to supplement my disability income by buying, renovating, and reselling cars.

In those days Volkswagen Bugs were popular with college students because they were inexpensive to buy and economical to operate. Mechanical things had always fascinated me. Even as a kid, I had enjoyed taking things apart and trying to put them back together again. At first I tinkered with old, broken-down bicycles and lawn mowers. Then, as a teenager, I started working on motorcycles and cars.

When I didn't have studying to do, Julie spread the classified section of the local newspaper on the tray of my wheelchair and I scanned the car ads. I had already supervised the restoration of about 30 VWs when I noticed an ad for a Bug with a burned-out motor. Since I had a spare engine from a previous renovation, I decided to buy the engineless Bug, hire someone to help me get it in running condition, then sell it for a profit.

School had just gotten out for the summer, and many of our friends had already gone home or to summer jobs. I had a little trouble finding someone who would agree to drive my van, pulling a rented trailer, to take me to purchase the Bug and then haul the crippled car back home. (Julie didn't like to drive the van when it was pulling a trailer.) As it turned out, Jonathan, the young man I eventually hired, was neither mechanically minded nor an experienced driver. But of course, that wouldn't be apparent until later!

We arrived at the owner's home and haggled briefly over the price. We finally agreed on a reasonable figure, and the man helped Jonathan load the little Bug onto the two-wheel trailer. They locked it in place, and Jonathan and I left. The problems began after we pulled onto the freeway. The trailer started whipping back and forth, jerking the van, rattling Jonathan, and terrifying me.

"We'd better pull over and check the hitch," I told him. "Can you do it alone, or do you want me to get out too?"

"The freeway's no place for a wheelchair," Jonathan said, pulling onto the shoulder. "You stay in the van."

Jonathan hopped out, walked to the rear of the van, did a little poking around, then got back into the driver's seat. "I can't see anything wrong with it," he said with a shrug.

As soon as we got up to freeway speed again, the van and trailer resumed their shimmying dance over the pavement. Jonathan slowed the van to a crawl, incurring angry looks and beeping horns from the impatient drivers around us.

We almost made it through the experience intact, but then, just as we arrived at our destination, calamity struck. Jonathan parked the van and trailer on a slight slope and then hopped out to unload the Bug. But as soon as he unhooked the VW from the trailer, it slid off the edge and started rolling. With a sick feeling in the pit of my stomach, I cringed as I watched the little, engineless car pick up speed on the slope and crash full force into the side of another student's parked car. Only then did I realize the Green Bean—with me still in it—was rolling too.

"Help! Jonathan! The van is moving! Quick! Get in! GET IN! SET THE BRAKE!" All I could do was scream—but I did some of the loudest screaming of my life.

Jonathan—flustered and breathless, his face as red as a stoplight—made a wild dash to catch up with the runaway van and finally was able to grab the emergency brake just before we hit the wall of the college gymnasium.

Such moments of mayhem broke the routine, the ordinariness, of our years at CHC. But the proud moment came in 1988 when I graduated with honors.

The work had been hard for both of us—difficult for me as the disabled college student and car mechanic, and exhausting for Julie as the constant caregiver. She was a wonderful wife. Her loving support was an ever-present blessing that I soon took for granted.

Only later—too late, really—would I realize how much she had sacrificed to help me get my education and how fortunate I was to have her as my partner.

21

Dreams Achieved...and Lost

$\sim$

"Auto mechanics?"

Harold Grove, the principal of East Linn Academy, the Christian school in Brownsville that I had attended as an eleventh-grader, had graciously offered me a job as a counselor and teacher. But when Mr. Grove outlined what he expected me to teach—Bible, English, and *auto mechanics*—I was flabbergasted.

"My degree is in the humanities, Mr. Grove," I told him. "Bible will be no problem, but I'm a little skeptical about teaching English. And auto mechanics? How can I show the kids what to do? Do you really think I can hack it?"

"Ron, there were lots of doubting Thomases around these parts when you started college. Only your family and a few close friends ever expected you to graduate. But you did. Right? Well...with your determination and ingenuity, I'm sure you'll find a way, and you'll do a good job. If I didn't believe you would have a positive impact on these students, I wouldn't be offering you a contract."

I floated home on cloud nine, repeatedly bragging to myself, *Harold Grove has confidence in me!*

"Honey, you're married to a schoolteacher!" I just had to say it out loud again that night as we reviewed the day's events.

"Ron, this is wonderful! I'm so happy for you." Julie's face lit up in that warm, familiar way.

"Happy for *us!*" I reminded her.

"I'm proud of you, honey!" She sat on my lap and snuggled her face close to mine. I cherished the feel of her cheek resting against my skin. *It feels so good to have her close to me. We used to sit and snuggle like this all the time,* I thought. *But it's been weeks since we've had a chance to focus on just the two of us, our marriage, and how we feel about each other.* I vowed to be more attentive to Julie now that the pressures of studying and surviving our meager college-student existence were over. Now, I told myself, our "real" life together could begin.

Soon after we returned to Oregon, my dad purchased and renovated a small house adjacent to my family's home, turning it into a cozy country cottage Julie and I could afford to rent. We settled into our new home, enjoying a carefree summer together—until another setback occurred.

Julie, my cousin Rhonda, and I were visiting Julie's parents one rainy evening when the three of us decided to go out for dinner. When we returned home and I rolled onto the Green Bean's lift, the mechanism developed a stubborn streak. It took repeated attempts to get the lift to work, and when it did, none of us noticed the malfunction of the end gate that was supposed to raise automatically and keep me from rolling off. Before Rhonda and Julie could stop it, my 350-pound electric wheelchair tumbled off the lift. As Julie shrieked in horror, I was launched across the driveway to land face first in the gravel. The impact loosened a tooth, broke my nose, and cut gashes in my mouth. My glasses had shattered, and pieces of the lenses were embedded in the abrasions in my face.

The two women hurried to my side and gently rolled me over, then gasped as they saw the bloody mess my face had become. Julie sat in the mud, cradling my head while Rhonda rushed inside to get help. Mr. Richards drove us to the hospital in his car while Julie held me and sobbed. "Ron, I'm so sorry, I'm so sorry! It's my fault. I should have checked the lift."

"It wasn't anyone's fault," I insisted. "That darn lift just broke, that's all. I'll be fine. Don't worry."

The truth was that the pain from my broken nose and badly cut mouth was excruciating. But even worse was the frustration that welled up in my spirit like a cauldron boiling over. *Why did I have to fall flat on my face, for heaven's sake, the only part of me that has any feeling?* I asked myself—and God. *Just once, why couldn't I bang up my back or chest or legs, where I feel nothing? Haven't I been through enough, Lord?*

Then, turning my head to one side to look into my loving wife's face, I remembered something to be thankful for. *Well, at least I didn't break my neck again. The fusion held. And Julie's here. She's always right here with me whenever I need her. Thanks, Lord!*

"Ron," Julie's urgently whispered words made me wonder if she'd been reading my thoughts. "I hope you'll be all right, because, darling, if anything ever happened to you…I…don't think I could stand it."

Gradually the cuts healed, the bruises subsided, and the plastic surgery the doctors had said might be needed to repair my nose turned out to be unnecessary. For the remainder of that summer, I studied my teacher's manual, brushed up on memorized Bible verses, honed my mechanical skills—and enjoyed being with Julie.

On the opening day of school, I was there early, filled with enthusiasm and a desire to be one of the best teachers East Linn Christian Academy had ever had. I considered my new job a God-given opportunity to show the world that a quadriplegic is capable of contributing something worthwhile to society. I also wanted to prove to one certain gentleman that I could support my wife and myself without asking for financial assistance.

As I expected, auto mechanics proved to be my biggest challenge, but also the part of my job that gave me the most satisfaction. I thoroughly enjoyed teaching my students all the things my dad had taught me through the years. Since it wasn't possible for me to physically show my students what to do, I guided them verbally through all the steps necessary to change fan belts, test spark plugs, work on valves and pistons, rebuild engines, and do general tune-ups. First we studied pictures of all the engine parts as I explained the procedures they were going to learn. Then I supervised their projects from my wheelchair. When the class ended, I decided they had learned much more by their intensive hands-on experience than they would have if I had merely demonstrated the work and let them watch.

When I wasn't teaching, I was in my office, where students with problems came for counseling. I was surprised one day when Ann, one of my homeroom students, appeared in the doorway. The classroom clown, Ann had a talent for keeping the homeroom in an uproar. She repeatedly dreamed up antics to entertain her classmates—and try my patience. To see her sitting in front of me struggling to hold back tears seemed completely out of character.

"What's the problem, Ann?" I asked.

She drew in a deep breath and shrugged. "It's…" She let out her breath and let her shoulders drop. "It's my grandpa. He's got cancer, and…it's so hard, Mr. Heagy! They don't think he's gonna make it."

"Oh, Ann, that's hard to handle, isn't it?" I sympathized.

We talked quite a while, and Ann came back several times as her grandfather's condition grew worse. Ann was absent from school for several days when he died, and when she returned, I made it a point to let her know I was available to talk anytime.

Determined to be an inspiring teacher and effective counselor for all the students, I spent most of my time that year either at the school, attending school activities, or working on lesson plans and grading papers at home. As I had done during the four years of college, I began focusing more and more on myself and my career and less and less on my marriage. I simply took for granted that Julie understood my motives. It didn't occur to me that she could be lonely during the long hours I spent away from home—or that she might resent the time at home I spent focused on schoolwork. While I was being stimulated by outside activities and enjoying plenty of praise and positive feedback from students and their parents, Julie was home alone, feeling deflated, unneeded, unfulfilled, and unappreciated.

Looking back on that time, it's hard to believe that I—someone who was working as a professional counselor—could be so insensitive. But I was. Totally unaware of the festering problem that was eating away at our marriage, I arrived home one day, found Julie in tears, and didn't have a clue why she could be so unhappy. It took a lot of coaxing before she was able to put her feelings into words.

"I…I feel so useless, Ron, like the last five years have been wasted. You've gone ahead and gotten an education while I've stayed home and accomplished nothing."

"But that isn't true, Julie! You've helped me accomplish my degree," I argued. "I couldn't have done it without you."

"Not really. Anyone could have done what I did; I was just a caregiver, nothing more. Now most of my friends have earned degrees, and they're working and doing something interesting. I'm bored, Ron, and I feel so useless, so…so unfulfilled."

"Julie, I had no idea you felt this way. Why didn't you tell me before?"

"You're so busy. You work hard, and when you come home, you're tired. I don't like bothering you with my problems. And the fact is, we hardly talk about *anything* anymore."

She was right. Somewhere along the way we had simply lost the thing that had brought us together—the sharing of our feelings and thoughts and dreams. In my eagerness to prove myself to the world, I had neglected to prove my love to Julie. We had drifted apart; a chasm had developed in our relationship, unnoticed by me but devastating to Julie.

Instantly, I promised to change. "I'm so sorry, Julie! This is my fault, and I want to make it up to you. Tell me what to do. Tell me what will make you happy. Would you like to go back to college…get a job…have a child? Whatever your goals are, I'll help you pursue them just like you've helped me achieve mine," I said.

She sat there on my lap, her head hanging forlornly, her tears falling on my shirt.

"That's part of the problem. I don't know, Ron. I really don't know what I want. Since we've been married, I've…I feel like I've lost my own identity. Besides, if I started something and failed, you'd blame me for it."

"Julie!" I was stunned. "You know me better than that."

"Do I?" she asked.

Why did she feel this way? How could things have deteriorated to this point?

"Julie, please forgive me for being insensitive to your needs. More than anything in the world, I want you to be happy. Whatever you'd like to do, you can count on me for support."

She lifted her head but kept her eyes averted. "I shouldn't have said anything," she lamented, pushing herself off my lap.

"Of course you should have! I want to know when something's bothering you. You're my wife, Julie. I love you!"

Reluctantly she smiled and gave me a passionless kiss. I suggested she make us dinner reservations for the following evening. "Let's go someplace romantic, just the two of us," I said.

The next afternoon when my student driver dropped me off at our cozy little cottage, I rolled up the ramp with a smile on my face, eagerly anticipating our dinner date. I was surprised to find the front door standing ajar.

I pushed the door open with my wheelchair and went inside, thinking Julie might be in the shower or the bedroom, getting ready for dinner.

"Julie? I'm home."

The little house had an inexplicably strange silence.

"Julie?" I rolled into the kitchen, then into our bedroom. Seeing the closet doors standing open, I felt my heart begin to pound. Julie's clothes were gone. In slow motion, I backed into the center of the room and wheeled around slowly in a tight, jerky orbit, the bursts of the wheelchair motor's whining the only sound. Pictures were missing, perfume bottles were gone, her shoe rack was empty.

Julie had left me.

22

Hitting Bottom

~

I found a letter on my desk in the den—a simple, yellow sheet of paper covered with words that crushed my spirit and changed my life forever.

Dear Ron,
I have decided that the time has come for us to go our separate ways. Believe me, this is the hardest decision that I have ever made, but it is one that I think is best for both of us.

There was more, much more. Julie said she loved me. But she asked me not to look for her or try to contact her.

I sat by the desk, empty and afraid, reading and rereading her letter until the words disappeared in the gathering darkness that filled the house. Too stunned at first to comprehend that Julie had no intention of returning, I tried to focus instead on the part of the letter that said, "I'll always love you, Ron..."

But she's left me.

It didn't seem possible. I rolled again into the bedroom, now filled with black shadows pierced by light from the hallway. I stared again at the empty closet, the bare tabletop where the pictures had stood, the dresser where her perfume bottles had been...and I cried.

Hot tears coursed down my cheeks. No one was there to wipe them away.

Never had I felt so lonely and dejected. After all the pain, all the difficulties, all the grief and struggles and regrets I'd been through, I'd hit bottom. Surely, I told myself, this was the worst thing life could hurl at me.

I blamed myself. I'd been too shortsighted, too selfish, too focused on my own needs and goals. Living in an idyllic bubble of self-absorption, I had neglected the person who mattered most to me. Now, after five years of unselfishly meeting my needs, Julie felt burned-out, unappreciated, empty. She wanted her freedom, and no one could fail to understand why.

Please, Lord, I prayed, sitting there alone in the darkness, my shirt soaked by tears, *help Julie see that I just need another chance. I know this is my fault; I want to make things right. Please, Lord, send her back to me…*

If Julie would just come back, I fantasized, I would show her how much I appreciated all she had done for me. I would make sure she knew how much I loved her.

Gradually, reality set in. I was alone, and I needed help. I dreaded telling my family—and not just because of the pain I knew it would generate in them. Any disappointment they might feel about the breakup of *my* marriage would intensify the heartache they had felt when Pennie left her husband.

With remorse, I realized how judgmental I had been of Pennie, thinking that nothing like that could ever happen to me. Not to *my* marriage. Now I regretted the unkind things I had thought and said to my sister. And again I had no one but myself to blame for my narrow-minded insensitivity.

I didn't want to call home, didn't want to hear the pain in my mother's voice, nor the comeuppance in Pennie's.

But who else was there? Who would be willing to help a paralyzed man with his most intimate personal needs, feed him dinner, change his catheter bag, undress him, and lift him into bed? My mind quickly ran through the short list of possibilities without stopping. Then I thought of someone…

My Uncle Dave and his family had recently moved back to Oregon after his retirement from the military. I called Dave's daughter, my cousin Brenda. Her cheerfulness as she answered the phone made a lump rise in my throat. "Hi, Ron. How are things going?"

"Rotten."

"Oh? Why?" she asked, surprised.

"Julie has walked out on me, and I didn't know who else to call. Could you…I'm sorry to ask…could you possibly come over and spend the night?"

Brenda didn't hesitate, didn't ask any more questions. "Of course, Ron. I'll be right over." She came immediately, listened to my sad story, and cried with me. Then she fixed my dinner and put me to bed. I was emotionally spent and physically exhausted, but sleep wouldn't come. Again and again, I replayed in my mind the passionate speech I would say to Julie, if only she would come back. Again and again, I prayed, *Please Lord, bring her back to me.*

By the time I needed to be turned over, I had dozed off. As a matter of habit, I called out to Julie. Brenda's face soon appeared over mine.

"It's me, Ron. Julie's gone, remember? But don't worry. I'll stay as long as you need me," she said, gently rolling me over. She patted my back then padded silently into the other room.

Somehow I made it through my classes the next day, but it was obvious to my students that my heart wasn't in it. "Is something wrong, Mr. Heagy?" one of them asked.

"I'm just not feeling well today, Shannon," I answered. "I'll be okay."

As the student driver turned the van onto our street, I closed my eyes and prayed again that Julie's little car would be waiting in the driveway. But it wasn't. I kept hoping she would come back, but in my heart I knew she was gone for good. Julie was not an impulsive person. She probably had been mulling over this move in her mind for a long time without telling me. Now, knowing what a determined person she was, I didn't really expect her to come back.

Still, I waited, hoping every time the phone rang, every time a car passed on the street, that it might be Julie. But it wasn't. She didn't come, didn't call.

After a few days, I called Jim, her disabled brother, the member of her family to whom I felt closest. He didn't know where Julie had gone. Her friends told me the same thing. I even tried to get in touch with her old boyfriend, the man she'd been engaged to before we met. But no one knew where my wife was. She apparently had vanished without a clue.

Pride got in the way of my telling others what had happened. I didn't want my colleagues and the students at school to know that my marriage had failed—that I had failed.

For the past five years I had been on an intellectual mind trip. Earning a degree, making good grades, and proving to the world that disabilities can be overcome had become my top priority. Now, without Julie, those things no longer seemed important at all.

Mom and Dad were shocked when I finally found the courage to tell them what had happened. They both loved Julie, and they worked hard not to take sides while offering unquestioning love and support. Only Mom could see how crushed and empty I felt. When we were alone, she put her arms around me and cried, just as she had done the night she had arrived at my bedside in the California hospital. "I don't understand why God has let you go through so much heartache, but nothing happens without a reason. You'll be a stronger person for this. You'll understand how painful it is for a marriage to end, and you'll be able to help others work through their misery just as you're going to have to work through yours now."

"I know you're right, Mom. All things work together for good," I agreed. "But right now, all I can think about is how much it hurts."

23

My New Companion

~

I needed a permanent caregiver, but the Social Services agency had no nurses available for live-in assignments. When the staff ran an ad in the local newspaper, only one person responded. The agency gave Daniel Webster Doe my number and suggested he call me.

When my student driver dropped me off at my home on the day of our interview, I found a rough-looking man in his fifties waiting on my front porch. He was half aging hippie, half Hell's Angel; a big, burly man with long hair and a bushy beard. A leopard tattoo peeked out from under the sleeve of his faded T-shirt, and his blue jeans sagged. An old, beat-up bicycle leaned against the porch steps.

Great! I thought, morosely checking our Mr. Doe's disheveled appearance and shabby clothes. *They must have advertised for a bar bouncer or a companion for a paralyzed Hell's Angel.* For a moment I regretted that I hadn't locked my front door before leaving that morning. *He's probably already been inside and robbed me blind,* I decided.

I wondered how quickly I could get rid of him. It would be impolite just to roll up to the porch and say, "Hello, nice to meet you. Please leave." But obviously, this guy would never do.

As if to contradict my first impression of him, the huge man quickly rose and hopped off the porch when he saw the van pull in. Stepping to the side door, he lifted the door handle, reached inside, and deftly lowered the lift.

"Hello," he said with a merry twinkle in his eye. The friendly smile beneath his beard instantly transformed him from an intimidating hulk to Santa Claus.

Starting to reach out for a handshake, he quickly shoved both hands in his pockets instead. "I'm Daniel," he said, eyes still twinkling.

Surprising myself, I liked him instantly.

His background was as mottled as his appearance: An abused child, teenage runaway, military veteran, and former alcoholic and drug abuser, he had been married and divorced twice and had even served time in jail—the perfect companion for a completely dependent, single, Christian schoolteacher trying to recover from a broken heart.

Ours was an odd-couple arrangement that somehow worked. Once I finally adjusted to his shortcomings in cooking and housekeeping, I grew to admire and appreciate his more important characteristics: staunch loyalty and great dependability. Daniel's heart was as big as his body. He would do anything for me, and he never once complained, no matter how many times I called him during the night. Like Mike, he didn't always wake up right away, and he sometimes crashed around in a sleep-induced stupor, trying to find me. But once awake, he was a lucid and caring companion.

Daniel had one shortcoming—he didn't drive a car and refused to learn. Instead, he had become a speed demon on his old bicycle. When he first came to work for me on a temporary basis, Daniel held down two jobs. During the day when I was at school, he rode his bike to Corvallis, a distance of 34 miles round-trip. When I returned home each evening, he was always there waiting for me—rain or shine. And in Oregon, there's a lot more rain than shine!

It was a relief to have my physical needs so ably managed, but emotionally, my life was in shambles. It shamed me to realize how callous I'd been to heartbroken friends and relatives who had grieved after ruined marriages. I'd certainly not sympathized with them as they struggled to put their lives back together as divorced and broken people.

Now I understood. The guilt, shame, rejection, remorse, and self-incrimination that endlessly swirled through my psyche left me weak and devastated. Eventually I became physically ill and suffered heart palpitations. My doctors blamed the problem on stress.

"You need to slow down, Ron. Relax! Take time to smell the roses," the cardiologist said.

My ophthalmologist's diagnosis was similar. "Your optic nerves were damaged by the severe blow you received to the head, and stress has a tendency to make the pressure in your eyes go up. Unfortunately you've developed glaucoma, and you may have to have surgery someday. You should stop pushing yourself, Ron. Learn to relax and take life easy."

The doctors thought stress was a side effect of my constant work activities. What they didn't know was that I worked constantly to try to take my mind off my broken heart.

Daniel was a spark of hope in that dismal, dark period. He had become a better cook, but the real source of his nurturance was his ridiculous sense of humor. He made me laugh when I felt like crying.

He also offered his rather casual philosophy on life. For example, he equated marriage partners with flies on a window pane. "Those on the outside want in," he mused. "Those on the inside want out. So why not open the window and let them go their own way?"

I didn't share Daniel's easy-come, easy-go philosophy. Instead, I considered the vows Julie and I took at our wedding as sacred and thought she felt the same. I wrote long letters to her, recommitting myself to those vows, telling her how much I loved her and promising to do anything she suggested.

My letters came back unopened.

24

The Next Step

~

E verything in our little home reminded me of Julie. Staying there was killing me. I had to get away, to make a new start. I finally contacted her by phone, but despite all my pleading and promises, she refused to reconcile.

I decided to go back to school, hoping the challenges of studying toward an advanced degree would be a good distraction. I applied for admission to the graduate program at San Diego State—and was promptly rejected. The university wasn't equipped to handle students with a disability as extensive as mine, the admissions officer's letter explained. I fired back a reply, citing discrimination and urging the university to reconsider my application. A couple of months later, I was a college student again.

Daniel agreed to go with me to San Diego—but only temporarily. All the hustle-bustle of traffic would get on his nerves. Hating to lose him, I reluctantly agreed to look for another caregiver as soon as he helped me get settled in San Diego.

The next difficult thing I had to do was give Harold Grove my resignation from East Linn Academy. I dreaded it, but he responded kindly and said a job would be waiting for me when I completed my master's degree.

My cousin Brad drove Daniel and me to San Diego in the Green Bean, then flew back to Oregon. We settled into a place with a bedroom for each of us and kitchen privileges shared with Ron and Theresa, a young, compatible couple who had advertised for roommates. We didn't have much privacy, but knowing the young couple would be around in case of an emergency gave me confidence that the arrangement would work out.

My first visit to the local vocational rehab agency was about as successful as my first application to San Diego State. I had hoped the agency would be able to provide some financial assistance, but their focus was on young drug or alcohol addicts, who they believed could be rehabilitated. In contrast, the agency considered a quadriplegic as a dead end, a lost cause with an irreversible condition. After repeated requests for help, the rehab counselor finally told me if I could find four companies who agreed to hire me after I had a master's degree, the agency would reconsider my request.

"Are you kidding?" I asked in disbelief. "Even a student without disabilities couldn't find four companies who would *guarantee* employment two years in the future!"

"Sorry, Mr. Heagy, but we can't award grants unless we're assured that the final results are worth the risk."

I rolled out of his office feeling discouraged but determined. As soon as I got back home, I made an appointment with a different counselor at the same agency, and again my persistence paid off. The compassionate professional helped me get my request for financial assistance approved.

Two down, two to go, I told myself when the rehab agency's financial support came through. I'd persuaded San Diego State to take a chance on me, and I'd won financial assistance. Now all I had to do was find a competent caregiver and earn my degree! Ruefully, I admitted that the first two steps, as hard as they had been, were easy compared with the next two challenges I faced. Soon I would decide that graduate school was a snap compared with finding a good caregiver.

First there was Wally, a character who turned out to be as undependable as Daniel had been faithful. He took off the first weekend, leaving me stranded and completely dependent on my kind roommates, then reappeared late Sunday night, dead drunk. In the wee hours of the morning, he wove his way up the ramp to the porch, stumbled through the door, and fell on the floor twice before finally flopping onto his bed, fully clothed.

The next day, Wally was hung over—and extremely sorry. "My wife ran out on me a couple of months ago," he said, sitting at the kitchen table and holding his aching head in his hands, "and I've had a hard time getting over it."

Join the club, pal, I silently agreed.

"Thought a few beers might help me forget," Wally continued. "So I stopped at a bar…and that's the last thing I remember. Sorry, Ron. It won't happen again. I promise."

It wasn't as if I had a dozen competent contenders standing in line to work for me, so I forgave Wally and reluctantly agreed to give him a second chance. Greatly relieved, he popped some aspirin and declared that his hangover was under control. He loaded me into the Green Bean and helped me complete the errands I had planned on doing over the weekend. One of them was withdrawing some cash at an automatic teller machine, where Wally persuaded me to increase the amount I'd told him to withdraw so that I could give him a cash advance on his salary.

Okay, I admit it. I was stupid. That became abundantly clear when a school assistant brought me back home later that day, and I discovered Wally and my ATM card were both missing. I never saw him again. The card eventually showed up in the mail, but not the $400 Wally had withdrawn from my bank account.

Helen, my next caregiver, was even worse than Wally, if that's possible. Crude and slovenly, she read my mail, used obscene language, and swore at me whenever her patience grew thin. Her coarseness and her rough treatment of me made me long for Julie's tender touch again. Then Helen decided she was infatuated with me and made sexual advances while taking care of my personal needs.

Next came Ned, an 18-year-old student who quickly proved to be incompetent. He was followed by Thomas, whose bungling ways I almost thought I could endure—and then he dropped me as he was rolling me off the bed one day. Wedged between the box springs and the wall, I was fortunate that my roommates had not yet left for work. It took all three of them to finally get me back onto the bed.

While trying to survive the string of killer caregivers, I was finding that graduate school in a secular setting was a far harsher challenge than I had anticipated it to be. Many of my professors began our relationship with the same, pointed question: "Mr. Heagy, how do you expect to earn a master's degree in your condition?"

Even though I came to expect it, the question always caused my heart to thump a little harder in my chest, but I managed to look each one of them in the eye and answer resolutely, "One day at a time, that's how. I'm just gonna take it one day at a time."

Some instructors weren't willing to make any concessions for me. They insisted that I take tests with the rest of the class or complete spoken exams with a prompter. Some of them probably thought they were doing me a favor by having a good-looking coed sit close to me and ask me the test questions. Instead, I often became flustered; inevitably my mind went blank, and the material I had studied thoroughly and knew well went flying into outer space. Despite these limitations, I was determined to make straight As. Anything less was unacceptable.

In contrast to the many instructors who were unwilling to go out of their way to make anything easier for me, one professor showed an exceptionally compassionate attitude. Instead of delivering stern ultimatums, Dr. Harris asked me how she could help meet my needs. She understood that my disability made it difficult to accomplish even the simplest tasks, and her warm and nurturing instruction was a godsend to me that first year.

Between my caregiver blues and struggles to complete my coursework, I had little time for socializing. I rarely left my apartment except to go to my classes. It seemed that every minute was devoted to solving problems—either homework assignments or caregiver crises. I was lonely, and there didn't seem to be any remedy. I had few opportunities to make new friends. I missed my family. But most of all, I missed Julie. As hard as I tried, when my assignments were finished and I was lying alone in the darkness, I couldn't help but think of her, how we'd talked and laughed together, the crazy things we'd done, and the intimacy we'd shared. I had thought in San Diego I would be able to get over the hurt; I had prayed that the pain of losing her would finally diminish, but it didn't.

There was one spark of hope deep down in my heart that refused to be smothered. It was that stubborn part of me that thought maybe, just maybe Julie would come back to me.

Then came the day when I rolled to the front door to answer the doorbell—and found Julie standing on the porch.

25

What Might Have Been

~

Julie stood on the other side of the screen door, silhouetted by the sunlight glowing behind her. Seeing my startled expression, she smiled. "Hi, Ron. May I come in?"

"Uh…Sure!…Of course!" I stammered. "Why…I mean… what are you doing in California?"

"My parents and I are here on vacation; I decided to drop in and see how you're doing. How is everything? You're looking good."

"Great! Yes, I'm doing great…just fine, no problems." I fought the impulse to tell her the truth. As long as we were here talking, smiling, chitchatting, maybe she wouldn't leave—and with all my heart, I wanted her to stay.

She played the game with me. We exchanged trivial conversation, tossing empty phrases back and forth like a beach ball. *Just keep the conversation going,* I told myself. *Don't get into the heavy stuff. Don't break the mood. Don't tell her how much you love her and need her. Just keep the small talk flowing.*

And we did—talking, chuckling, reminiscing, and bringing each other up to date on our friends and families until the sun went down and the stars came out. I braced myself for the moment when she would stand and say good-bye, but she seemed in no hurry to leave. Finally, I gathered up my courage and asked if she'd like to stay.

"There's a spare bedroom just down the hall," I quickly added. "You're welcome to stay as long as you like."

141

"Thanks," she said simply. "I'll go get my suitcase; it's in the car."

Much to my surprise, Julie stayed the next day...and the next. It was wonderful being near her again. For one fleeting moment, I hoped that being together might make her reconsider our separation. But things were not the same. The magic had disappeared from our relationship. Julie's eyes no longer sparkled when they met mine.

Still, she stayed a week, and I suggested again that we go see a counselor to try to work out our differences.

"It's too late for that, Ron," she said gently.

"Then why did you come, Julie? You must have had a reason."

She hesitated. "I...I really don't know. Maybe it was just to make sure...to make sure this separation was the best thing for both of us."

"Well, it's *not* the best thing for *both* of us," I answered, the frustration rising in my voice. We were both quiet then, empty and finished. Finally I asked the question that had been bothering me since she first left. "Julie, is there someone else?"

Julie looked away and didn't answer. Instead, she picked up her suitcase and carried it to the door.

"'Bye, Ron," she said.

A few weeks later, the divorce papers arrived.

While my marriage was coming apart, my sister, Pennie, whose own divorce had caused me to be so judgmental of her, was in the process of marrying again. By the time I'd completed my first year of graduate school, she and her husband, Sean, were the parents of a handsome little son.

In many ways, Pennie had been my soulmate as we were growing up. We had been very close to each other all our lives, so I knew my sanctimonious preaching had hurt her when her first marriage ended. Now that I was divorced myself, I was a lot wiser about the kind of pressure and pain that follows a failed marriage. I called Pennie in the middle of the night after a bad dream in which I'd seen her lying hurt and abandoned on the beach. Haunted by the memory of how harsh I'd been toward her, I scared her with my late-night call—when all I needed was to apologize.

"Oh, Ron, I understand," she said when I told her I was sorry. "People don't know what it's like until they go through it, do they? I love you, Ron. Good night."

Now, as the school year ended, Pennie and Sean were inviting me to spend my summer vacation with them and baby Jacob, and Daniel agreed to come and take care of me as soon as he was free. It was a perfect arrangement.

I enjoyed getting to know little Jacob. Sometimes Pennie would set his carrier on the tray of my wheelchair and tape his bottle to my mouth stick so I could feed him. Watching him gurgle and coo as he concentrated so intently on my face, I longed to hold him and felt sad thinking about what might have been…if only Julie hadn't left me…

Seeing Pennie so happily married made me wonder if my own marriage might have survived if Julie and I had started a family. Surely she would have been more committed to our marriage if we'd had a child, but it was too late now for second-guessing.

It was an idyllic summer. I relished being back in Oregon among my family and friends, and after the series of inept caregivers I'd suffered with in California, having Daniel with me again was a true blessing.

The only thing that marred my homecoming was a crazy rumor circulating among my former East Linn Academy students. The kids had been told by some unknown culprit that I had left my wife for another woman.

"How could anyone believe such a thing?" I asked Pennie, astonished that anyone would start a rumor so far from the truth. "I tried to be a good example for those kids. Now they must think I'm a hypocrite as well as an unfaithful husband."

"Your friends know the truth, Ron," she said. "It really doesn't matter what others believe."

"It matters to me! It matters what those kids think of me. I held myself up before them as a Christian, someone they could trust to do the right thing. I can't stand by and let them think I deliberately went against my own values," I argued.

"Well, what are you going to do about it?" Pennie asked.

"I'm going to talk to the kids and tell them the truth."

As I mentally went through my student roster, trying to think of someone who might help me set the record straight, a student's name popped into my mind. Ann Stone, the fun-loving classroom clown who had made sure there was never a dull moment in my homeroom—she would help me.

26

Ann

~

"Who is this?"

"Ann, it's Ron Heagy. Remember me? I was your homeroom teacher at East Linn Christian Academy."

"Oh! Hi, Mr. Heagy." On the other end of the line, Ann Stone hesitated, wondering, no doubt, why her former teacher had called. Now attending Chemeketa College on a volleyball scholarship, she sounded older, more confident and poised than when she'd kept my classroom in a constant uproar.

"There's something I'd like to discuss with you, Ann, but I'd rather not do it on the telephone. Could we get together for a few minutes in the next day or so? It shouldn't take long," I said.

Despite her more mature voice, Ann was still impetuous and enthusiastic. "Hey, I'm free tomorrow. A friend and I had planned on driving over to the coast to hang out for a couple of hours at the beach, but something's come up and she can't go. Would you like to go with me instead?"

"Well…" The beach sounded nice, but I didn't want to give her the wrong impression. After all, she was still a kid, just out of high school. Yet, it would be enjoyable to relax on the beach for a while. "Are you sure it wouldn't cramp your style to have an old, incapacitated schoolteacher tag along with you?"

Ann laughed. "You aren't that old and decrepit, Mr. Heagy. And you aren't my teacher anymore either."

145

Something in her tone made me pause a moment before continuing. "In that case, maybe you should call me Ron," I suggested.

"All right, Ron. Shall I come pick you up tomorrow?"

I gave her Pennie's address and asked if she would mind driving the Green Bean. "No problem," she said confidently.

I was ready and sitting outside the next morning when she arrived. The sight of her left me momentarily speechless. In just a year she had somehow been transformed from a bouncing, lanky, ponytailed teenager to a graceful young woman. Her long blonde hair framed her pretty face. Sporty sunglasses were perched on her cute, pixieish nose, and the brightest smile I'd ever seen nearly blinded me as I tried to think of something intelligent to say.

"Hi!" I finally managed.

"Hello," she replied easily. "I see you're all ready to go."

Ann helped me lower the lift and roll into the Green Bean, then she closed the door, stepped around the front of the van, and slipped into the driver's seat. I couldn't take my eyes off her.

"Is anything wrong?" she asked, seeing my dumbfounded face in the rearview mirror.

"I was just noticing how much you've changed in the last year," I confessed. "It's hard to believe you're the same girl who tried my patience every day for a solid year. I keep thinking about the day you stuck Cheetos in your nose and tried to imitate a walrus."

She laughed. "Yeah. I was pretty talented at stuff like that, wasn't I?"

We both laughed. The day was getting off to an interesting start—certainly it seemed to be heading along a far different tack than the one I'd expected.

At the beach, Ann pushed my wheelchair on the boardwalk as we continued to talk about trivial things. Finally, I decided to tell her the reason I had called. "Ann, you've probably heard a rumor that's been circulating about why my marriage ended," I blurted out.

"Yes, as a matter of fact, I have heard something about that," she replied evenly.

"Well, it isn't true, and I don't have any idea how such a thing got started in the first place."

She looked at me, smiled, and shrugged her shoulders. "Don't worry, Ron. No one believed it. We just considered the source."

"Oh." I felt a little embarrassed that I'd assumed my students would blindly believe the worst of me without checking the source. *I should have given them more credit than that,* I realized. And that was that. Our "business meeting" was over, and the rest of the day stretched before us.

At lunchtime Ann fed me as we both chattered away like magpies, laughing, joking, and enjoying our shared love of mischief. Once during the day, she even drained my leg bag, and it amazed me to see how she took everything in stride. She accepted my disability without reservation or embarrassment. By the time we had shared a pizza for dinner and were on our way back to Pennie's, I'd completely forgotten about the rumor that had irritated me the past few days.

That night in bed, I relived the day in detail, smiling again at Ann's wit and sense of humor. I realized it had been a long, long time since I'd laughed so much and had such fun. I also realized how attracted I was to Ann, and it disturbed me.

27

The Incredible Journey

~

Summer slipped by much too fast. I dreaded leaving my family and
friends—especially Ann. But the moments we had shared over the
past months were captured in my memory for future reminiscing.
I was relaxed and refreshed, ready to finish my master's program. Only
one problem remained: Daniel still refused to go with me to San Diego,
so I had to find a new caregiver.

Pennie suggested advertising for an attendant who could also drive
the Green Bean and take me back to California. She helped me interview
and screen applicants, and we finally agreed that the most likely candidate was a pleasant, 48-year-old lady with a Ph.D. She told us she was
a credentialed teacher by profession but had recently been working as a
practical nurse. Shane sounded sincere, and I had no reason to doubt her,
nor did we have time to thoroughly check the references she gave us.

Once we were on the freeway, it pleased me to see how well Shane
handled the van, even though we were pulling a heavily-loaded trailer.
She was also a pleasant companion and an interesting conversationalist.
We chatted amicably, sharing some of our experiences as teachers, and
with each mile we covered, my confidence in Shane increased. I would
no longer have to fear being mistreated, robbed, or abandoned.

Several times along the way, we stopped for rest breaks and fuel.
Shane offered me some of the fried chicken and potato salad she had
brought along, but I opted for a sandwich Pennie had packed for me.

Each time we stopped, Shane took care of my needs and then hopped out to stretch her legs.

When we stopped in Bakersfield for gasoline, Shane went to the restroom, carrying a tote bag with her, while an attendant filled the tank. Several minutes passed, and I began to be concerned when Shane finally reappeared, swaying unsteadily as she walked, both arms clutching the tote bag. She approached the driver's side of the van, slipped off the step, and grabbed the steering wheel for support, accidentally honking the horn.

Thinking she might be sick, I asked, "Are you feeling okay?"

Shane nodded. "Sure, I'm fine."

The stimulating conversation we had carried on before suddenly stopped. *She's probably tired*, I thought. *After all, it's been a long drive. I feel pretty washed out myself.*

We slipped back into the stream of traffic and soon started winding down the Grapevine, a steep and treacherous stretch of highway that truck drivers dread. The Green Bean swung a bit wide on several turns, causing me to fall forward. I could smell rubber every time Shane stepped on the brakes a little too forcefully. Deep ravines lay just beyond the guardrails, and I was relieved when we reached the bottom of the grade without catapulting over the edge.

We had just rounded the last curve, weaving slightly over the center line, when I heard a loud bang that sounded like a gunshot. The van swerved, first right, then left. I cringed, expecting the trailer to jackknife and whip us off the road any minute.

"Stop, Shane!" I shouted over the screech of the tires. "Pull over. Sounds like we've blown a tire." She jerked the wheel to the right, and we came to an unsteady stop on an unpaved shoulder. "You'd better get out and check the tires."

Shane stared at me as though in a stupor. I had to repeat my words before she finally grabbed the handle and pushed the door open, missing the step again as she stumbled out of the van.

"Shane, are you all right?" I asked again.

She didn't answer, but merely cocked her head and stared at me, her eyes bleary and unfocused.

Seeing she was not going to be much help, I asked her to open my door and lower the lift.

For several seconds she struggled with the levers while I waited impatiently. Once the ramp was lowered, I rolled out and back to check the trailer. Sure enough! One of the trailer tires was in shreds.

"What're we gonna do now?" Shane's question came in a slur.

"Good question," I answered. "The only spare we have is for the van." I glanced at her again. "Shane, what's wrong? Are you ill?"

"I feel...sick. Must...have been...the chicken." Without another word she clumsily climbed into the backseat and closed her eyes.

"Shane?" I called to her.

No answer. The van was silent except for Shane's heavy breathing.

Turning my wheelchair in a circle, I surveyed the surroundings. Ahead lay the beautiful San Fernando Valley and a service station a mile or so down the road. Behind us sat a small motel we had passed shortly before the tire blew. Figuring the motel was closer, I headed there, steering my wheelchair with my chin as it rolled bumpily along the shoulder of the road.

When I reached the parking lot several minutes later, I spotted a man unloading his luggage. "Excuse me, sir," I said. He seemed not to hear me. "SIR!" I repeated, causing him to turn around. "My trailer has blown a tire. Could you possibly come give me a hand?"

Without a word and with obvious reluctance, he followed me back down the road to the van. "This spare won't fit your trailer wheel. It's too big," he said after examining the spare.

"Yes sir, I know that," I answered as patiently as I could. "But if you could take the tire off the trailer and strap it onto my lap, I'd be much obliged. There's a service station ahead. Maybe I can buy a new tire and have the mechanic come put it on for me."

The man heaved a disgusted sigh, then went to work with the jack. When he got the tire off the trailer, he carried it over to me, laid it on my lap, fastened it in place with a strap, then turned and walked off without another word. He didn't offer to take me to the service station, and I didn't press my luck by asking.

Once again I was bumping along the shoulder of the freeway, now in deepening twilight. Motorists sped by, the draft from their speeding vehicles nearly toppling me and my wheelchair. "Should have had lights installed on this hot rod," I mumbled to myself.

The service station was farther away than it had appeared, and the attendant was preparing to close for the night when I rolled in. He seemed annoyed by the interruption. He didn't speak English, and I knew only a few words of Spanish.

Nodding toward the shredded tire in my lap and then the rack of new ones overhead, I asked "Cuanto?"

"Sesenta y cinco," he answered. When I shook my head, he scribbled some numbers on a scrap of paper: $65.

I had less than $50 in my wallet.

I shook my head. "Mucho grande."

"Sesenta y cinco," he repeated with finality.

Discouraged, I rolled back to the van with the shredded tire still on my lap.

During my absence, Shane had apparently roused long enough to lock all the doors of the van. I yelled her name and bumped my wheelchair against the door several times. No response, except for her snoring.

I shut my eyes. *Hello, Lord. It's me, Ron. I'm here in the wringer again and need help. Could you please…*

Just then an old, beat-up Chevy truck with one headlight out and a coat hanger for a radio antenna pulled up alongside my wheelchair. A scruffy-looking guy with a bandanna tied around his head shouted out the window, "Hey, buddy. Need some help?"

I didn't know how to respond. Yes, I did need help, but I didn't expect the Lord to send a knight in shining armor who looked more like a thug. No telling what this guy might do. All of my possessions— clothes, computer, TV, books—were in the trailer.

As his hippie-looking girlfriend blew smoke rings out the window, he slid out of the truck, hitched up his blue jeans, and walked over to me. He glanced at the tire on my lap and smiled, showing a gap where one of his front teeth had been. "A blowout, huh? If you've got a spare, I'll change it for you."

"Thanks. I do have a spare, but it's too big."

He dropped his cigarette and ground it into the gravel before answering. "In that case, guess I'll have to find one for you." He untied the tire and threw it into the back of his truck. "Shouldn't take long," he said, slamming the door and driving off in a cloud of black smoke.

Good-bye, wheel, I lamented. *That guy's probably going to trade it for a six-pack of beer.*

Shane was still dead to the world.

Thirty minutes later, the old truck returned in its cloud of smoke, and my Good Samaritan friend hopped out and proudly retrieved a new tire from the back. "Got it!" he announced with a grin.

In record time, the new tire and wheel were on the trailer, and the lug nuts were securely tightened. "Hey, man, you're a godsend," I told him. "How much do I owe you?"

"Nothing, pal. If you ever see me sitting beside the road in trouble, you can return the favor, okay?" With that, he got back into the dilapidated Chevy and took off.

Where did he find a trailer tire this late at night? I wondered, watching his taillights shrink in the distance. *Guess that really doesn't matter, Lord. The important thing is that You found him, and he found me! Thank You, Father!*

I bumped the van door repeatedly with my chair until Shane finally sat up. "Where are we?" she asked in a groggy voice.

"We're in the middle of nowhere, and I'm chilled to the bone," I said impatiently. "Are you feeling any better?"

"Uh-uh."

"Sorry," I responded, "but it's too dangerous to stay here. We're lucky someone hasn't smacked us already. Lower the lift, and let me in."

Once she got me back inside and secured my chair to the floor, I wondered if my decision had been a wise one. She started the engine with a roar, and without looking pulled onto the freeway. She wove through the traffic, totally unaware of honking horns, flashing headlights, and screeching tires responding to near misses.

Eventually I spotted a shopping mall on our right and told her to pull into its well-lighted parking lot. "Shane, let's stop for the night," I suggested. "Maybe you'll feel better in the morning."

Shane's answer was a blank stare and, "Huh?"

I didn't bother to explain again. "Take the next off-ramp. Okay?"

As soon as the car came to a halt and the ignition switch had been turned off, Shane slumped over the steering wheel and was asleep again. I lowered my wheelchair to a reclining position and tried to sleep too, but it was hopeless. Shane's incessant snoring kept me awake. I closed my eyes in an effort to relax, then opened them at the sound of approaching footsteps. Several teenagers wearing baggy pants and baseball caps were sauntering toward the van. *Great!* I thought. *All we need to make this day perfect is to be robbed by a gang of kids!*

"Shane, wake up!" I yelled.

She stirred and pushed herself away from the steering wheel. "Huh? Whatcha want?"

"We've gotta get out of here! And quick."

My urgent tone must have startled her into action. Shane peeled out of the parking lot like a demon-possessed maniac. Feeding back onto the freeway, she weaved in and out of lanes with abandon as angry drivers swerved to avoid being sideswiped by the careening trailer. All I could do was hold my breath and pray.

After more than three hours of highway horror, we arrived in San Diego at 2:30 in the morning—unnerved but otherwise unharmed.

Shane collapsed on the couch while my roommates, the married couple who had befriended me so many times during the previous year, put me to bed. Theresa even offered to stay home from work the next day to fill in until my nurse was back on her feet. Three days later, when Shane's condition still hadn't improved, I finally—and reluctantly—called Helen and asked her to come take care of us both. She was still rough and loud, but at least she was alert.

Only then did we discover Shane's problem. It *wasn't* food poisoning.

28

Life Rolls On

~

Shane was drunk. Helen found six empty vodka bottles under her bed. It thoroughly disgusted me to see my caregiver sprawled on the floor, still lost in a drunken stupor. Yet at the same time I felt sorry for her and wanted to help. Wondering if I was repeating the mistake I'd made with Wally, I told Shane if she would enroll in Alcoholics Anonymous and stick to the program, I wouldn't fire her. "But one relapse, Shane, and you're out of here," I warned.

Theresa and Ron were not happy with the arrangement, and I couldn't blame them for not wanting to share their home with a quadriplegic and an alcoholic. I rented two rooms from someone else, and Shane and I moved.

True to her promise, Shane joined Alcoholics Anonymous, and for a few weeks she stayed sober. Then, after an especially stressful day at school, a friend drove me home to find the house a mess and Shane back on the bottle.

When I confronted her, she made threats and verbally abused me before collapsing onto the couch in another one of her drunken stupors. Asking her to leave would have been ridiculous when she couldn't even stand up; on the other hand, I wanted her out *right then!*

I called the police department and asked if Shane could be taken into custody. The dispatcher replied that as long as she was not in a public place and was not disturbing the peace, there was nothing the police could do. I was disgusted with Shane and with myself. I had gotten myself into this mess by being too softhearted, and it wasn't the first time!

"Well, there's nothing I can do but wait for her to sober up," I told the friend who had driven me home. "But in the meantime, I'll need some help." I paused, hoping Jim might volunteer. He didn't.

"Uh…Jim, is there any chance you could feed me some supper and lift me onto the bed before you leave?"

Jim was one of the men from the Bible study I had helped lead since first moving to California. He was not a college student, but I considered him to be a friend I could confide in. His response shocked me. "Ron, you don't seem to realize that we all have problems and responsibilities. You should hire someone dependable to take care of you and not impose on your friends every time there's a problem."

I couldn't have been more stunned if he had suddenly slapped me. Nodding curtly, I thanked him for driving me home and said good-bye, wondering as I watched him leave if all of my buddies felt the way Jim did—and if I had any friends at all.

With my mouth stick I dialed the number of another Bible study friend. "Jon, I'm in a real bind tonight," I told him.

"What's the problem?"

"My nurse is out, and I need some help. There's food in the refrigerator, but I can't get to it. Is there any chance you could come over to feed me and lift me into bed?"

There was a brief pause, then Jon answered, "Uh, Ron, several of the guys from church are coming over for a Bible study tonight, and it's my turn to lead the discussion."

"Hey, that sounds great," I said, terribly relieved. I knew those guys. "Why don't you meet here instead? This has been a really trying day for me; everything that could go wrong *has*. I could use some Christian fellowship right now."

"Sorry, Ron. It's too late to change our plans," Jon replied breezily. "The guys are due to arrive in 15 minutes. But we'll pray for you."

I hung up, shocked and hurt by the reaction of men I had considered my friends. I glanced over at Shane, still sprawled on the sofa in a most unladylike position, an empty vodka bottle clutched in one hand and her crumpled dress stained with urine. I bumped my wheelchair against the couch in an effort to rouse her. "Shane, wake up. *Wake UP!*"

Silence.

"Shane, it's time to fix supper." She opened her bloodshot eyes, stared into space for a minute, then promptly snapped them closed again. If this binge was similar to her previous one, she would be a zombie for days. In the meantime, my only option was to call an agency and ask them to send over a nurse, an expensive alternative on such short notice.

That night after the agency assistant had fed me and put me to bed, I lay awake a long time. I had never felt so alone.

A few days later, I received a letter from Jim. He called me selfish and overbearing and said I had taken advantage of casual acquaintances.

So I lost some "casual acquaintances" that second year in San Diego, but I also gained a real friend. Dave Woods liked many of the same things I did. We enjoyed some lively discussions about our Christian beliefs, and we also had fun hanging out at the beach on weekends. Dave was willing to be there for me when I needed him. If I had an accident, soiling my clothes or overfilling my leg bag, he took care of it with good humor. After my hurtful experience with Jim and the others, Dave's friendship turned out to be one of the best things that happened to me that year.

Even better was my relationship with Ann. Since the day we'd spent together on the beach in Oregon, she had rarely been out of my thoughts. Ann was beautiful, vivacious, popular among her peers, and always fun to be with. I was instantly attracted to her, but told myself she was hopelessly out of my reach. I was ten years older than Ann, divorced, and unsure whether remarriage was an option for me.

The summer before I had been surprised—at myself and at her response—when I asked her to go out with me on several occasions and she said yes.

We had seen each other frequently throughout the summer, going to parties, movies, and concerts in Portland. But I kept telling myself we were just friends, nothing more. We never spoke of our feelings or discussed our relationship until the weekend before I was to leave for California. We had gone camping with my cousins, and on the way home, I started thinking about going back to San Diego—without Ann.

Driving the Green Bean expertly through the mountain pass, Ann also seemed lost in thought.

"Tired?" I asked her, finally breaking the silence.

"No, just thinking."

"What about?"

She turned toward me with a wistful smile. "I may as well tell you, Ron. I was thinking about you...about us. I've had a lot of fun with you this summer, and I'm going to miss you."

Her reference to "us" gave me hope. "Ann, I haven't dared tell you before, but I've come to have some very strong feelings for you, and that bothers me."

"Bothers you? Why?"

I nodded. "You're young and beautiful, Ann. I'm ten years older, and I've been married before. It's crazy to think you could feel anything more than friendship for me."

Even in the darkness, I could see the pleased expression on her face as she turned to glance at me. "Do you remember the first time we went to the beach together?" she asked.

"Sure. I remember every moment."

"So do I. That was such a wonderful day I didn't want it to end. Most of the guys I've met are on ego trips. All they think about is themselves—what they want and how they're going to get it. You're different, Ron. I can be myself with you; I can share my feelings and be confident you won't put me down."

In the movies, at that point the car (no doubt a sporty convertible) would have pulled to the side of the road, and the man would have swept the young woman into his embrace, kissing her passionately.

Instead, we kept rolling along in the big green van, both of us smiling into the darkness, a single, shared thought forming in our minds: *Wow!*

When Shane and I left the next morning on what was to be our harrowing trip back to the university, Ann, Daniel, Pennie, and little Jacob watched from the driveway as we prepared to leave. Daniel winked and told me to behave myself. Pennie cautioned us to be careful and told me to keep in touch. And Ann...well, Ann cried.

"I'll be praying for you, Ron," she said, her voice breaking, as she stood at the door of the van.

"Thanks, Ann. Take care of yourself while I'm gone, okay? I'll see you at Christmas."

Something was different—better—about my second year of graduate school. The difference was Ann.

Living on a very limited budget, I always had more bills than money, but I became an expert in cutting corners and scrimping on nonessentials so I could indulge in my one luxury—small gifts and long-distance telephone calls to Ann.

The first thing I did after returning home from campus each day was to check my mailbox, then my answering machine. Finding a letter or a telephone message from Ann always made my day.

I enjoyed buying little surprises to send her—a card with a sentimental message, flowers, candy, a bottle of perfume. No matter how trivial the trinket, she responded as if it were the Hope diamond, gushing, "Oh, Ron, I love it! Thanks! You're sweet! I miss you so much, and I can hardly wait for us to be together again."

I couldn't help but notice, though, that she always stopped short of saying those three magic words, "I love you." I suspected she was waiting for me to say the words first, and they were certainly ready to spring out of my heart. But despite my growing feelings for Ann, my past still stood in the way. I was a divorced man and a Christian, and I wasn't sure what that meant for my future. The Bible has some pretty strong declarations about divorce and remarriage. I needed help understanding how they applied to my situation.

I hoped it would be possible for my relationship with Ann to continue. She made me feel happy and complete, like a 16-year-old in love for the first time. Julie had needed me, and I certainly had needed her, but that hadn't been enough. In contrast, Ann was self-confident and determined, a young woman who knew what she wanted and went after it enthusiastically and purposefully. I was less needy than before, or so I thought, because I had succeeded—albeit tenuously—at living on my own. I had proven that I could fend for myself. Although it was a struggle at times, I had become fairly self-reliant. I didn't need a wife to take care of me. I wanted someone to share my life with, have fun with, cry with, struggle with through whatever challenges life threw at us. I could now take care of a wife's needs.

With these feelings growing stronger every day, I was delighted when she called one night and said she was coming to California.

"Our volleyball team has some games in Pismo Beach. How far is that from San Diego?" she asked.

"About a five-hour drive. I'll be there."

Bethel Baptist Church
P.O. BOX 167
AUMSVILLE. OR 97325

"Ron, wait. I have to stay with the team. I just thought you might like to come see one of our games."

"I'll be there," I repeated. "Maybe Dave can bring me. If not," I added with exaggerated gallantry, "I'll make the trip in my wheelchair."

Ann laughed. "Knowing you, Ron Heagy, I wouldn't be at all surprised if you tried."

Luckily, Dave eagerly agreed to join me on a two-day getaway, so I didn't have to make another freeway trek in my wheelchair. Early one morning, he loaded my chair into the back of a pickup truck I had purchased for resale, and we took off for Pismo Beach. The Chemeketa Community College team was already in the middle of a spirited game when we arrived.

Even in her uniform, soaked with sweat and her hair pulled back in a braid, Ann was beautiful. When I told Dave which one she was, his eyebrows lifted in stunned admiration. "Man, Ron, you really know how to pick 'em," he said. When Ann saw us and waved, my heart started racing.

After the game, Dave and I followed the team's bus to the motel, then the three of us went out for hamburgers and french fries at a fast-food restaurant. After dinner, Dave knew we wanted to be alone, so he lifted me into the truck and buckled the seat belt around my shoulders, then walked around to the driver's side and closed the door behind Ann.

"Think you can drive this Cadillac?" he asked Ann.

"Sure!" she answered, revving the engine and shifting gears. We headed for the beach, where we watched the sunset and chatted away as gentle waves swept over the sand. It was a warm, Indian summer night. Before we knew it, shafts of silver moonlight sparkled on the water as though the ocean had been sprinkled with stars.

I studied Ann's profile while we sat in silence, listening to the surf.

"You know, it won't be long until Christmas break," I said finally.

"Yeah, I can't wait," Ann replied.

"I was hoping you'd come down and drive me back."

"Well…"

Before she could say no, I hurried to give her all the details. "I'll send you a plane ticket, and I have some friends you could stay with in San Diego—that is, if your parents approve."

"Don't worry about Mom and Dad," she said. "They trust me, and they think you're a real great guy."

"Ann, I've never even met your parents."

"Maybe not in person, but they remember seeing you at East Linn Christian Academy when you were teaching there. Besides, both Mom and Dad have read about you in the newspaper."

"They don't mind having their daughter date a quadriplegic?"

"Ron, I don't think of you as disabled. Neither does anyone else, once they get to know you. You don't focus on your disability. Instead, your ability shines."

The next few hours passed much too quickly. We talked and talked, neither of us wanting the evening to end. The rhythmic sounds of the surf were mesmerizing, and eventually we both dozed off, Ann's head resting on my shoulder.

"Oh, no! Look what time it is!" Ann suddenly said, sitting up straight. "We'd better go back to the motel before I get in trouble."

Ann's coach was waiting for us when we arrived, pacing the sidewalk in front of the motel. We could see at a glance that he was furious. "Miss Stone, where have you been?" he asked sternly as she slid out of the truck.

Ann was scared, thinking her volleyball scholarship was about to be revoked. She started to cry. "I'm sorry, Coach. I'm so sorry. I didn't mean to be gone so long. I was with my friend, and I hadn't seen him for a long time, and we drove to the beach, and the time just got away from us."

"Sir, please don't blame Ann," I said in her defense. "It was thoughtlessness on my part. I should have asked your permission before we went for a drive." I explained that we were "old friends" and that Ann had once been my student when I taught at East Linn Academy. He finally calmed down, but not before giving her a stern lecture.

Ann slunk away to her room, glancing back quickly over her shoulder as she opened the door. The next day she stood by the truck's open window as Dave and I prepared to leave. Impulsively, I asked her, "Ann…would you kiss me good-bye?"

Without a moment's hesitation, she leaned into the cab and pressed her lips to mine. It didn't matter to either of us that our first kiss occurred with my buddy and all her teammates looking on. We weren't thinking about the others; we were thinking that this kiss felt like a promise of things to come.

On the drive back to San Diego, I confided in David my mixed emotions concerning Ann. "When we're together, she makes me almost forget about being strapped into a wheelchair. I'm afraid I'm falling for her, Dave. I feel like a 'normal' man when I'm with her…like she needs me, man."

"Afraid? Why?"

"I'm ten years older than she is, and I've been married before. Besides, I'm a quadriplegic, remember?"

"Does Ann know how you feel?" he asked.

"Not really," I admitted.

"What's holding you back?"

"I guess I'm just afraid where it might lead. I've been walked out on before; I don't want to go through that again. And besides, Ann's so young. This could be nothing more than a schoolgirl crush."

"Oh, come on, Ron. You aren't that ancient. If you're in love with Ann, tell her how much she means to you. See how she reacts. After all, that doesn't necessarily mean you have matrimony in mind."

"But I do, Dave. I do want to marry her. That's what scares me, because I'm not sure what truly motivates me."

29

Facing the Inevitable

~

When the holiday break began a few weeks later, Dave and I met Ann at the airport. As she walked down the ramp, smiling at me with those sparkling blue eyes, my pulse pounded like a jackhammer.

Being together again was nothing short of wonderful. I wanted to show her around campus and introduce her to some of my friends before we left for home. We spent a couple of carefree days on the now-quiet campus and the nearby beach, then left for home. It felt good to be on the freeway, heading north, with Ann beside me.

It was time for the next step, and I believed it was my role to take the lead. "Ann, I'd like to meet your folks while I'm home for Christmas break," I began. "I need to talk to your dad, discuss some things with him."

"Why?"

Guess she's not going to make this any easier for me, is she? I thought, seeing the mischievous gleam in her eye.

"Well, I…I've told you that I care a lot for you. Before things go any further, it's important for me to know your parents approve of our relationship."

When we got back home, Ann quickly arranged an invitation for me to come meet her parents. I wanted to meet them, but at the same time I was dreading the evening, remembering the awkward scene with Julie's dad all those years ago. I had no idea what to expect from Ann's father, but I did know he was the chief of police and an important man in their community. That didn't make things any easier! I had visions of him towering over me and ordering me out of his house—maybe even out of town! Worse yet, he might laugh at me. By the time I arrived at the Stones' comfortable home, I had conjured up a whole repertoire of ugly scenarios.

Dinner was easy. Ann kept up a steady stream of entertaining chatter as she easily fed me and herself. Her parents greeted me warmly and made me feel at home. Still, I was dreading the moment when Ann and her mother would leave us, and I'd face Chief Stone man to man. When the moment came, I plunged right in. "Mr. Stone, I'd like to know how you and Mrs. Stone feel about my dating Ann."

He didn't respond, didn't say a word, so I blundered on. "As you can see, I'm a quadriplegic…" *Oh, Ron, this is great. Why don't you also tell him you're a natural blond while you're at it? The man isn't blind!* "And well…I've been married before, and I am ten years older than she is…"

Gee, don't hold back, buddy, just spill it all in one big breath. This wasn't coming out the way I'd planned at all; the horrible plague of motor-mouth I'd experienced in front of Julie's dad was suddenly starting to replay itself in my memory.

"Do…do you object to Ann and me seeing each other?"

There, I'd said it. The worst was over…I hoped.

Chief Stone, still unsmiling, suddenly stood up from his chair. I tried to bend my neck to look up at him, to meet his stern gaze. "And if I do object?"

"Without your approval, sir, I won't see Ann again."

The serious expression on his face gave way to a broad, friendly smile, and he grasped my shoulder with an outstretched hand. "I like your straightforward attitude and honesty, Ron. If you and my daughter enjoy each other's company, you have my wholehearted approval and I'm sure my wife agrees with me. Ann's told us a lot about you, and now that we've had a chance to meet you ourselves, I can see why she likes you so much."

Later that night when Ann drove me home, I looked her in the eye and said the words I'd felt so long, "I love you." They fell easily off my tongue and seemed to swirl around in the air between us.

"Say it again," Ann instantly demanded.

"Huh?"

"Say it again," she repeated. "Tell me you love me again."

"Why?"

"I just wanna make sure I'm not dreaming," she said with a smile, her face glowing in the moonlight.

After Christmas break ended and I returned to San Diego, we saw each other just once before the spring semester ended. Dave drove me up to Sacramento during spring break, and Ann and a girlfriend met us there for a little R and R. For two days the four of us cruised around the city, sightseeing, picnicking, and just being together.

One of the things that made Dave a good companion was his unpredictable sense of humor. Many times his lighthearted banter eased the tension, instantly putting what might have been an embarrassing situation into proper perspective. For example, he emptied my leg bag one day, then, as he and Ann were trying to lift me into my truck, they both stepped in the puddle and slipped, launching me headfirst toward the car seat. I landed, face first, in the lap of Ann's friend Tammy. She was embarrassed, and I was humiliated. But Dave thought it was hilariously funny, and when he started laughing, the rest of us did too.

Another time, something I'd eaten didn't mesh well with my digestive system. After Dave and I checked out of the motel on the last morning, I kissed Ann good-bye. "See you in three months, hon. I'll miss you."

Ann's eyes were glistening with tears when she looked at me. "It's too early to start home yet. Can't we stay a little longer? " she asked.

"You have a long drive ahead of you, and so do Dave and I," I insisted.

"Just a cup of coffee, then we'll go," Ann said. She smiled across the seat at Dave. "Please?"

He grinned. "It's okay with me. Hop in."

We had no sooner pulled away from the curb and turned toward the coffee shop when Dave started sniffing. He looked at me suspiciously. "Ron, something tells me you've got a problem."

It was a big problem, one that required a shower and a complete change of clothes. We had already checked out of the motel, and the local rehab hospitals Dave called were unwilling to accommodate us. We finally ended up at the YMCA, where Dave took me into the locker room, stripped off his own clothing as well as my own, pushed me into the shower, wheelchair and all, and soon had me cleaned up and looking spiffy again.

Now there was no time for a lingering good-bye over coffee. We all had to get on the road. Ann kissed me good-bye before slipping behind the steering wheel and turning her little car north out of the parking lot. Dave and I watched her car turn a corner and disappear into the distance. I heaved a sigh. "Dave, thanks for everything you did for me this morning—and during this whole trip. You're a great friend."

Dave shrugged off the compliment. "It was the least I could do. Besides, I felt sorry for you having an accident in front of Ann. I'm sorry."

"Don't be. If we're going to have a future together, she has to know what it's really like. Caring for a quadriplegic is a 24-hour-a-day job, and not always a pleasant one. Ann knows that now, for sure."

Seeing Ann again and then returning to my lonely room in San Diego made me even more dissatisfied with being a bachelor. I wanted to be sensitive to the Lord's leading; the issue of divorce hadn't been resolved in my mind. I was still torn between proposing to Ann and breaking up with her. My heart urged me to take a chance and pop the question, but my mind cautioned, *Take your time. Don't rush into something you will regret.*

If I was able to find a job as a counselor in a public school system, my marital status would not be an issue, since the secular world accepted divorce as par for the course. But would a twice-married man be accepted in Christian circles? My heart's desire was to be a role model, not a stumbling block, for both Christian and non-Christian young people. I also wanted to encourage the physically impaired, just as Joni Eareckson Tada and little Jimmy had encouraged me.

I searched the Bible for an answer to the questions that bothered me. In the New Testament, I read what the apostle Paul had written to the church at Corinth: "To the married I give this command (not I, but the Lord): A wife must not separate from her husband. But if she does, she must remain unmarried or else be reconciled to her husband. And a husband must not divorce his wife."

Jesus' words to the notorious Pharisees were even stronger: "I tell you that anyone who divorces his wife, except for marital unfaithfulness, and marries another woman commits adultery."

Adultery! The word leapt off the page and slapped me in the face. I sat there a long time, stewing over what I knew I had to do. *Okay, I've dodged the issue long enough. If I'm to have any peace of mind, it's time to bite the bullet,* I told myself.

I called Julie's brother and, as kindly as I could, asked if Julie was seriously involved with someone else.

"Yeah, Ron. She's…they're…Yeah, you could say she's seriously involved," Jim replied.

Knowing Julie had found a man who made her happy affected me differently than I had feared. I had expected to be devastated all over again, feeling the old wound rip open in my heart. Instead, a sense of peace and closure swept over me. Suddenly I realized I had completely relinquished my past. Buoyantly free for the first time in ages, I was ready to move ahead into the future.

My pastor also encouraged me. "Ron," he said, "I don't advocate divorce, and it grieves me that couples today take their wedding vows so lightly. But a marriage is never successful unless both partners are willing to work at it. If your wife left you and wasn't willing to reconcile, then you didn't have much choice in the matter."

"That's true," I said, "but I don't want to give the impression that it was all Julie's fault. I should have been more appreciative and not taken her efforts for granted. We were together for five years. Without her care and support, I wouldn't have gotten my bachelor's degree. It's not easy to be married to a quadriplegic; I don't want to imply Julie didn't have any reasons to leave."

"I'm sure it wasn't easy for either of you, but such issues should be resolved *before* marriage, not after the fact. Ask any pastor, and you'll hear the same thing. There are more broken hearts and shattered marriages in the Christian community than most people realize. And even if infidelity is involved, when there is repentance, do we have the right to turn our backs on fellow Christians who are hurting and not make an effort to help them? If God forgives, why can't we forgive each other? I'm afraid the problem with you, Ron, is that you haven't forgiven *yourself.*"

"I want to be a Christian role model," I said slowly, thinking about his words. "I want to serve the Lord in whatever way He wants to use me…and I would like to do it with Ann by my side."

The minister smiled and patted me on the shoulder. "Ron, I think you will make Ann a good, loving husband. And because of your own experience, you will be a far better counselor."

I left his office feeling greatly relieved but knowing there was one more person I needed to talk with. I wanted Dad's affirmation. The church he and Mom attended took a more legalistic stance, and because my family had been so supportive of me in the past, I didn't want to do anything that would hurt them now.

When I called him, Dad agreed with the pastor. "Son, if you decide to ask Ann to marry you, it will be with my best wishes and blessing," he said, his voice sounding firm and encouraging.

Suddenly I couldn't wait to pop the question!

30

Surprise Proposal

～

After finally deciding to pop the question, I wracked my brain trying to think of a way to make my proposal spectacular. Gradually, a complicated scheme took shape in my mind, and I asked my health care internship supervisor, Betsy Carey, to help me pull it off.

I asked her to type a letter on official stationery letting Ann know about a contest the San Diego Rehab Institute was sponsoring to encourage persons with disabilities. The purpose of the fictitious contest was "to remind those who are physically challenged that happiness is within their reach," the letter explained. Contestants were to write a four-page, double-spaced essay describing "How I Fell in Love with a Disabled Person."

"Ron, you should be ashamed of yourself!" Mrs. Carey said with a devilish laugh. Then she added, "Should I ask what the prizes are?"

"Well, first prize will be a shopping spree at Nordstrom's with the winning entry published in the institute's monthly newsletter. I plan to give that award to a fictitious, 50-year-old couple who are both in wheelchairs. Second prize, which Ann Stone will win, is limo service to the most exclusive restaurant in her local area and a candlelight dinner for two."

By now my cohort was completely caught up with the idea. "Don't leave me hanging, Ron. What happens after that?"

"I plan to drop into the restaurant unannounced and ask Ann to marry me. Do you think she'll be surprised?"

"Shocked would be more like it," Mrs. Carey said, nodding. "I hope she says yes; otherwise, she'll probably strangle you for tricking her into writing a four-page essay!"

The only hitch in my plan was finding a way to get from San Diego to Oregon on the big night. Then, out of the blue, Dave surprised me by saying, "I want to ask Leanne to marry me, but I'd like to talk to her father first, and he lives way up in Bend, Oregon."

I looked at him in amazement. "What a coincidence! That's near the town I'm hoping to visit—and for the same reason. Wanna make it a double engagement?"

We planned our trip, Betsy Carey drafted the phony contest announcement, and we waited for the inevitable telephone call that was sure to follow. It came on schedule. Ann's voice sounded even more effervescent than usual, for she had taken our bait—hook, line, and sinker. "Ron, I'm going to enter the contest."

I feigned ignorance. "Contest? What contest?"

"You know, the one about falling in love with a disabled person."

"Hmmm. Tell me about it."

She read me the letter, word-for-word. "I'm going to win the first prize. You know how much I love to shop." If she could have seen my face via the telephone, my plan would have been blown then and there, because I was grinning like a possum.

A few days later, Dave and I went shopping for engagement rings. I bought the diamond I could afford—used but shiny—and Dave bought a beautiful ring for Leanne. Now, with both of our bank balances nearing zero, we still needed to find free transportation to Oregon. It was then that Pennie called and asked me to be present for the birth of her second son. "I'm having a C-section on February 20," she said. "Can you come?"

"I wouldn't miss it," I assured her. "Just don't tell Ann."

When my brother, Mike, learned that I planned to be there for Pennie's C-section, he asked if I would buy a used pickup for him and bring it to Oregon. Everything was falling into place: I had a truck, a driver, a beautiful diamond ring, and a gorgeous fiancée-to-be waiting at the end of the road.

As expected, Ann's entry came in right on time. "We have a winner!" I exclaimed when I read her beautiful, love-filled prose.

Mrs. Carey and I sent Ann a congratulatory letter announcing her second-place finish in the contest, and Ann promptly called me.

"Ron! Guess what! My entry won second prize in the contest!"

"Contest? What contest?"

"You know. The one sponsored by the San Diego Rehab Institute. I wrote an essay about falling in love with a disabled person. They sent me two tickets for dinner at O'Callahan's, the most expensive restaurant in Corvallis. And I even got a hundred-dollar bill in lieu of limo service. Can you believe it?"

"Wow, that's nice," I answered warmly. "Congratulations! Who are you taking to the dinner?"

"I was hoping you could come home and go with me. Will you be finished with your midterms by February 20?"

"Sorry, honey. That's right in the middle of exam week."

"Oh." She sounded so dejected I almost gave in and told her I'd be there.

"Why don't you ask my dad to go with you instead?" I suggested. "I'm sure he would feel honored to be my proxy."

"That's a good idea," she answered, "but I wish it could be you."

While I was planning my big event, Dave was working on his own surprise. He told Leanne he would be gone for a few days on a backpacking trip. Then, after taking our last midterms, we packed our gear in the pickup I'd bought for Mike and left for Oregon on the eighteenth. I wanted to talk to Ann's parents' and get their permission before I surprised her at the restaurant.

Everything went fine until Dave and I reached San Francisco the next day. Then the rain started, first a mere sprinkle and soon a blinding downpour that continued as we crossed the state line into Oregon. My motorized wheelchair, riding uncovered in the back of the truck, was getting drenched. To make matters worse, the winding highway that led to Ann's parents' home was treacherously slick. More than once we nearly slid into the ditch. We even had to go around a couple of downed trees. But we finally made it—only to find their house dark and deserted.

"They're not home!" Dave said, looking at the windows. "Now *there's* something we hadn't planned on."

"Let's try the police department; they'll surely know where the chief is," I suggested.

We rushed into town and found the police station. "They're at a police officers' convention," the clerk told us.

"Oh no!" I couldn't believe it. *Why didn't I just call them?* I raged silently at myself.

"They're in Bend," the clerk continued. "At some big resort."

"Let's call it a night, Ron. I'm exhausted," Dave said when we left the police station. "How about finding a motel and getting some rest?"

"We can't, Dave!" I exclaimed. "Pennie's C-section is tomorrow morning at 7:00. We'll never make it unless you keep driving."

So weary we could hardly keep our eyes open, we arrived at my parents' home at 2:00 in the morning, bleary-eyed and exhausted from the long drive. Dave was able to sleep in the next morning, but Mom and Dad got me up at 6:00 so the three of us could join Pennie and her husband at the hospital. When we drove by the house where Ann was living at that time, I insisted they cover my head with a blanket, just in case she happened to glance out the window. I had to tell Dad about my plans because he was taking Ann to dinner that night, but I made him promise not to even hint that he knew what was going on.

Thirty minutes later, I sat in my wheelchair wearing a surgical cap, gown, and booties and watched the doctor deliver my nephew Seth by cesarean section. What a joyful experience, witnessing the miracle of birth! I was so pumped up about seeing little Seth, it was hard to pull myself away and get on with my big scheme. But when Dave showed up a little later, I reluctantly said good-bye, thanking Pennie for sharing such a wonderful moment with me.

Soon Dave and I were back on the road, heading for the resort in Bend where the police conference was being held. Dave was in a hurry, too, and he literally tossed me into my wheelchair when we got there and hurried me into the building. As I nervously approached the part of my scheme I'd been dreading, I realized that after two days of traveling without a shave or shower, I looked more like a disaster victim than a man who wanted to make a good impression.

Mr. Stone was in a private meeting when we arrived, but after I told the hotel desk clerk this was an emergency concerning his daughter, both he and his wife came rushing into the hotel lobby. They quickly sized up my disheveled appearance and assumed the worst. "Ron!" Ann's mom exclaimed. "Is Ann all right? What are you doing here?"

"Yes, she's fine. I'm sorry to upset you. Everything's fine, really; there's no problem. It's just that we were hoping to catch you at home and then my sister had a baby and we had to rush over here to Bend and now I've got to get to Corvallis because Ann won the contest and my dad is taking her to dinner and—"

"Ron, Ron! Slow down! Here, let's sit down," Chief Stone said, thankfully ending my running monologue. As he led his wife to a nearby chair, he said, "Now, just start at the beginning and tell us what you came to say."

I took a breath and started over. "Mr. and Mrs. Stone, your daughter is a prize of great peril...I mean, a pearl of great prize, a...she's really wonderful..."

They turned their heads toward each other slightly and smiled knowingly.

"I love her," I said earnestly, "and with my Masters Degree, I could give her a great life! I would like to ask Ann to be my wife, that is, if you approve."

After a brief pause, Chief Stone smiled and said, "Ron, even before our daughter was born, we prayed that she would someday marry a godly man. We weren't concerned about whether he would be able-bodied or wealthy, only that he would love her and love the Lord. We would be proud to have you for our son-in-law. Welcome to the family."

Wow! I wanted to kiss him. "Thank you, sir! You don't know how much this means to me. I'll do my best not to disappoint you."

It seemed insensitive then to leave so quickly, but that's what I did. Dave threw me into the pickup, and we tore off for O'Callahan's in Corvallis. We were way behind schedule, and I was a nervous wreck. I finally suggested that Dave stop and call the restaurant. "Explain our situation to the *maître d'* and ask him to delay dessert. If Dad and Ann leave before we get there, it will blow the whole thing."

Five minutes later Dave returned to the truck where I was impatiently waiting. "Okay, buddy. It's all set. But the *maître d'* said for us to hurry. He can't stall them much longer."

We finally screeched to a stop in O'Callahan's parking lot. We had arranged to meet Mike and his wife, Bobbi, there, and he was immediately ticked off when he saw us—irritated that we were late and upset to see how dirty his new truck was.

"Sorry, Mike. But the mud will wash off. No big deal."

"Sure! No big deal for you—you're not the guy who'll have to wash it!"

"Mike, I'm sorry! I'll explain later. Dave and I have to get to the restaurant, and we don't have time to stand around talking."

"O'Callahan's? How do you expect to get there, fly? The restaurant is on the second floor, up a flight of steep stairs, and there are no elevators."

I wasn't about to let anything stop me now. "You and Dave will just have to pull me up the stairs."

"In your wheelchair?"

"Yeah, in my wheelchair."

"No way! That thing weighs 350 pounds even *without* you in it."

"Come on, Mike. It's important. Please? You and Bobbi can join us for dessert. Something big is about to happen, and you won't want to miss it."

"Oh, all right," he groused.

Mike hadn't exaggerated. The stairs were steep, but somehow, with a lot of grunting, groaning, pulling, and straining, the two of them managed to drag me up to the restaurant, one terrifying step at a time. In the restaurant's doorway we nearly collided with a waiter carrying a tray of fancy pastries over his head. "Oops! Sorry, sir," Dave apologized.

"Hey! Take it easy, you guys," I said. "All I need now to make this a total disaster is to have a tray of gooey desserts dumped on my head."

"Quit complaining, buddy," Mike retaliated. "We got you up here, didn't we? What more do you want?"

"My hair combed. With a two-day beard and my clothes a wrinkled mess, I must look like we've come through a hurricane."

Mike grinned. "That's right. You do."

"Thanks, little brother. You're a big encouragement."

Ann looked up just as I rolled through the door. She blinked her eyes as though not believing what she saw, her mouth dropping open in stunned amazement. "Ron, is it really you? What in the world are you doing here?"

"Dave and I finished our finals early, so we decided to drop in and join you for dessert," I said as nonchalantly as possible while Dave and

Mike, now soaked with sweat and red in the face from all their effort, stood huffing and puffing behind me. I didn't exactly look like Mr. Clean myself, but Ann didn't seem to notice.

I glanced around the dining room. All eyes were on Ann and me. Even the waiters and waitresses, who had been clued in by the *maître d'*, were discreetly watching from the sidelines.

I cleared my throat and began. "I guess you all know why Ann and Dad are here celebrating tonight. A candlelight dinner for two was her prize for writing an essay describing how she fell in love with a disabled person."

I read Ann's beautiful essay, then shared the poem I had written in response. Finally I said, "I'm sorry I can't propose to you on bended knee, but since that is impossible, I'll ask you in plain, simple words. Will you be my wife?"

It took a few seconds for her to recover from the shock of the whole scene. In the silence, Dad quipped, "Well, Ann, what's your answer? Do you still want to break up with him?"

My bride-to-be ignored the teasing and looked at me with tears in her blue eyes. "Ron, I would *love* to be your wife."

Only later did I confess that the contest was phony and I had orchestrated the whole affair. This was the beginning of my deceitful, macho heart. I planned, I conquered, I felt in control. By then Ann was too happy to be mad at me.

The following morning, I returned to San Diego, an engaged and very happy man.

31

Daniel Webster Doe

~

Although my love life was taking a definite turn toward happiness, my domestic situation continued to be chaotic. I still hadn't found a dependable caregiver. After interviewing several disappointing prospects, including a man who had just been released from prison, I hired Stan, a clean-cut young fellow who had good references and a pleasant personality—at least until something ignited his hair-trigger temper. That was the end of Stan!

While the rehab agency helped me find a permanent replacement, I had to undergo eye surgery to treat my worsening glaucoma. After the surgery, I returned to my apartment discouraged and dejected. When Mom called me that night to ask how I was getting along, I first answered, "Fine, just fine," then suddenly broke down and bawled like a baby.

"Son, if you need me, I'll fly down first thing in the morning," she said quickly. I imagined she was reaching for her suitcase with one hand and the phone book with the other, ready to look up the airline's number.

"No, Mom, really. I'll be fine; I was just feeling sorry for myself." She listened to me outline all the problems that had caused me to feel so low, then she quietly asked, "Son, is getting a master's degree worth all the pressure you're going through?"

"Yes, Mom, it's worth it. I'm not about to give up now. Sometimes I get discouraged, but I'm not defeated. Sorry I came unglued just now. Don't worry about me. I'll be back on track in a day or two."

Ann also called that night. "Ron, just say the word, and I'll come take care of you myself."

"Thanks, Ann. It's kind of you to offer, but the last thing I want is for you to quit school on my account," I answered.

What I really needed, I thought, was Daniel. So it seemed like nothing short of a miracle a few days later when the phone rang, and I heard his deep, resonant voice on the other end of the line. He was visiting relatives in Southern California, he said, and was just calling to say hello.

Obviously, God had brought my trusted friend to me; now the ball was in my court. Whatever it took, I was going to persuade him to come live with me.

"Daniel, I'm in a real bind. You wouldn't believe the problems I've been having..." I started in, prepared to recite the whole litany of crises.

"Hey, man, would you like for me to come stay with you?" he interrupted.

"Are you putting me on?"

"Now, Ronald," he answered with exaggerated sweetness, "would I do that?" Then he laughed, that old familiar belly laugh that I remembered so well filling my heart with hope. "Hang in there, buddy. I'm on my way."

Stunned to have him pop back into my life, I'd forgotten to ask where he was calling from or if he was traveling by bicycle, but three days later he rang my doorbell. I was mighty glad to see him. After that, I never worried about coming home to an empty house, never wondered if there would be food on the table or clean clothes in the closet, never wondered if I would be robbed or mistreated or abandoned. It was wonderful to have my buddy with me again.

He was more than a caregiver. Daniel cheered me up when I was down, never complained when I called him to roll me over in the night, and even turned the pages of books for me. My big, burly nurse didn't look like the sentimental type, but underneath his rough exterior was a soft heart. I wasn't at all surprised to discover that he had an insatiable love for poetry. When my eyes were tired from studying and I needed a break, we sat outside, and he read to me for hours at a time.

Daniel did all the shopping, which gave me more time for studying. He carefully carried everything home on his old bicycle, and sometimes he came back with more than I had ordered. To put it bluntly, Daniel was a Dumpster diver. One day he found 200 chocolate bars in a supermarket bin, all in their original wrappers, a trifle melted but still in good condition. They had been discarded because their shelf date had expired.

"Hey man, look what I found!" he exclaimed when he got home with his bounty. "They're really good—a little soft maybe, but they'll harden up once I put them in the freezer."

There was seldom a dull moment after Daniel came to live with me again. His overall demeanor was a cool, laid-back facade; the truth was, it didn't take much to put him in a dither. One afternoon I returned from school to find him agitated and antsy. I was sure something disastrous had happened. His blue jeans were streaked with dirt, his hair was askew, and one sleeve of his denim shirt was torn. "What's wrong, Daniel? You look like you've been chased by a banshee!"

"Worse than that, man. I locked my keys in the garage."

"Okay, well, that doesn't sound so bad. What happened?"

"Had to break a window and crawl in to get at 'em."

I started to laugh. "Is that all? You had me scared to death!"

"What will the landlord do? Throw us out?"

"Calm down, Daniel. It's no big deal. We'll buy a new pane of glass and have it installed. The landlord will never know it happened."

Daniel heaved a sigh of relief, but he didn't breathe easily again until that windowpane was replaced.

When he wasn't worried about something, my first mate's wacky sense of humor knew no bounds. Because Daniel was an avid reader, at least once a week he bicycled to the public library and brought home an armload of books. He checked out anything and everything that caught his fancy at the moment, from Bugs Bunny to Shakespeare. Once he purposely left one of his borrowed volumes on an end table where I would be sure to see it. He mischievously watched from the kitchen as I rolled over to the table and read the title: *Nurses Who Kill*.

"Hey, what's this?" I said, knowing it was a joke.

"Just thought it might give me some ideas when you get out of line next time," he wisecracked.

I had no such worries about Daniel. He was such a softy, I sometimes wondered if it hurt him to swat a mosquito.

Knowing that I could count on Daniel not to walk out and leave me in a lurch made the last year-and-a-half of my master's program far less stressful. He was a godsend in every sense of the word. My classmates liked him too and often dropped in just to chat or to study with me on weekends.

With Daniel taking care of me and a beautiful young woman in love with me, my life settled into a calm, reassuring routine leading toward graduation. My only pressing concern was the van. The Green Bean's odometer registered a whopping 150,000 miles, and the old van was overdue for a major overhaul. The lift frequently malfunctioned, sometimes stubbornly refusing to open and other times failing to retract. When it wouldn't fold back into the van, my driver, Celia, had to drive with the door open and the metal platform protruding—not just a hazard but a calamity waiting to happen!

The end came after Celia had driven me home from school one afternoon and attempted to lower the lift. The instant she touched the switch by the steering wheel, the lift started smoking and shooting sparks in all directions. She jumped out the driver's side, ran around, and tugged with all of her strength on my door. But the metal platform wouldn't budge. By that time the van was completely filled with smoke, with me helplessly trapped inside.

"Get me out of here!" I yelled frantically as my lungs filled with the black, foul-smelling smoke. "I can't breathe. Break the window, Celia! Do anything. Just get me out!"

Man! What a way to go! I told myself. After all I've been through, to die because of a short circuit in the stupid lift. As I coughed and gasped, Celia continued to work determinedly at the latch. Just as I thought I couldn't last another minute, the door opened, the lift lowered, and I rolled out onto the sidewalk. The smog-filled California air had never seemed so sweet.

I was still frazzled by the close call, and Celia was hysterical. "Ron, if you don't get this lift fixed *now*, you'll have to find another driver. I can't take this!"

"Yeah, it wasn't too pleasant for me either," I quipped. "I'll call the rehab agency and see if they can help. I don't have the cash to pay for repairs myself."

The rehab agency first said no to my request for help. Determined to investigate my options, I read the state's book of vocational rehab rules and regulations and gleefully discovered that as a disabled student I actually qualified for a new, fully equipped van.

It took six months for the agency to process my paperwork, plus a few weeks to send me another rejection notice. As a last resort, I took my case to the board of appeals, with my friend Dave Woods coming along for moral support. Fortified with a briefcase filled with petitions signed by school officials and other leaders, I presented my arguments during a board hearing.

At the end of my appeal, I had Dave hold up one of my mouth paintings. "Ladies and gentlemen," I concluded, "this seascape at sunset shows you where I am right now—my wheelchair is at the water's edge without a boat. I hope you can see how eager I am to get an education, and I hope you'll find it in your hearts to assist me."

The board's decision was unanimous. Yes, another victory! I got the van.

32

Accolades and Attacks

~

For two years I had been the recipient of an annual monetary award given by the Blanche Fisher Foundation. The grants—along with profits from cars that I had purchased, refurbished, and sold—helped me pay my living expenses and tuition and buy textbooks and supplies. So when I was asked to speak at the foundation's annual awards banquet, I accepted immediately, eager to give something back to this group that had helped me so much.

And, well, I also accepted because I thought it was a chance to show off for Ann—and I did. I invited her down, sent her a plane ticket, then picked her up at the airport in a limo before whisking her off to the banquet. The evening was a grand success—and we still had a few days to be together.

I wanted to spend all my time with Ann while she was in San Diego, but I had term papers due in several classes and didn't dare fall behind. Typing with a mouth stick was extremely slow, and I sometimes worked late into the night to finish my assignments, then spent every free minute of the day with Ann. So I was exhausted when Dave called and said he and his girlfriend, Leanne, were going to the beach to "mellow out" for a couple of hours. He asked Ann and me to join them.

"Sounds great. I could use some time on the beach right now," I replied.

It was a warm, sunny day—the kind of weather that attracts tourists to Southern California's beautiful beaches all year, and the kind of day that those who can't come here dream about. After Dave parked the van, I rolled up and down the sidewalk, looking for wheelchair ramps.

"Guess there aren't any," Dave commented, his tone far more positive and pleasant than I felt.

"How do they expect people with wheelchairs to get down the bluff?" I grumbled. "If you ask me, that's discrimination."

"Relax, Ron. I'll carry you down. We couldn't get your wheelchair through that loose sand anyway."

"Uh-uh. I don't think so," I barked.

"Why not?"

"Why not? What would that look like, you traipsing across the sand with me like a groom carrying his bride. There might be someone here we know. I don't want anyone to get the wrong idea. Besides, I can't sit in the sand without being propped up."

"We already thought of that. Leanne and I brought a lawn chair. The gals can set it up in the sand while I carry you down." He was already unfastening the straps that held me in the wheelchair.

"Hey, wait a minute," I protested when he slipped one arm under my legs and another around my shoulders and lifted me up in an "over-the-threshold" embrace.

Resigned to this humiliating posture, I decided I might as well go along with the scene. I stretched my neck toward Dave's face and planted a big old kiss on his cheek.

Dave struggled to keep his composure, but I could see that he was ready to crack up. "Honey, you wanna be dropped on your *derriere?*" he quipped in the most serious tone he could muster.

"Oh come on, sweetie," I answered in a high falsetto. "Surely you wouldn't drop me."

"Then forget the kissing, okay?"

Dave plopped me into the lawn chair. Then, while Ann strapped my shoulders against the backrest, he crisscrossed my legs at the knees. "What are you doing?" I yelled. "Cut the comedy, man. You've got me fixed like a girl. Uncross my legs."

He let me protest and sputter for another few seconds before finally straightening my legs.

"Okay, *now* are you happy?" he asked. When I smiled and pursed my lips into another kiss, he said, "Do you mind if the girls and I go down by the water and throw this Frisbee around for a while?"

"Of course not. Go ahead. I'll wave my chin to all the bikini-clad babes who pass by."

"I'd better not catch you flirting, Ron Heagy," Ann threatened playfully.

"Don't worry, hon. I'll be right here when you get back. I'm not goin' anywhere; that's for sure."

I watched them walk down to the water's edge, then closed my eyes and let the sun warm my face. The sunshine, plus a lack of sleep from staying up too late, made me drowsy. I closed my eyes and didn't open them again until the raucous laughter of a group of volleyball players awakened me. Waves were lazily washing over the sand, coming and going at the tide's bidding and leaving behind an assortment of seashells, sand crabs, and twisted strands of seaweed.

A pelican lifted off of an offshore buoy. I had never seen one in flight before and was awestruck by its magnificent wingspread, which must have been six or seven feet from tip to tip. It flapped its huge wings to gain some altitude then soared inland, toward the beach. *Toward me.*

There were hundreds of people on the beach that day, so why did this particular pelican dump his payload on the head of the only *paralyzed* man on the beach, the only one who couldn't hop up, run into the surf, and wash the pelican poop off his head? All I know for sure is that it scored a direct hit—right in the middle of my forehead. *Splat!* I felt the stinky, slimy stuff trickle down my face, dripping into my eyes.

"DAVE!" I shouted at the top of my lungs. Of course he was nowhere in sight, but several other people did turn to look at the man with the bird poop on his head. I decided it would be better to keep quiet and attract less attention.

Maybe if I smile and nod to people who walk by, they won't notice the mess, I decided. Probably there were at least a few who wanted to stop and say, "Uh, sir, did you know you have a big glob of bird poop on your head?"

But no one said a thing.

After what seemed hours but was probably only a few minutes, Dave and the girls returned, took one look at me, and burst into laughter. "Hey, stop laughing. Wipe this stuff off my face," I said. "Hurry! Before the sun bakes it on."

33

Finding My Niche

~

S am, a tough-looking teenager, glared at me defiantly. It was the very first day of my internship at an inner-city junior high school, and the school principal had asked me to substitute in a detention study hall for an absent teacher. I had asked Sam to please sit down and be quiet so the other students could study, and he wasn't taking kindly to my suggestion. He sauntered over to me, bent down to sneer directly into my face, and said, "Hey man, I don't hafta sit down. I don't hafta do nothing you say. You couldn't even stop me if I decided to walk out of this stupid study hall."

I was tempted to say, "Try it, buddy, and I'll run you down with my wheelchair," but basically Sam was right. There was no way I could physically restrain him. All I had at my disposal was words.

"You're right, Sam," I answered calmly. "There's nothing I can do to stop you."

Thinking he had me buffaloed, Sam came closer and threatened me with a clenched fist. "I might even decide to poke you in the nose."

"Yes, you could. But what would that prove, that you can hit someone who can't fight back?" I paused a moment, then shifted gears. "You know something, Sam? I feel sorry for you, because you've got a disability, same as me."

"No way, man! I ain't got no disability. You don't see me strapped in no wheelchair." He flexed his muscles and strutted around like a peacock on parade. In the meantime, all the other students were watching intently.

"You may be strong, Sam, and you aren't in a wheelchair, but you are disabled just the same. Your disability is the kind that doesn't show."

He glared at me defiantly. "What you talking about, man?"

"You have a learning problem." I nodded my head toward his desk. "See that math book over there?"

"Yeah, what about it?"

"If you aren't retarded, if you know how to study and aren't learning disabled, then prove it. Do your math assignment and show me whether you have the ability to learn."

He didn't move a muscle, just stared at me, but I could tell he was thinking about my challenge. The other students ducked their heads and snickered as Sam slipped into his seat in sullen silence, picked up his pencil, and started to write. Thirty minutes later when study hall was over, he laid his completed assignment on my desk. "See? I *ain't* retarded, man."

"Well how about that! You *can* learn! Nice going, Sam. Keep up the good work." His paper was covered with erasures and smudges, but at least he had tried.

Sam never caused me any more problems. He even stopped by my office occasionally just to rap. His bravado and tough talk were only a facade hiding a fatherless young man who longed for acceptance and was looking for a masculine role model.

That episode with Sam was one of many learning experiences during my internships. First, I was at a local rehabilitation hospital. Then, when I shifted my focus to acquiring a Pupil Personnel Credential that would qualify me to counsel in a public school system, I served at an elementary and a junior high school. I was on the home stretch, closing in on graduation and eager to prepare myself for a counseling job in a public high school.

As I'd had to do with Sam, I'd learned to talk my way out of threatening situations and to challenge obstreperous students on an intellectual level. Because I didn't pose a physical threat to them, many listened to me. And each time one troublemaker had a change of attitude, my self-confidence increased. My struggle to get a Pupil Personnel Credential would be worthwhile if I thought I'd made a positive, permanent impact on just one gutsy guy like Sam.

One of my biggest challenges was Rahau, a gang leader who smart-mouthed the teachers, didn't show any respect for authority, and seemed to trust no one. When he was sent to my office the first time, he was extremely wary, never looking at me when he spoke, and refusing to talk about his feelings. Gradually, as the weeks went by, he seemed to drop his guard a little, and I was just starting to believe we had made some positive inroads when Rahau dropped in to tell me good-bye.

"Why? Are you leaving, Rahau?"

"Yeah. I'm being transferred to another school."

I studied his face. Rahau's expression was impassive and emotionless. "What happened?"

"I got busted for gang violence. But honest, I didn't do nothin' wrong."

"I believe you, Rahau. I'm going to miss seeing you on campus."

He turned his face to the wall but not before I saw a tear trickle down his cheek. "Yeah, I'll miss you, too, Mr. Heagy." Rahau never returned to our campus, so all I could do was pray for him and hope he remembered some of the things we had discussed during our brief encounters.

Shortly before my junior high school internship ended, the mother of a student I had not met called me, very distraught. "Please, Mr. Heagy, will you talk to my boy?"

"What's the problem?" I asked.

"Tommy is upset. Real upset." Her voice broke, and she started to cry. "He's…he's threatening to commit suicide. Rahau told me about you, Mr. Heagy. He respects you. Will you please talk to my boy?"

"Of course, Mrs. Turner. Send Tommy in. I'll be glad to help him if I can."

The next day her son came to my office wearing baggy jeans and a baseball cap turned backward. Before sitting down, he pulled the bill around to cover his eyes, and I simultaneously sent up a quick prayer. *Lord, this youngster is desperate. Please give me the right words to say.* "Hello, Tommy. I understand you and Rahau are friends."

He didn't look up. "Yeah, Rahau told me to come."

"Are you having a problem?"

"I ain't got nothin' to live for." Keeping his head down, Tommy slid his hand into the pocket of his baggy jeans and pulled out a razor blade. "Might as well cut my wrists and end it all."

I tried to keep my voice calm, but inside my chest my heart was going bonkers.

"You must have lots of problems, Tommy, to think about taking your own life."

"It's bad, man. Real bad. You don't know how stinkin' bad things can be."

"Oh really? Well, I do know life can be tough. Look at me for instance, Tommy. Every morning I wake up and have to yell for someone to come get me out of bed, take me to the bathroom, give me a shower, shave my face, brush my hair, put on my clothes, feed me breakfast, and drive me to school."

I inclined my head, grabbed the mouth stick out of its holder, and continued talking with my teeth clinched around the stick. "Have you ever seen me type on the computer? This is the way I do it, one letter at a time." He watched with wide eyes but made no comment as I bobbed my head over the keyboard, pecking out a couple of words, letter by letter. "Do you still think I don't know about problems? Would you like to trade places with me?"

He shook his head.

"Okay, I've told you about my problems. Would you like to share yours with me? I care, Tommy, and I'd like to help you."

"My...my..." His voice broke, and he swallowed several times before going on. "My father molested me when I was a little guy. It was terrible, and I can't forget...Sometimes I still have nightmares."

"I'm sorry, Tommy. But it wasn't your fault. Bad as that experience was, you can't let it destroy your future."

"What future? I told you, man. I ain't got nothin' to live for."

"You have a mother who loves you and is concerned about you, Tommy."

"You're wrong. My mom married a druggie who smacks me around when he's high on cocaine. I'm afraid to go home when she ain't there. I'm a nobody, man. And nobody cares what happens to me."

"I care, Tommy, and so does God." At that point, I forgot about rules and regulations prohibiting me from mentioning religious beliefs. This youngster's life was at stake, and he needed to know that God cares.

Still holding the razor blade in his hand, Tommy looked at it and in a hollow-sounding voice said, "I'm still gonna check out."

There was no way I could disarm Tommy. On the spur of the moment, I tried another idea: "Well, okay, maybe that's not such a bad idea after all. You and I both have problems. Why don't we commit suicide together?"

For the first time, he looked me straight in the eye. "No! You can't do that, man!"

"Why not? We've both been given a bum rap in life, so let's take the coward's way out. You can use your razor blade. I'll just drive my wheelchair in front of a truck, and it will all be over in a jiffy."

His mouth dropped open. "No, man. You're needed here. You help people. My friends say they've been showing up at school just to chill with you, man."

We sat in silence for a minute. Then I said quietly, "Take a look at yourself, Tommy. You're strong. You can walk and hold a pen and drive a car. You're good looking, and you have the whole future ahead of you. You can help people too. You just need to change your attitude, change the way you look at things. Sure, you've had some bad breaks, but you've got to look at the positive side."

Tommy hung his head, took aim, and tossed the razor blade in my trash can. "If only I could forget what my dad did to me."

I drew in a big breath, blew it out in a great sigh of relief, and smiled at Tommy.

"Maybe you can't forget, but you can remember that it wasn't your fault. It *is* your fault, though, if you choose to let your past destroy you. Life isn't easy. Unexpected tragedies come our way. Believe me, that's one rule of life I know very well! But in the end we are stronger, better people because of it." I nodded toward the sunset painting that hung on my office wall. "Do you know how I painted that picture"?

Tommy shrugged.

"I held a paintbrush in my mouth."

He stood up and took a closer look. "Hmmm. It must be a paint-by-number picture."

"No, Tommy," I said, laughing. "It's an original."

"That's hard to believe, man."

"I want you to have it, Tommy. Take that painting off the wall and hang it in your room. Whenever you're feeling down, look at that painting and remember what we've talked about today. Think of all the things you have to be thankful for and all the things you can accomplish if you try."

As Tommy left my office that day with my painting tucked under his arm and a smile on his face, I thought, *This is real stuff, not just textbook examples, and I like it. Maybe I've finally found my niche. Lord, if you want me to spend the rest of my life being a school counselor, just push the buttons, open the doors, and guide me through them. I'm ready.*

34

Moving On

~

T he final week of school was another one of those bittersweet experiences. Saying good-bye to professors who'd invested so much into my life and telling classmates farewell—friends that in all probability would never cross my path again—was like closing one chapter of a book and opening another without knowing what was in it. I hadn't landed a job as yet and had no idea what the future held for me. But of one thing I felt certain—David Woods and I would always stay in touch. Ours was the kind of friendship that distance couldn't destroy.

The long-anticipated hour arrived at last. It was May 23, 1992, graduation day for more than 9,500 of us who were to receive our diplomas at San Diego State University. Mom, Dad, Pennie, Mike, Ann, and Daniel Webster Doe were all sitting in the audience as I rolled up the ramp that had been specially built so I could cross the stage like all the other graduates. When the dean announced, "Ronald Charles Heagy Jr., *summa cum laude*," my family proudly burst into applause. Then others started to applaud too. My classmates popped to their feet, cheering and clapping, and soon the whole auditorium was filled with standing spectators. The university president laid my diploma on the tray of my wheelchair, and I rolled back to my place among the other graduates, the sound of the applause ringing in my ears.

After three years of frustration and hard work, I had finally proved to the naysayers that a Master's Degree was within my grasp. Television cameras and newspaper reporters were waiting to interview me when the graduation ceremony ended. I told them all that Daniel Webster Doe's name should also be inscribed on my diploma. Without him, none of this would have been possible. My old buddy, his beard trimmed and wearing a new maroon suit (the first one he'd ever owned), had a smile that extended from ear to ear.

One reporter wrote, "This was a big weekend at San Diego State University for more than 9,000 graduates. But Ron Heagy Jr. stole the show. He well may be the only student who has ever 'mouthed' his way through the master's program." Boy, did that stroke my ego.

With my college goals accomplished and new challenges ahead of us, Ann and I cruised up the freeway on our way back to the Pacific Northwest. It was a sunny May morning, the kind of day that made me glad to be alive. The pressure that I had been under for so long had suddenly slipped away. Disappointments of the past were behind me, the future looked bright, and it was good to be going home.

I glanced at Ann. The expression on my fiancé's face and the anticipation of our soon-to-be wedding filled me with elation. I watched with pleasure as she admired her diamond engagement ring, turning it from side to side so the facets of the marquis center stone would catch the sunlight and sparkle. So what if I had drained my savings account to buy it? Seeing Ann happy was worth any price.

"Well, hon, we did it. We both graduated. You have your business degree, I have my master's, and soon we will be moving into a cozy little cottage of our own. No more separations. Now we can relax and just enjoy being together."

"Maybe you can relax, but I can't," Ann said. "Not until the wedding's over. Do you realize how much there is to do before then? I've got to reserve the church, select the flowers, and plan the reception. I haven't even shopped for my wedding gown yet."

"Honey, you'll be a beautiful bride, no matter what you wear. And, after we're married, this man will be making the big bucks, and you can shop, shop, shop." Ann is a very spontaneous young lady, serious one minute, laughing the next, and I love to watch the changing expressions on her face when she talks. "Would you like to know what I'm thinking right now, Miss Stone?"

"Maybe. That depends."

"I was just thinking, *Ron old boy, you've got good taste. And you're a mighty lucky guy.*

She made a face at me. "Flattery will get you nowhere, Mr. Heagy."

"Well, now. I don't know about that, seeing as how the prettiest girl on the Chemeketa College volleyball team promised to be my bride."

She turned her head and smiled at me. "I love you, Ronald Charles."

On July 18, 1992, Ann and I were married in a simple ceremony at the Eastside Christian Church in Albany, Oregon. Her sister, Lynn, was maid of honor, and Mike was best man.

Following an informal home reception, my bride and I left for an extended honeymoon trip.

The first thing I did when we returned home was check the answering machine for important messages. There was one from Scott, the job placement professional in San Diego who had been helping me look for employment that would utilize the credentials I had struggled so long and hard to earn. Now that I had a wife to support, finding a job was of paramount importance to me.

A call to Scott was the first thing on my agenda. "Hi, this is Ron Heagy. What's up? Any good leads?"

"Sure thing Ron. I've found a counseling position that's right up your alley. It's in a school district that has around 800 children with disabilities."

"Wow! That's exciting. Just what I'm looking for. Please fax me an application."

"Will do. It's as good as there."

I mailed a comprehensive resume along with my portfolio by Airborne Express. As a follow-up, I called to reaffirm my interest in the position and asked if I qualified for the position. "Yes you do, Mr. Heagy, and we are looking forward to an interview." The lady I talked with didn't ask questions about my physical condition, and I didn't volunteer the information.

After that reassuring telephone conversation, I told Ann, "Honey, pack our bags. Your husband is a candidate for school counselor. We're heading for the Golden State again."

On the morning of my interview, I was jittery and my stomach was tied in knots as Ann went through the daily ritual of giving me a shower, shampooing my hair, shaving me, brushing my teeth, and feeding me breakfast. After pressing my pants and jacket, then getting me dressed, she pushed my chair up to a mirror. "Well, what do you think?"

"Thanks, hon. You've made me look my professional best. If I get this job, it will be because of your care."

We left the motel later that morning in a euphoric mood. And why not? We were young, in love, and idealistic newlyweds. Ann told me how handsome I looked, that she loved me, and that she felt certain the school superintendent would hire me on the spot. Even though what she said was a gross exaggeration, her words did wonders to build up my confidence.

When we arrived at the school, I was pumped up and ready for anything—except the shocked look on the receptionist's face when she saw my wheelchair.

I flashed her my biggest smile. "I'm Ron Heagy," I said cheerfully. "I have an appointment for an interview."

"Yes, yes, of course," she stammered. "Please follow me. Interviews are being conducted in the boardroom."

The members of the search committee may have been as shocked as the receptionist was to discover that a quadriplegic was applying for the counseling position, but they were courteous and seemed impressed by my credentials. When the interview ended and I returned to the outer office, Ann was waiting, her face wreathed with a smile. "Did they hire you?" she whispered.

"Not yet," I answered. "They won't announce their decision until next week, but it went well. I think your husband is about to land his first counseling job."

To celebrate our impending employment, we treated ourselves to frozen yogurt while scanning the apartment rental ads in the newspaper. That afternoon we found a cozy little duplex that was wheelchair accessible. After a quick visit, Ann excitedly made a list of the things we would need to furnish it.

The phone call came several days later. The search committee chairman's voice was warm and kind. "Mr. Heagy, your credentials qualify you for our counseling job," he said. Then came the lightning bolt. "But under the circumstances, we aren't able to offer you the position. I'm sorry."

"What circumstances?" I asked. "Why can't you hire me?"

"Because of your immobility."

I was so stunned that for a moment I couldn't answer. Finally I mumbled, "Thanks for calling," and then said good-bye.

I was crushed; Ann cried.

"It isn't fair!" she sobbed. "Why didn't they tell you that to start with? And who would be a better counselor for disabled kids than a disabled counselor? How blind can they be?"

"It's my fault. I shouldn't have gotten my hopes up; that wasn't very realistic of me," I said apologetically. "We might as well pack up and head for home."

Scott, my employment counselor, was indignant when he heard the news. "Immobility is not a valid reason, Ron. Let me see what I can find out. Don't leave until you hear from me, okay?" Ten minutes later he called back. "This is discrimination, pure and simple. I think we should protest their decision."

Ann and I talked it over and agreed. She dialed the district office and held the telephone to my ear while I talked with the district superintendent. "Sir, I'm not convinced that the reason your committee disqualified me for the position of school counselor is valid. It may be in the district's best interest for us to have another conference."

My boldness paid off. Scott accompanied me to my next appointment and asked members of the upper echelon why the immobility issue disqualified me. The committee supervisor contended that I would be unable to make house calls or complete paperwork without an assistant.

"Have you forgotten that I just completed a master's degree and internship? Do you realize how many reports I've already written?" I asked. "I can write reports as well as anyone! I may run the race differently, but that doesn't keep me from reaching the finish line. All I need is a chance to prove what I can do."

The superintendent calmly answered me. "I am sure you are quite capable, Mr. Heagy, but those are district policies."

I wasn't ready to throw in the towel without one last try. "Do you realize the message your judgmental policies are giving your students? In essence you're saying, 'Go ahead. Get an education. We'll help you go through school, but you're just wasting your time. We still won't hire you.'"

After Scott pointed out that the law mandates employers make reasonable accommodations for qualified, disabled applicants, the superintendent turned to his subordinate and said, "I think the committee should reconsider Mr. Heagy's application."

Scott and I left the office feeling a little more optimistic, but we never heard from that school district again. At the time, I wondered why. Now I realize that God had bigger and better plans for Ann and me.

We returned home to Oregon, discouraged and worried. To break the gloomy mood, I suggested we go out to dinner. That evening as we dined at our favorite restaurant, my old football coach, Percy Benedict, came over to our table. "Ron Heagy! It's good to see you. How's the world treating you?"

"Oh…okay I guess," I answered.

"No. It's been lousy," Ann corrected.

"Really? What happened?" Coach Benedict asked.

"I applied for a counseling position in California and got turned down. We're feeling a little rejected right now," I told him.

"Uh-uh, we're feeling a *lot* rejected right now," my wife candidly added.

"I know how that feels; I've had a few big rejections of my own. But don't let it get you down, Ron. You're a guy with lots of grit and determination. You sometimes limped off the football field feeling so stiff and sore you could hardly move. But after a couple of minutes on the bench, you'd say, 'Coach, get me back out there!' Sometimes life is like a football game, Ron. When you get knocked down, you've gotta get up and keep running with the ball."

"Yeah, you're right, Coach. Trouble is, I don't know which direction to run."

Percy slapped me on the back. "For starters, how about coming to Central Linn High School and giving our kids a pep talk? They need to hear what you've got to say."

Two weeks later I sat in the gym of my alma mater, recognizing the old, familiar smells and sounds. Nothing had changed much, it seemed, except that the students looked a lot younger than they had when I was a student there. For 30 minutes, I spoke to those kids from my heart, and much to my amazement the students listened intently. When I finished, they rose to their feet and applauded for a full minute.

The wonderful feelings that swept over me as I sat there, smiling into their applause, were the same ones that had surged through me all those years earlier when I'd spoken to the campers at Cannon Beach Conference Grounds where Pennie was working for the summer. They were feelings of gratitude and fulfillment and accomplishment and confidence. *I can do this,* I told myself emphatically as the students stood, cheering, before me. *This is how I can make a difference, touch a life with my story, and give a hurting heart hope.*

My ministry as a motivational speaker had begun.

I had lots to learn about public speaking, but I'm a big believer in the adage, Anything worth doing is worth doing poorly—until you can do it well.

The first year of my new itinerant career, Ann and I struggled to make ends meet. We spent lots of time on the road and were barely able to cover our traveling expenses. And not all of the audiences were receptive. On one occasion, I spoke to a public school audience of 600 students ranging from kindergarten through senior high. Because of the age differences, it was difficult to hold the students' attention. Many of them were rowdy and inattentive, and afterward I thought, *I blew it! My speech was one huge flop. What am I doing here? Maybe I should go home and forget about a speaking ministry.*

I looked up from my immersion in self-doubt to find a timid, 12-year-old girl awkwardly hobbling over to my wheelchair, dragging one leg as she walked. "Thanks for coming, Mr. Heagy," she said. "I really liked your talk. You…you've given me hope."

"Really?" I asked, amazed that anyone had been able to hear what I'd said above all the ruckus. "How's that?"

"The other kids think I'm a freak."

My heart went out to the thin, freckle-faced adolescent. "Don't you believe it, honey. I think you're pretty special, and I love your smile."

Her face brightened. "Your paintings are *rad,* Mr. Heagy. And seeing you in a wheelchair with a smile on your face made me realize I'm not so bad off after all. Mama says when I was six I had a brain aneurysm. It left my left side paralyzed, and they said I'd never walk." She gave me another big smile. "But I do."

"You sure do, and you've got a great attitude, honey. Never give up," I told her.

When she hugged me, I said, "Thanks. That's exactly what I needed right now."

After that experience, whenever I faced an unruly or inattentive audience, I tried to imagine that there was just *one* person out there whose life I might touch, and I spoke as though focusing on that one lonely child.

Gradually, the invitations to speak came more frequently and from more distant places. Eventually, a tour of several cities in Texas was organized for me. Just before we left, however, additional sites were added to the tour, and the itinerary was expanded to include California, Arizona, Alabama, Louisiana, and Florida.

I was thrilled, but Ann didn't share my enthusiasm. "No way, Ronald Charles," she argued. "We would be living out of a suitcase for two months!"

"But honey, we promised to go wherever the Lord leads. This is my passion, my purpose. I can feel it deep in my soul."

She looked at me and shook her head. "I don't think God is sending us the same message." Little did I know the future impact of this statement.

I was surprised and disappointed by her reaction. It made me wonder if I was being fair to her. I told her I'd reconsider the expanded tour, but a few days later, Ann hugged me and said, "Honey, it's just that I'm scared. I wish I could get a normal job, you know, nine to five. Traveling is so hard, but if you believe we should go, I'm willing."

Time proved that Ann's intuition was well-founded. The tour was a strenuous two months—and a logistical challenge. Sometimes we stayed in private homes, a stressful situation for Ann and a great inconvenience for our hostesses, but due to a shortage of cash, we had no other choice. When we did have money to pay for accommodations, we found that wheelchair-accessible motels were few and far between. One night after Ann had driven 12 exhausting hours, sometimes on unpaved roads, we arrived at our destination only to discover the room they had reserved for us was on the second floor, and the motel had no elevators. As weary as she was, Ann had to drive another two hours before we found suitable lodging.

Church congregations always received us warmly, and sometimes they gave love offerings that were more than adequate to take care of our traveling expenses. But at secular schools, we were usually given a small gratuity that barely paid for our meals. At one particular school with an enrollment of 1500 students, the youngsters listened politely, but we sensed a negativism on the part of faculty members. In fact, one teacher was so openly critical of us that Ann left the campus in tears. I felt equally frustrated, certain we'd wasted our time and energy on this out-of-the-way stop.

It was nearly a year later when my secretary, Cindy, laid a letter and several snapshots on my desk. "Look at this, Ron," she said, showing me a picture of a mangled Camaro. "How could anyone survive an accident like this?"

The letter she read to me was from a 16-year-old girl, a student who had attended the school assembly that I had decided was a waste of time. "My boyfriend and I were involved in an accident shortly after you spoke at my school," she wrote. "Ron, if I hadn't met you, the crash that left me paralyzed and in a wheelchair would have been more than I could cope with now. But when I get down, I remember your words, and they give me the courage to go on. Thanks, and keep up the good work." The letter was signed, "Your friend, Lisa."

Cindy and I looked at each other and had the same thought: *Nothing is wasted in God's plan. Everything works together for good.* We had that confirmed once again when Jack West, the director of the National School Assemblies, said, "Ron Heagy's attitude has deeply affected the lives of many thousands of young people in the schools we serve throughout the United States."

Slowly our ministry expanded from a focus solely on youth work to include motivational speeches at business seminars, churches, colleges, seminaries, prisons, detention centers, law-enforcement organizations, and groups like Promise Keepers and Christian Berets. I also became involved with various disability organizations and was extremely honored when Governor John Kitzhaber named me the 1995 Disabled Oregonian of the Year.

As our work expanded, Ann and I occasionally found ourselves in some awkward or even frightening situations, but without a doubt, the most unnerving experience was at a juvenile detention center where the young inmates' offenses ranged from petty theft to murder.

A couple of hours before my presentation, we were having breakfast in a small café near the detention center when our waitress asked us, "You folks passin' through?"

We nodded.

"Where ya headed?"

"We're from Oregon," Ann answered. "My husband has come to speak at the detention center."

"Yipes! I wouldn't want to be in your shoes. No way I'd go near that place! A couple of weeks ago one of the guys grabbed an officer's gun and shot him in the head. A bunch of bad boys, they are. That's why they've got 'em behind bars."

Ann looked at me, I looked at her, and without words we read each other's thoughts: *Are you sure, Lord, this is where You really want us to go? Maybe we should reconsider, huh?*

But when we'd had a moment to think things through, I knew this was *exactly* where we were supposed to be. As we paid our bill and left the café, I told the waitress, "If what you say is true, those kids *really* need to hear what I've got to tell them." Still, as we drove to the center, I asked Ann to wait in the van. I couldn't bear the thought of anything happening to her.

The administrators settled me in the room where I was to speak, and the young inmates filed in, several of them staring at me suspiciously as they took their seats. Some were sullen, and others were downright rude, mouthing obscenities and rolling their eyes. But after I started talking, the room quieted down, and the boys gave me their undivided attention. I could actually see their expressions soften as they listened to the challenges I presented them. Incredibly, I even spotted tears in the eyes of some before my message was finished.

Later several of the young men gathered around my wheelchair. Now it was their turn to tell me *their* stories. Most were unloved and from broken homes. The only family they had, the only people they could confide in and trust, were fellow gang members. They put on the tough-guy act to cover their hurts and insecurities.

When it was over, I rolled back to the van where Ann was anxiously waiting. "How did it go?" she asked quickly.

"It went great," I told her. "The only thing that bothers me about this place…is that I can't stay longer."

35

Kevin

~

S ometimes our schedule gets pretty hectic. On one particular occasion I was scheduled to speak at a Promise Keepers breakfast in Southern California at 7:00 a.m., be interviewed on a television program at 8:30, address three school assemblies during the day, and deliver the keynote address at a banquet that evening. Our travel alarm went off at 5:30 a.m., and as I watched Ann stretch and roll sleepily out of bed after only a few hours of rest, I realized again how hard she works and how many difficult sacrifices she's had to make to keep our ministry on track.

As we pulled into the parking lot where the breakfast was being held, we saw a man taking a small wheelchair out of the rear of his truck. Next he lifted a little boy out of the cab and gently eased him into the tiny chair.

I rolled over to the youngster and greeted him. "Good morning! How are you?"

The boy blinked his eyes rapidly but made no sound. "Kevin is paralyzed from the nose down," the man explained. He introduced himself as Allen and said, "When I told him you were going to speak at Promise Keepers this morning, he wanted to come hear you."

Remembering how I'd been hurt long ago by the stranger who spoke to my dad, rather than me, when we'd made our first wheelchair trip out of the hospital, I kept my eyes focused on the little boy's face and spoke directly to him. "I'm glad you came, Kevin; it's good to meet you. Maybe we can get together a little later, okay?"

After breakfast, seeing Kevin sitting at the table where some of my artwork was being displayed, I rolled over to join him. "I'd like to give you a picture, Kevin. Which one do you want?"

His eyes lit up, and he spoke in unintelligible sounds. "Kevin is trying to say he likes the lighthouse, and he wants to hold it on his lap," Allen translated.

"Right on, young man! It's yours." Ann put a pen in my mouth, and I autographed it for him. We posed for pictures together, and I asked, "Kevin, instead of going home in your truck, how would you and Allen like to ride in my van?" He couldn't smile or speak, but the little boy blinked his eyes twice in rapid succession. Above his head, Allen smiled and nodded yes.

Allen drove the van, and Ann followed in their truck. The man said Kevin had been born with a disorder known as Floppy Baby Syndrome and that his own father had abandoned him at birth. As a result, Allen had become something of a surrogate father to the little boy. "I enjoy working with Kevin, and my children love him. He's always happy and never complains, no matter what happens. Kevin can't eat or taste regular food. He gets all of his nourishment through a tube, but after hearing the other kids rave about their chocolate milk, he asked me to make his brown. He wanted to think he was having chocolate too."

"What an inspiring young man you are," I told Kevin as we said good-bye. "I'm so glad we met; I'll never forget you, Kevin."

His eyes twinkled merrily. I can still see them now in my memory.

Meeting Kevin had a profound effect on me, much like little Jimmy had years earlier when he gave me hope through his simple words, "I love you, Ron." Kevin couldn't say those words, but he loved me too, and his love, like Jimmy's, would help pave the way for the next chapter of my life.

When I said good-bye to Kevin at the Promise Keepers rally, I impulsively invited him and his mother to visit us in Oregon the following summer. At the time, I really didn't expect them to accept the invitation. But six months later, I received a phone call.

"Hello, Ron?" the caller asked. "This is Susan, Kevin's mother. Do you remember me?"

"I surely do," I answered. "How's my little buddy doing?"

"Kevin's fine," Susan answered. "He wants to know if the blackberries in Oregon are ripe yet. If so, he'd like to come pick some."

I laughed. "Are you serious?"

"Kevin's sitting beside me in his wheelchair right now and blinking his eyes yes. In fact, if Kevin could speak he would tell you himself how much he's been looking forward to visiting you."

Along with Kevin and his mother, Kevin's caretaker Allen and his family arrived a few days later.

Despite Kevin's limitations and the cramped quarters of our small mobile home, my new buddy's visit was a memorable one. The entire week, although a bit hectic at times, was filled with fun and first-time experiences for Kevin. Although he couldn't laugh or verbally express his thoughts, the sparkle in his eyes said far more than words ever could. Things that other active children consider no big deal were an absolute delight to him.

As an example, one day Susan and Allen loaded Kevin and his wheel-chair into a trailer attached to our ride-along lawn mower. Then they took him for a merry-go-round ride, circling our property until they were all exhausted. On another occasion we took Kevin to a children's playground in the park. It was there that he experienced the thrill of whizzing down a slide for the first time. Susan carried Kevin to the top, laid him on his back, and Allen was waiting with open arms when he slid to the bottom. Each time they asked if he wanted to do it again, Kevin blinked yes.

Because *Free Willie* was one of Kevin's favorite movies, we took him to see the famous Orca, Keiko, in Newport, only a couple of hours away. Along the wheelchair-accessible beach like a couple of so-called "normal kids," the two of us had a wheelchair race and played tag with incoming waves. I wanted to buy something special for Kevin as a memento of the trip, so while he and Allen's two little girls watched Keiko perform in his specially-built tank, I asked Susan what her son would like to have. I expected her to name some small trinket, maybe a miniature replica of Keiko or a Free Willie pin.

She surprised me by saying, "What Kevin really wants, money can't buy."

"Oh, what's that?" I asked.

"A smile."

I blinked back tears. Susan's comment made me more grateful than ever that I could smile. I was thinking in terms of material things, and all Kevin really wanted was the ability to do something that the rest of us take for granted. I made a resolution then and there that no matter what happened in my own life, even if glaucoma took my sight as the doctors once predicted, I would still keep on smiling.

Before our guests returned to their California home, the Albany *Democratic Herald* newspaper asked me and my little buddy for an interview. When they published our story, along with a colored photograph of the two of us together, Kevin felt like a celebrity.

Several months later, Kevin's special education teacher called me from Modesto, California. "Mr. Heagy, we're having a fundraising auction to finance the purchase of an Eye-Gaze Computer for Kevin. Would you be willing to donate one of your limited edition paintings to the cause?"

"Of course," I replied. "There's nothing I'd like to do more. Kevin and I are buddies."

"I know. He thinks you're pretty special."

"If Ann and I can help in any way with the auction, we'd be happy to fly down to Modesto for the event," I offered.

"Wonderful! I was hoping you'd say that," she enthused. "How would you like to be the master of ceremonies and keynote speaker?"

Kevin was so excited when Ann and I arrived that he followed me everywhere—like Mary's little lamb. When his mother and I wheeled around the school's auditorium on auction night to check out articles that people had donated, I noticed that one item was a San Francisco 49ers T-shirt with a $10.00 price tag attached. *Hmmm. Wonder who donated that?* I thought.

As though she had been reading my mind, Susan smiled and said, "That's Kevin's T-shirt. It's his most prized possession, besides the lighthouse picture you gave him," she hastily added.

"And he was willing to contribute it to the cause?" I asked.

She nodded. "Kevin's excited about the school getting an eye-controlled computer, if and when they raise enough money. Then he'll be able to communicate with his classmates and play computer games."

Later, Kevin—with Allen as his spokesman—introduced me to the audience. After I had challenged them with a few inspirational words, the auction began. My limited edition brought in the first $600, and Kevin's $10 shirt went for $480. Although the final goal of $23,000 wasn't met that first night, the drive was well on its way.

Before I left the stage, Kevin and his teacher brought the program to a dramatic conclusion. With his immobile hands held in hers, she helped him sign the words to a well-known melody: "Do you know that you're my hero? You are everything that I would like to be." I felt so undeserving of his tribute! Because if the truth be known, Kevin's *my* hero.

36

Mountain-Moving Faith

~

Have you ever wondered how a small seed can lay dormant in the ground for a long time without taking root? Then, one spring day when conditions are just right, a tender green shoot may poke through the soil. If watered, fertilized and properly cared for, that fragile shoot eventually produces succulent fruit or it becomes a fragrant flower that is a joy to behold.

In my case, the seed for a camp where children in wheelchairs could come and enjoy God's great outdoors was first planted in my mind way back in sixth-grade when our class went on a campout. While we were gathered around a crackling fire roasting marshmallows the very first evening, someone asked, "Where's Johnnie?"

"He couldn't come because of his wheelchair," our counselor explained.

Johnnie was a close friend of mine, and it made me sad that he was missing all the fun. I remember thinking, *It isn't fair for him to be left behind. Someone should build a camp where kids like Johnnie can go.* I never forgot that incident, but I had no idea at the time that a decade later I would find myself in the same situation—sitting at home alone in a wheelchair while the rest of my friends were out enjoying themselves. Not until then did I realize how frustrating it is to feel you are drifting downstream in a canoe without a paddle, especially when it seems that no one really cares whether you reach your destination or not.

In the intervening years, as my public speaking ministry expanded, I became even more aware of the need for a facility with full wheelchair accessibility where the able-bodied and disabled could get to know and appreciate each other. On one such occasion, as I was waiting to be introduced at a school attended by several students with disabilities, my attention was drawn to a sporty pink wheelchair that came rolling into the gymnasium with a pretty teenage girl operating its electric controls. She smiled at me while passing, and I noticed that the young lady had apparently been born with a normal, well-developed torso, but she had no legs, and only one arm. I watched in utter amazement and with a great deal of admiration as she lowered herself onto the floor in an upright position. By swaying her torso and twisting her hips, she reached the bleachers. Then, with her one arm holding on to the top of each bench, she pulled herself up, unassisted, to the third row where a group of able-bodied friends were waiting to welcome her. After sitting down, she smiled and waved at me with her one arm.

I thought, *What courage! That spunky little gal has risen above her limitations.* Her tremendous self-esteem enabled her classmates to accept her as though she were no different than them.

After the program was over, several youngsters with disabilities gathered around my wheelchair. I invited them to join me in an informal gabfest and encouraged each one to talk about his or her pet peeves. "Tell me what bugs you the most about having a physical disability," I asked.

One little guy, whose body and limbs were twisted because of cerebral palsy, had difficulty communicating because his mouth and head were pulled to one side. He was upset, and rightly so, over the way people stared at him. "It's not my…not my fault," he told me haltingly. "I was born like this."

"Of course it isn't your fault," I agreed. "God made us all different. That's why no two people look exactly alike, unless they're identical twins. Some babies are born with brown eyes, some with blue. Some are skinny, some are fat, but that doesn't make one better than the other. It also helps to remember that *everyone* has a disability of some sort. Ours are visible. Others hide theirs—but deep down inside they may be hurting too."

One shy little girl asked, "Even the Homecoming Queen?"

"Yes, even the Homecoming Queen," I answered.

Several of the older students complained about not being able to find part-time jobs. One girl who was a paraplegic with a sweet smile told me she had applied for a cashier's job at a fast-food restaurant. "The manager turned me down without looking at my application, because he said his customers might feel uncomfortable around me. He also said I couldn't reach the register from my chair, and they couldn't afford to lower it."

"Don't be discouraged, honey," I said. "That man's the loser, and what he did is actually illegal. There are lots of kind, understanding people in this world who can see what lies beneath the surface. In fact, if I had been that restaurant manager, your sweet smile and outgoing personality would have won me over right away."

She blushed, but seemed reassured by the compliment.

A freckle-faced, red-haired junior higher was ticked off by the lack of recreational facilities for those with disabilities. "Every summer my big brother goes to Scout Camp, but I gotta stay home because there aren't ramps to the dorms and dining room. It isn't fair."

I agreed. "You're right, buddy, and something should be done about it."

Several years before, I had been booked to speak for an entire week at a church-sponsored summer camp. As a support, I asked my sister, Pennie, to come along. When we arrived, the dorm manager directed us to our rooms—up a flight of stairs. Since there were no elevators and the nearest motel was 50 miles away, he offered to make pallets on the ground floor for me and Pennie to sleep on. "Sir, do you realize how hard it is for someone to lift me into my wheelchair from the floor?" I asked. "Although she probably would be willing to try, I can't ask my sister to do that for an entire week." I stayed only to speak at their campfire that evening, and then reluctantly, Pennie and I drove home.

Not until becoming a quadriplegic myself did I learn that our attitude—*my* attitude—determines how high we will fly in life. Some individuals soar, while others never get off the ground. Although my motionless body is strapped into a wheelchair, my mind dares to take flight, and sometimes it soars to dangerous altitudes.

The longer I thought about a disability camp, the more determined I became to do something about it. Perhaps you could say the seed that had been sown years before was finally germinating. After doing considerable research, I discovered there aren't many facilities in the United

States that can accommodate all types of disabilities, and none of the few that do are located in our vicinity.

It was then that my prayers became more fervent. *Lord, You know that all of Your children, even those who can't walk, should be able to experience the thrill of going to camp in a majestic mountain setting where they can enjoy Your great creation. Please help me find someone who can make that possible.* Maybe if I had known that someone would be me and if I had realized what an enormous undertaking it would be, I might not have been so eager to become involved. At any rate, I continued to pray that a wealthy individual or a charitable organization of some sort would also see the need and would make my dream come true.

One day as Ann and I were driving to Bend, Oregon, during a snowstorm, we passed a For Sale sign posted on a 34-acre parcel of prime land near the small town of Sweet Home. I saw at a glance that ancient oak trees and stately pines grew around a large flat meadow and that the South Santiam River snaked its way along one side. With the exception of two old, weathered buildings that looked as though they had been built in the late 1800s, the land was undeveloped. In the distance, majestic mountains seemed to be standing guard like silent sentinels.

"Ann," I exclaimed. "Pull over on the next shoulder and stop."

"Why? Is something wrong?"

"No—far from it. Everything is right about this place."

"Right?" She looked puzzled.

"Yeah, wouldn't this be a *great* spot for a summer camp?"

She eyed me skeptically. "Okay, Ron. Tell me what's on your mind."

"Ann, someone should buy this land and build a retreat for kids who are disabled. I can already see it. The meadow is flat and large enough to accommodate yurts and lots of log cabins. A bathhouse with roll-in showers and an all-purpose clubhouse could be built in the center, and…"

She interrupted my daydreams and brought me back to reality while easing onto the highway again. "Forget it, Ron. You're supposed to speak in Bend tonight, and we're behind schedule."

As much as I tried, it was impossible for me to forget that piece of property. I was already hooked by its potential. That night I went to sleep thinking about what an idyllic setting it would be for the project uppermost in my mind, and in my dreams I saw a boy on a skateboard being pulled by a little guy in an electric wheelchair. They were both laughing and having a great time. In the activity center, a group of giggling girls were having a wheelchair race, while a bunch of boys fished in a small pond near the river. That dream seemed so real that even after awakening, I could still hear the sound of childish laughter. From that point on, I felt confident that if a camp was meant to be, yours truly was the man to get the job done.

When I told Ann about my decision, she brought me back to reality. "Ron, you're a dreamer. Where would we get the money?"

"Honey, God owns the cattle on a thousand hills, and if He wants a camp to be built, He will supply the financing," I answered hopefully.

I called the realtor who had listed the property, and he told me what the owners were asking for the acreage. To a poor guy like myself, struggling to survive, barely meeting traveling expenses, the price sounded like a fortune. "Would the owners consider selling it on a contract with a small down payment and small monthly payments?" I asked.

"I'm sorry, Mr. Heagy, but they need the full amount up-front," he replied. "To buy the property, you'll have to apply for a bank loan."

"Well I guess that leaves me out then," I said. I knew I'd never qualify for a loan. At that time we had only a few hundred dollars in savings, our credit cards were maxed, and my cash flow fluctuated from month to month. My chances of getting a bank loan were less than zero. Next, my move was to call an influential businessman who I hoped would not only give me some good advice, but who also might be interested in taking on the project personally.

He advised me to forget it. "You'd be getting in over your head financially, Ron, and it would be too gigantic an undertaking for one man to handle alone—especially someone in your condition."

He was right, of course. Still, I wasn't willing to give up that easily, so I called other friends. They all gave me the same advice—everyone but Uncle Bruce who had single-handedly turned his nearby country property into a beautiful wilderness park. He said, "Go for it, Ron. You can do it!"

So, stepping out on faith, I wrote to the owners, telling them about my dream of building a disability camp and asking if they would be willing to sell me their property on a contract. For several weeks I waited…and waited for a reply. In the meantime, I kept praying that God would touch their hearts and perform a miracle.

And He did! One day the realtor called and told me his clients were willing to go along with my proposal.

I was relieved, but also scared. *How can I raise that much money?* I thought. *Maybe I should follow my friends' advice, Lord, and forget it. Even if I sell all of my personal possessions and convert everything we own into cash, I can't possibly come up with the amount it will take to swing the deal. So I'm going to make a counteroffer of $40,000 less than the asking price. If You really want us to have that land, Lord, please perform another miracle.*

Once again, He did, and the owners accepted my offer. Next, I checked with the Building Department and learned that, subject to the approval of other landowners and the County Board of Supervisors, the property was properly zoned and could be used as a campsite. But before the hearing could proceed, I had to come up with approximately $1,000 for a Conditional Use Permit and had to provide proof of a source of drinking water on the property.

"That shouldn't be any problem," I assured the Building Inspector. "There is a spring on this particular piece of property."

"Sorry, springs are not acceptable for drinking purposes," he replied. "You'll need to drill a well and have a supply of water available for emergencies, such as a fire."

"How much will it cost to drill?" I asked.

"Somewhere between $3,000 and $5,000, depending on how high the water level is," he said. "However, there's no guarantee that you'll strike water or that it will be acceptable for drinking purposes. Several landowners have recently had wells come in with high levels of strychnine."

I went to sleep that night with dollar signs dancing before my eyes. Probably anyone with more experience, expertise, and good sense would have backed away. But, as Ann will tell you, I can be an extremely determined man.

The following morning, I called the realtor with my final ultimatum. By that time we were conversing on a first name basis, and although he didn't say so, I suspected that Jim was pulling for me. "Tell your clients that I'm willing to move forward on one condition."

"What's that?"

"That they will provide us with potable water."

He laughed. "I think you're pushing it too far, Ron, but if you insist, I'll try."

"Nothing ventured, nothing gained," I reminded him.

He called me a short while later. "The Man Upstairs must be on your side."

"Why?"

"Because, believe it or not, the owners agreed to your terms. However, they specified that you'll have to make a nonrefundable deposit in advance."

"Great! It's a deal," I said.

That the owners should be so cooperative was miracle number one. The second was that they struck good, clean water at 160 feet on the first try. Even though it drained our savings account to pay for it, I applied for a permit and asked the county to schedule the necessary hearings. Everything had gone so smoothly that I felt confident all the major hurdles were behind us. But I was in for a big surprise! At the hearing, one landowner vehemently opposed having a campsite adjacent to his property. Other landowners, however, approved of our project, so the Board of Supervisors voted unanimously to give us the necessary clearance. That was the third miracle, because several days later, legislation was passed prohibiting construction of any more camps on forest land. If I had applied for the permit one week later, it would have been denied.

Thank You, Lord!

In an effort to get money for the down payment, I converted everything we owned that was negotiable into cash and started telling friends and supporters about my commitment. They all thought I was crazy. But everyone knew better than to tell me a man in my condition couldn't accomplish something worthwhile, because I would do everything possible—short of breaking my neck again—to prove they were wrong.

I finally raised the necessary down payment, went into escrow, and closed the deal. It wasn't until then that reality hit me full force. The old ramshackle buildings were about to fall down. There were no roads into the property, and the meadow was overgrown with thistles, blackberry bushes, brush, and decaying tree stumps. A 400-foot span of the river needed to be fenced off for safety's sake because the bank down to the water was steep and slippery. In addition, I didn't know the first thing about building a camp. For a man who couldn't dig a ditch or swing a hammer, I had taken on more than I could handle alone. I would have to depend on God to provide the funds and other folks to do the manual labor.

As Ann and I drove to a home schooler's conference being held at a large church in Portland, I mulled the problems over in my mind and wondered what to do next. In addition to being on the conference program, I was also booked to speak at a Sunday evening church service. When we arrived and saw that the auditorium seated several thousand people, I thought, *Great! In a church this size, there should be lots of individuals willing to give us a hand.*

But my euphoria was short-lived. The conference director told us the church he had booked me in was some distance away, and that the 60-member congregation met in a small Grange Hall. As we drove over winding country roads, I grumbled and complained to Ann all the way. "I wouldn't have accepted this engagement if the guy had told us in advance that we'd be going to a remote little church in the wildwood. Guess we can forget about getting any help for Camp Attitude from a congregation this size. Why, they don't even have a church building of their own."

God had given me the name for the site—Camp Attitude—and yet I'm sorry to say, my own attitude was still remarkably fickle, even though God had come through every step of the way so far. Clearly the first attitude that needed to change about Camp Attitude was my own.

When we reached the church, I saw cars and trucks parked all around the Grange Hall, and inside the place was packed from wall to wall. More than 150 people turned out for the meeting. As soon as the music started, I felt the presence of God in the midst of this warm, responsive crowd of believers, and I remembered something that Jesus had once said: "Where two or three are gathered together in My name, there am I in the midst of them."

Before starting to speak, I asked God to forgive me for my negative attitude, and I thanked Him for bringing us to this amazing little church instead of the large one I had anticipated. During the service, I barely mentioned my building project, but the Lord had already prepared hearts in advance. At the conclusion of the program, I was presented with a love offering of $2,500—enough money to pay for the gravel needed to make a road from the highway to the meadow.

But God wasn't finished with my attitude adjustment that day. When a man with major disabilities approached me and said he would like to help, my first thought was, *What can a guy who walks with crutches and doesn't have the use of his hands do? He's almost as helpless as I am.* The would-be volunteer told me that he had broken his neck during a construction accident. "I fell off of a scaffold," he explained. "Been a walking quad ever since. Even though my hands are paralyzed and most of the muscles in my legs, I can still operate a back-hoe with shoulder muscles and these attachments on my arms. If you need any ditches dug or trees uprooted, I'll be glad to do the job for you."

I was amazed at God's provision and said, "Thanks! Maybe we can rent a back-hoe and…"

He interrupted me with, "That won't be necessary. I'll bring mine."

God was at work again, supplying needs. "Brother, you're just the man I've been hoping to find," I said. "We need to have trenches dug for our underground electrical lines, and the Building Department wants us to dig several soil compaction test holes before installing our sewer system. They've got to be six-feet deep, and I didn't know how we could get the job done."

"That won't be a problem. Leave it to me," my new friend said.

True to Oregon weather, it rained on the Saturday morning when we met with our volunteers at the property. It wasn't a gentle sprinkle, but a heavy downpour. "No one will be able to work in weather like this," I grumbled to Ann. "Guess we may as well turn around and go home."

Just then we rounded a bend in the road and saw a conglomeration of cars, trucks, and campers. I turned to my wife in amazement. "Can you believe it? They've actually put up tarps, and they've already started working. There must be more than a hundred people…It looks like…like Woodstock!"

The volunteers had brought their own equipment—shovels, wheelbarrows, rakes, hoes, and chain saws. The gals were working as hard as the guys. My new quadriplegic friend was there, and I watched in amazement as he yanked scrubby trees up by the roots and started digging the first of nearly 400 feet of trenches. Wow! What a guy! I thought. *He's a living example of determination and true grit, and doing it all without the use of his hands!*

In one day's time, that group of volunteers actually accomplished what it would have taken an ordinary crew more than a month to do. And as an added bonus, when they cleared the meadow, beneath the brush they discovered an old abandoned pond that could be filled with water again and used as a backup reservoir. That took a big load off my

mind, because I was concerned about meeting the fire hazard require-
ments.

Before they left, I tried to thank all the volunteers, but words were
inadequate. "You'll never know how much I appreciate all that you've
done. I just wish I could have gotten out there with a shovel and a hoe
to help."

The pastor patted my shoulder. "You're an inspiration to all of us,
Ron, and we are committed to this project. You need a fence along the
river bank because there's a 50-foot drop down to the water. We'll not
only raise money for the material, but we'll be back to put the fence up
for you."

These wonderful people returned, not once, but many times to do
the necessary odd jobs that needed to be done.

And not only this small church, but many, many others helped
turn this rough land into my dream come true for disabled kids. Several
members of my family moved their motor homes onto the property and
worked long weekends from dawn till dusk. Others who had a part in
Camp Attitude were a result of God's divine appointments, scheduled by
the Lord Himself to accomplish what needed doing on the property.

After much hard work, many donations, frequent bullet prayers
to heaven, and plentiful miracles from God, Camp Attitude became a
reality.

We opened our "impossible" dream in August 2000 with more than
1,000 people from six different states who came to wish us well. It was a
fantastic time of victory, filled with fun, laughter, good food, music, and
great fellowship. Then, just before sunset, three colorful hot air balloons
arrived to take campers for a ride. As the crews inflated their balloons,
all eyes fell on me. The kids expected yours truly to be the first volunteer—me, a guy who's afraid of heights! But when Zachary, my four year-
old nephew, who loves Camp Attitude and insists that he will take it over
some day, said "Uncle Ron, you're the Camp Dude," I had no choice.

In an effort to not let them see how jittery I felt, while my brother
and dad lifted me out of my wheelchair and strapped me into one of
the baskets, I told the kids this would be the thrill of a lifetime—which
proved to be an understatement. It was an emotional moment and an
awesome sight for me to see from the air all that had been accomplished
in such a short period of time. Three years before, this meadow had
been nothing more than a barren, overgrown bramble patch without

electricity, sewage, or a source of drinking water. Now, thanks to a multitude of generous people who were willing to contribute their time, talents, and money, it was slowly but surely becoming a full-fledged wheelchair-accessible camp.

When I landed, the kids eagerly waited for their turns in the balloons. And guess who was first in line? Kevin—my little buddy who couldn't even smile and had once been excited about just zipping down a playground slide for the first time—was now ready to experience yet another thrill. Fortunately, his mother had brought along a portable air bag to use in case of an emergency, so Kevin was able to be taken off his respirator long enough to make the short flight. When he came back down to *terra firma* several minutes later, the sparkle in his eyes told far more than words ever could. Kevin had done something that most of his able-bodied classmates in California had not, and I knew he would soon be using his eye-controlled computer to tell them all about it.

I knew too that Kevin was just the beginning, that God had many more Kevins for whom Camp Attitude could be a blessing.

37

The Promise of a Child

~

Not long after Ann and I were married, we were visiting one of our favorite haunts—the Wild Animal Park in San Diego. It was a warm day, and as we watched couples stroll by with their children, I noticed that the kids were all eating ice cream cones. However, Ann's and my thoughts, as I was about to discover, were not in synch once again. "Hey, hon, let's have one too," I said eagerly.

Ann smiled. "Ron, I was sitting here thinking the very same thing. It makes me so happy that you suggested it first. When shall we start?"

"What do you mean start?" I asked. "Just go buy one. There's an ice cream stand over by the monkey's cage."

The wistful expression on her face changed immediately. "Oh, I thought you were talking about having a child."

I gulped. "Honey, you know we can't afford to start a family yet," I said. "We agreed to wait for at least five years."

"But I was hoping you'd changed your mind. I can hardly wait to hold a baby in my arms." She pointed to a cute, curly haired toddler. "Wouldn't it be fun to have a darling little Ronnie or Ann like that?"

"Sure," I agreed. "But right now I'd much rather have an ice cream cone."

"Okay," Ann sighed. "Stay here and watch the monkeys. I'll go get you a treat. What kind do you want?"

"Make mine a tutti-frutti."

Ann made a face at me before strolling over to the refreshment stand. Five minutes later she came back with two cones in her hands and a mischievous gleam in her eyes. "Thanks, hon." I stuck out my tongue. "How about a lick?"

"Okay, Ronald, you asked for it." Without warning, she squashed my nose into the melting ice cream. "Next time, don't change the subject when I talk about starting a family."

That day at the park was years ago, but it always remained very vivid in my memory. For a while after this exchange, Ann seemed content to babysit our nieces and nephews. She even volunteered to take care of children we met in our travels. I knew how much she longed to become a mother, but it wasn't until our fifth anniversary that she really pressed the issue. By then my ministry was expanding, we were buying a small but comfortable home in Tangent, Oregon, and all signals seemed positive about starting a family. So we began to explore our options.

Ann made an appointment with a fertility specialist who recommended that we have artificial insemination. When he explained that it is possible to extract and use a quadriplegic's sperm, Ann told him we wanted to start the special process as soon as possible. We left his office that day with high hopes and a great deal of excitement. Ann was absolutely euphoric. "Just think, Ron, we could have a child of our own by Christmas."

"Honey, you heard what the doctor told us. It's not that simple. Artificial insemination is complicated, especially for a quadriplegic, and it doesn't always take because of inactive sperm, particularly after sitting in a wheelchair for 17 years." By then, my wife was so emotionally involved that she didn't even hear what I said. As soon as we got home, she consulted the calendar to see when her next ovulation would occur. Then she made an appointment with the specialist for us both to go in for our first insemination. Ann came home from the doctor's office that day floating on cloud nine, and needless to say, for the next month all I heard was baby talk.

While we were enjoying one of Ann's delicious stir-fry dinners shortly thereafter, she jumped up from the table and disappeared. Minutes later, Ann returned in tears. "Ron! It didn't take! I've let you down! I'm a failure!"

"Honey, it's not your fault. We'll try again," I said. I knew the process would be painful and maybe prolonged, but neither of us was prepared for the many disappointments that were ahead. Each time our efforts failed, Ann became more discouraged and withdrawn. Even though I tried to be sensitive to my wife's emotional pain, nothing I said seemed to help. We even tried donor sperm—all unsuccessful attempts. After 14 unsuccessful attempts, I dreaded discussing the subject. Yet we couldn't go on avoiding such an important issue. Frankly our baby issues compounded our existing problems and our relationship took a serious dive. From the beginning, we had overlooked all the red flags. We wanted things to work out, but we never faced the problems head-on. Instead, we kept going without repair.

After praying for wisdom and the right words, I decided to share something I had heard on a local radio station. "Ann, I'm hurting too," I said. "Maybe it's time for us to consider adopting a child. There are millions of babies born who are unwanted. We could give an abandoned baby love and a happy home to grow up in."

For the first time in months, I saw a spark of hope in Ann's eyes. Her sister, Lynn, had been adopted and was as close to Ann as any two sisters could be.

Ann immediately began exploring various types of adoptions. We had heard that orphanages in foreign countries were overcrowded with unwanted children, so she contacted an adoption agency to inquire about that possibility. However, the expense involved, and the fact that Ann wasn't old enough to qualify, made us realize that such a child would be out of our reach. Next, we pursued closed adoptions where the birth-mother and adoptive parents were not in contact. Since we didn't want our child in later years to feel that it had been abandoned, an open adoption—where the birth-mother is sent pictures and knows who the adoptive parents are—seemed to be our best alternative.

Two months after we started searching for such a child, we heard about a 23-year-old single woman in California who was expecting an unwanted baby. I dialed the number that had been given to us, and the telephone was answered by a jail matron who said she would relay my message. When Martha returned my call that evening, I learned she had been arrested for passing bogus checks but would soon be released on probation.

Although we felt uneasy about her background, Ann and I talked it over and decided to send Martha a round-trip bus ticket to Oregon so the three of us could discuss the possibility of adoption in person.

Rather than invite her to our home, we made arrangements to meet the expectant mother at a restaurant in another city not far from our own. While we were waiting for dinner to be served that evening, Martha told us she was homeless and destitute. Her boyfriend had deserted her when she became pregnant, and in order to survive she had written several checks without funds in the bank to cover them. Her story sounded plausible enough on the surface, and naturally we felt sorry for her. But during the course of our conversation, I began to detect discrepancies in some of the things she told us. I glanced at Ann and saw that she shared my misgivings. When dinner was over, Ann handed Martha some money to pay for meals on her way back to San Diego. Disappointed, but at the same time relieved, we watched her walk away without a backward glance or a word of thanks.

Our eye-opening experience with Martha made us more cautious. We were also hearing horror stories about adoptive parents losing their children by court decision after they had bonded with them. In one case, the birth-mother had been awarded custody of her little girl after three years. The adoptive parents and the child involved were all heartbroken. We didn't want that to happen to us. I finally decided to avoid our strenuous circumstances, concentrate on building Camp Attitude and let time take its course.

I have often been called a dreamer, and no doubt for good reason. Sometimes I have restless nights and awaken every couple of hours. Because I need assistance to change positions, instead of disturbing Ann, who at times was annoyed by my interruption of her sleep, I sometimes planned the next day's activities and thought about the challenges that lay ahead. Other times I dozed and dreamed. On one particular occasion when I was half awake, half asleep, I either dreamed or imagined that I was talking with a teenage girl who had heard me speak about choices and consequences.

"Mr. Heagy, I'm pregnant." Tears rolled down her face as she spoke. "My boyfriend said he loved me. Now he's with another girl and he wants me to have an abortion. My parents don't know." The distraught youngster started sobbing. "What shall I do?"

"Don't worry, honey," I told her. "You made the right choice not to have an abortion. I'll talk with your parents and tell them my wife and I will adopt your baby. Everything will work out just fine."

Perhaps it was only wishful thinking on my part, but the next morning while Ann was getting me up and dressed, I told her about the dream, vision, or whatever you care to call it. "Ann," I said, "I'm really convinced that God has a special child for us."

"I hope you're right!" she said. "I guess we'll just have to wait and see."

We agreed to leave the future in God's hands and later I became so engrossed with my construction efforts at Camp Attitude that the months whizzed by.

After one of our summer barbecue fundraisers for the camp, we received a phone call from a woman who had attended the barbecue. "I'm sure you don't remember me, but my name is Jan. When you spoke at our church some time ago, my oldest daughter and I heard you, and we both cried. You see, she was in an automobile accident and broke her neck too, but thank God Melinda recovered. That's why we were so touched by your story. Mr. Heagy, you are a real inspiration."

"Thanks, Jan. I appreciate your encouragement," I said.

Jan went on to tell me that she had recently found the Lord, and since then her outlook on life had changed completely. Her next statement came as a surprise. "I understand that you and your wife would like to adopt a child."

"Why, yes. Yes we would," I admitted. "Why do you ask?"

"My 15-year-old daughter heard you speak at her school too, and Jennifer is pregnant. The boy responsible has told her to get rid of it." She paused. "I wondered if you and your wife would be interested in adopting the baby."

A red flag immediately went up. "Is this Jennifer's idea...or yours?"

"Well, to be honest with you, I haven't talked to her about it yet. But after seeing the way you and your wife interacted with the kids at the barbecue yesterday, I feel that you would give my daughter's child a good home."

"Thanks, Jan, but Ann and I have been disappointed before. Unless Jennifer calls us herself, we'd rather not become involved."

Several weeks passed before she contacted us again. By that time Jennifer was six months along and had definitely decided to give her baby away. We made plans to meet with both of them the following evening, but only Jan showed up. Jennifer, we were told, had gone in for a sonogram that afternoon and had opted to attend a football game with friends rather than keep her date with us that night.

"You said Jennifer had a sonogram. Is the baby a boy?"

"Yes. How did you know?"

"I didn't really. It was only a gut feeling."

Two days later when I was at home alone, Jennifer finally contacted me by telephone, and my secretary drove me over to see her. We sat in my van in front of her house for more than an hour talking about Jennifer's options. She could drop out of school and raise the baby herself, difficult as that might be, or she could choose to give it to a childless couple who were prepared to offer the baby love and a good home. I didn't want her to make a snap decision that she might regret later. So I suggested that Jennifer take a week to think about it. "If you haven't called me by next Wednesday, I'll know you've decided not to give your baby up for adoption."

I was disheartened when Wednesday came and went without a word from Jennifer. Then, on Thursday morning my secretary asked if I had seen the telephone message she had left on my desk the day before.

I hadn't.

Jennifer had indeed called and left a message: "I have decided to give you the baby." And for a moment I thought a baby would pull our marriage out of the rut.

When I told Ann, she was beside herself with joy. We decided to name our son-to-be Cody Michael. His middle name was to be a tribute to my brother. Ann immediately started calling all of our close friends and family members to share the good news with them. She also began painting and converting our guest room into a nursery with teddy bear wallpaper, baby pictures, and cute little doodads. When we were traveling, no matter what city or state we were in, Ann managed to locate the nearest mall and buy another outfit for Cody. His closet soon held clothes from size newborn to toddler 3. Everything seemed to be falling into place, and our excitement mounted with each passing day. Jennifer asked us to go with her to doctor appointments, and the first time we heard our baby's heartbeat, Ann and I were overwhelmed with anticipation and excitement.

Our request for a state-mandated home study was approved in record time, so we immediately had legal papers drawn up by our attorney. Meanwhile Jennifer and her counselor prepared the documents necessary for an open adoption, assuring the birth-mother that we would provide pictures and keep her informed of the baby's progress at least once a year.

In the beginning, Ann had been concerned about whether or not Jennifer would resent her involvement with the delivery. But those fears were forgotten when she was asked to attend Lamaze classes, act as Jennifer's coach during delivery, and cut the umbilical chord after Cody's birth. She also invited me to be in the delivery room—as long as my wheelchair never ventured beyond the head of her bed, and I promised not to peek.

Two and one-half weeks before D-day, the midwife informed us that Jennifer had developed toxemia. After performing a series of stress tests to see if Cody's heartbeat was normal, the midwife recommended complete bed rest.

Several days later, when Jennifer's blood pressure continued to rise and they found protein in her urine, the medical team in charge decided to induce labor. For 48 hours we sat in Jennifer's hospital room while waiting for the injections to produce the desired results. Nothing happened. Finally the midwife told us to go home and get some rest. She promised to call as soon as Jennifer started dilating.

We reluctantly agreed, but neither of us slept.

At 3:00 a.m. the telephone rang, and Ann answered it. "Ron!" she cried. "The baby isn't responding. They're getting Jennifer prepped right now for an emergency C-section." I've never seen Ann move so fast. She had me up, dressed, in my wheelchair, and out the door within ten minutes.

Jennifer had already been taken into surgery when we arrived at the hospital. We waited by the swinging door for what seemed an eternity before I gently nudged it open a crack with my wheelchair. "Ann, listen! Cody is here! I heard him cry!" Moments later, on January 17, 2000, a nurse came out of surgery and presented Ann with a *pink* wrist band. I gasped! "Pink? Wait a minute…"

The nurse smiled. "Congratulations, Mr. Heagy. You have a beautiful baby daughter."

Ann flung both arms around my neck. "It's a girl! Can you believe it? I've never been so happy in my life." When they handed her our 6-pound, 10-ounce bundle of joy, all wrapped up in a pink blanket, Ann broke down and cried.

"Okay, Mama," I said finally. "It's my turn now. Let me give her a smooch." Ann held her close to my face so I could press my lips against the newborn's tiny ear. Her skin felt as soft as satin, even though she was still covered with amniotic fluid. "Daddy wants to be the first one to say 'I love you,' honey. You are the answer to our prayers. And I will always be here for you."

The surgical nurse who had been watching us get acquainted with our new baby asked, "What are you going to name her?"

I grinned. "Good question. We expected a boy."

Ann responded without hesitation, "I would like to call her Roni, but we'll have to wait and see what Jennifer says before making it definite."

As soon as the good news spread, our friends and family came to share our joy. When my parents took me home for some much-needed sleep, Ann stayed at the hospital for several days to nurse little Roni and help care for her. On the evening we planned to take our baby home, my attorney came to finalize the adoption papers, but Jennifer's counselor said that because she was still heavily sedated, we should wait another 24 hours. We agreed, and the attorney promised to return the following afternoon.

I teased Ann about all the boys' clothes she had purchased as we made preparations to bring the baby home. When the telephone rang later that evening, I answered it. The call was from Jan. "Ron, I don't know how to tell you this," she said haltingly. "I'm sorry, but Jennifer has decided to keep her baby."

I was stunned! Disbelieving! Nauseated! Heartsick! All kinds of unanswered questions raced through my mind. *Am I dreaming? Is this for real? How will I tell Ann?*

When I finally mustered enough courage to break the news to Ann, she was devastated too. "She can't do this to us! Roni is our baby! Jennifer promised!" she cried.

Nothing I said or did seemed to console her. The pain we both felt was indescribable, but with the loving support given to us by our family, we were able to cope with the loss.

No doubt the thing that comforted Ann the most was her sister Lynn's offer to be a surrogate mother for us, so we could become parents without going through the trauma of another adoption fiasco.

I cried when Dad held my head against his chest as he had when I was a child. "Dad, I told Roni that I loved her. I promised to be here for her always. Now she's gone, and there's nothing I can do."

"Son, I'm sorry," Dad said. "Your mother and I are hurting too. We know how much you want to become a father. But remember that God is in control."

The loss of my entire body did not impact me as much as the devastating feeling of having a child torn from my arms. The Lord never ceases to amaze me. As a result of this experience, several people who had lost a child were able to bare their heart and soul with me.

The heartbreak Ann and I felt came back to my mind when several months later I spoke in Washington D.C. at a Senate hearing. Several well-known Hollywood celebrities were also there, one of them paralyzed and in a wheelchair because of an injury similar to my own. They all advocated the use of stem cells from frozen embryos for research purposes in finding a cure for spinal cord injuries and a number of other diseases.

Yes, I too would benefit if such a cure were to be found since I suffer from continual bladder infections, bed sores, cold sweats, and phantom pain—just to mention a few of my problems. But in all good conscience, because I strongly believe in the sanctity of life, I could not go along with the pro-choice advocates—especially the well-known actress who likened a human embryo to a "goldfish."

I did agree, however, with a scientist who said that adult stem cells could be used just as effectively and without sacrificing an unborn child's life. If such were the case, I would be the first to welcome research that might contribute to the cure of diseases, help those with spinal cord disabilities, and effectively control pain. But never could I condone the taking of one life to save another. Should such a procedure become legal and federally funded, what will stop scientists from cloning and harvesting human embryos to find the ideal stem cell?

There are so many childless couples in our country who long to become parents. Wouldn't it be far more productive, and humane, to implant these fertilized embryos into the wombs of women who are unable to conceive and want so desperately to become mothers? Looking back on the loss of Roni, I believe it was another chance for Ann and I to seek help stabilizing our marriage before we brought a little child into our rocky relationship.

38

Do Dreams Come True?

~

A s hard as it was for me after we lost our baby, I still had commitments to keep. I was invited to be the keynote speaker at a Disability Awareness Conference in Southern California, and because the other speaker had died very suddenly, it wouldn't be fair for me to cancel at this late date. Two of our friends volunteered to go along and be my caregivers, so Ann urged me not to change my plans.

My caregivers and I flew to California and were picked up the following morning at our hotel in Corona by a very gracious, likable lady from the Crossroads Community Church. Melanie's face radiated warmth, love, and understanding as she laid her hand on mine. "We appreciate having you come so soon after the loss of your baby, Ron. You and your wife must be heartbroken."

The opening session was attended by an enthusiastic audience of disabled individuals and their caregivers. Although I had come to challenge them to rise above their own limitations, as is often the case, they were the catalysts that God used to strengthen my own faith and to give me peace about accepting the loss of our baby. I needed encouragement just as badly as anyone at the conference—perhaps even more. So, instead of returning to the hotel after my presentation was over, I opted to attend a seminar called "Adopting Children with Special Needs."

Bob and Donna King were the leaders. What an amazing couple! Each of them held an adopted, disabled child on their lap when the session began. I thought, *Wow! They are raising two children with special needs.* But my admiration for them grew by leaps and bounds after learning they had opened their hearts and home to a total of *nine* unwanted children, six of them with very severe disabilities.

"Some people see the disability first," Bob told the crowd. "My wife and I see the *child.*"

Donna reminded us that God loves all children, *especially* those with special needs—children whom the world shuns because they're imperfect. As a little girl, Donna said, she had sometimes put her dolly on the front porch and had pretended it was an abandoned baby left there for her to cuddle and care for. Once again, an example of a seed planted by God in childhood germinating years later as a way of ministry to others.

The Kings had been high school sweethearts and were married at an early age. After having three "homegrown" children of their own, this incredible couple started grafting adopted youngsters onto their family tree. As of today, they have adopted nine children, most of whom have severe challenges physically and mentally.

At the seminar's conclusion, I had an opportunity to get better acquainted with Bob and Donna. I told them that my wife and I were really shaken up by the loss of little Roni. They could empathize because one foreign-born child they had hoped to take into their home had been reclassified as unadoptable because of brain damage shortly before her scheduled departure from South Korea. "But," Donna said with a smile, "God has rewarded us since then with all these wonderful kids. We really feel blessed."

I was literally blown away by this enthusiastic, energetic couple who had the capacity to love unwanted children that others considered unlovely. "You must have full-time help to care for so many with special needs," I said.

Bob laughed. "Life does get pretty hectic at times, but the kids all pitch in and help. Donna and I do the rest. My day starts at 3:00 a.m. When the alarm goes off, I get breakfast started and do as much as I can to help Donna before leaving at 5:00 a.m. for work. My wife's the one who carries the heaviest load."

"Don't you believe it," Donna chided. "Bob's just being modest. He actually does all of the cooking, besides holding down two jobs to pay our expenses. Housing has been one of our biggest concerns. Our place is very modest. We actually started out with two bedrooms, but as we've added more children, it's been necessary to add more rooms. We now have seven bedrooms, but only two baths." She laughed. "Believe me, it gets pretty noisy when someone is taking a shower and a couple of kids are standing cross-legged in the hall pounding on the bathroom door to get in."

I listened to her with wide-eyed amazement. "What a remarkable couple you are. It must cost a fortune to feed a family of 14. Do you haul food in by the truckload?"

"Not quite, but it does take eight to ten gallons of milk each week."

"What about doctor bills?"

"We can't praise Shriners Hospital for Crippled Children in Los Angeles highly enough. Our kids have had a total of 23 major surgeries in the past seven years, and they haven't cost us a cent."

"Do you and Bob ever have an evening out, just the two of you?" I asked.

"Yes, that's one of our top priorities," Donna said. "We have great support from our family and friends. Besides, we have built-in babysitters of our own. The older children help take care of the little ones when Bob and I have date nights. We also make it a point to take each child out alone occasionally to McDonald's so they will feel important."

"I don't suppose you ever have a vacation."

"Rarely. It's too expensive for us to do much traveling."

I told them about Camp Attitude and asked if they would like to come for a visit. One of the boys' eyes lit up like a Christmas tree with all the lights ablaze. "Wow! That sounds awesome! Can we go, Dad? Please?"

Bob shook his head. "Sorry, Adam. How would we get there? We don't have transportation for the whole family or a way to take Sarah's wheelchair."

"But, Dad," rising to stand on his two prosthetic legs, "we never get to go anywhere," Adam cried.

I wanted very much to help this deserving family, and suddenly a solution to their lack of transportation came to me. "Am I right in assuming that you don't have a van that's equipped with a hydraulic wheelchair lift?"

"Not yet, but we're praying about it. I'm hoping to find a hospital van that can be converted."

"Sir, your search is over, and your prayers are about to be answered. I have two vans, and nothing would give me more pleasure than to give one of them to you."

"Give us a van? Are you serious?"

"Never been more serious in my life. Maybe, Lord willing, I can raise enough money to bring all of you to our family camp in August."

Needless to say, Adam was one excited youngster, and the very first thing he did was tell all of his brothers and sisters. "We're going camping in Oregon! And Mr. Heagy is gonna give us a van." As far as Adam was concerned, it was already a done deal.

Sunday morning, the pastor of Crossroads Community Church graciously gave me the opportunity to speak at all three services. When I told his congregation about my desire to raise money for the Kings' transportation to Camp Attitude, they very generously gave me the largest love offering that we had received to date. And, as frosting on the cake, a very special lady who heard the message also volunteered to help drive the King family to Oregon in her motorhome.

I could hardly wait to tell Bob that another prayer had been answered. This time it was mine!

When I returned home, Ann told me, "I have peace about losing Roni now, but my heart still aches," she said. "I guess she wasn't meant to be ours, but I'm still concerned about what will happen to her in the future."

"I know," I replied. "The thing that hurts me the most is that she won't have a daddy to love her. We need to pray that God will watch over the little darling and protect her. Maybe Jennifer will stay in touch and let us know how things are going." I told Ann about what had happened to me while we were apart. "I wish now that you'd gone with me. Donna and Bob King, who led a seminar on adoption, are one of the most incredible couples I've ever met."

"Maybe God is knocking on our door."

"Do you think He wants us to adopt a child who is disabled?"

"Could be," she answered. "Let's see what happens." We both agreed to wait and see what doors God might open.

I then turned to the task of dealing with the mail on my desk that had accumulated while I was away.

But within five minutes Ann was back in my office. "Ron, we've got to talk. Now!"

"Okay, as soon as I'm finished here," I said slightly perturbed at being interrupted.

"Now!" Ann repeated. "This can't wait. Jennifer called! She wants me to come over right away."

"Why?"

"She didn't say, but maybe I should go and find out what's on her mind," Ann said.

"Honey, seeing the baby again will only make it harder for you to give her up," I said. "But follow your heart. Whatever you decide, I'm behind you 100 percent."

I watched Ann leave with a lump in my throat, and each time the telephone rang, my heart turned flips. One hour passed, then two. Still no call from Ann. It was impossible for me to concentrate on anything. I rolled my chair into the guest bedroom that my wife had converted into a nursery with such enthusiasm and joy a short while before. The crib was still there, a cuddly pink teddy bear in one corner, a fluffy blanket in the other. I rolled over to the closet's open door. Ann had returned the clothes we had purchased for Cody. Now there was a row of dainty dresses hanging there—dresses that Ann would soon be taking back to the department store. My heart ached for her.

Please Lord, don't let Ann be hurt again!

I had just returned to my office when my secretary informed me there was a call waiting on line one. I tapped the button with my mouth stick. "Hello, this is Ron Heagy."

Ann came straight to the point. "Jennifer's upset."

"What about?"

"The baby won't nurse! She cried all night, and Jennifer doesn't know what to do. I think she's having second thoughts about keeping the baby. Here, you talk to her."

"Honey, this is something you need to handle yourself," I said. "She called and asked you to come over, not me. Just remember, we're leaving for the desert tomorrow, and we will be gone for two months."

"Okay," Ann answered. "I'll call you back."

I waited…and waited! Finally, after what seemed like eons instead of only a few minutes, Ann called to break the news. "Ron, are you sitting down?"

"Of course I am. Stop joking. Tell me what happened."

"You are about to become a father. Jennifer has decided, after two weeks of trying to take care of the baby by herself, that we can offer little Roni a better life than she can."

I could hardly believe what Ann was saying. "Are you sure?"

"Absolutely. The attorney is coming at 7:30 tonight to finalize our adoption papers."

Words cannot express the joy or the gratitude we both felt that night when our precious bundle of joy was placed in Ann's arms and we knew for sure that she was ours. We finally had a baby to call our own—to love and cherish, and raise to love God.

We will someday tell Roni what a generous choice her birth mother made in putting her baby's welfare before her own. It's our prayer that other unmarried teenagers will be encouraged to follow Jennifer's unselfish example.

39

Onward!

~

As I said earlier, sometimes life dumps on us and we have two choices...get bitter or better. God says consider it joy when you encounter various trials knowing that the testament of your faith produces endurance...if anyone lacks understanding, let him or her ask God for insight. (James 1).

One thing, I've decided is not to keep my wheelchair rolling on fast-forward indefinitely. Ever since I first dreamed of Camp Attitude, I've had a tendency to take on too much. I've truly burned the candle at both ends.

Fatigue, burnout, or whatever you wish to call it, has recently caused me to ask myself some serious questions. Is life really meant to be a race...or a joyful day-by-day journey? If the latter, then I think it's time for me to pause and enjoy the scenery.

Now that Camp Attitude is nearly completed, I'd like to slow down and spend more time with my friends and family. Our little Roni is growing daily. And as she continues to grow, I want to be there for her—after all, I made a very special promise to her the day she was born. I intend to keep that promise.

Of course, there's still work to be done at Camp Attitude. Before construction started, I asked God for one millionaire to help us build our facility. Instead, He chose to send us many ordinary, hardworking, generous people to get the job done in record time.

How can I possibly put into words my gratitude to every one of the wonderful friends who have helped my dreams become a reality? On behalf of myself and all the campers, both children and adults, who have been blessed in the future by Camp Attitude, I'd like to offer a truly heartfelt thank you and a prayer that God will richly reward you for your prayer support, unselfishness, and unbelievable generosity. More than a million dollars in private and corporate contributions, along with a great deal more in volunteer labor, provided for the improvements now in place.

I still maintain a heavy public speaking schedule, traveling from one end of the country to the other. Sometimes my trips offer unexpected turning points in my life. Such was the case when I met Kevin, and such was the case when I flew to New York City to attend the premiere of Martin Luther King III's documentary miniseries, "The Wisdom of Dreams," in which my story is a featured segment.

The date was September 11, 2001 and the hotel where we were staying was only a mile from the World Trade Center. I'll never forget that morning when our world changed forever as the airplanes hijacked by terrorists struck the Twin Towers. The sight was horrific. Spirals of smoke and clouds of dust blackened the sky. People were screaming, crying, running—trying to find shelter from the falling debris and searing flames.

Sirens pierced the air as fire trucks, police cars, and ambulances screeched past on their way to Ground Zero. Firefighters rushed into action at the risk of their own lives. Strangers helped strangers. Volunteers worked frantically to rescue the injured and those still trapped inside.

As I watched, I thought of all the changes that would happen in the days ahead to so many families—and especially to the children in those families. I thought of the fathers and mothers, grandparents, and aunts and uncles who would never come home again. I remembered how close our family had come to being changed forever as we nearly lost our Roni in the adoption fiasco. Children were the least visible victims of September 11—not just those who were killed that day, but those who will face the rest of their life without a loved one.

My heart was also moved when I heard about other less visible victims of the tragedy—the disabled men and women who were stranded in their wheelchairs at the tops of Trade Center stairwells, hoping for someone to carry them down to safety. One dear able-bodied man, a newscaster reported, stayed behind, unwilling to leave his quadriplegic friend in the building alone.

It was from this great tragedy that God gave me an additional burden for the wheelchair-bound. When the air flights resumed several days later and I was able to go home, I started my "Freedom to Move Fund." This campaign is designed to give individuals who experience mobility challenges greater independence by eliminating the barriers that hinder their "freedom to move."

I see a three-pronged strategy to accomplish this goal. One is education. If we can provide more adaptable equipment, including high-tech computers and other modern technology to the disabled, we can eliminate the intellectual decay that many disabled suffer simply because of their mobility restrictions.

The second strategy has to do with transportation. By providing accessible vehicles to the disabled, we can give them more freedom to work, attend school, play, grow, and travel. We need more wheelchair accessible automobiles, aircraft, and vehicles for businesses who provide services for the disabled.

The final strategy concerns the disabled's residence. Buildings need to be structured to provide safe and adequate emergency exits, requiring minimal assistance from others. All rooms on the first floor of apartments, condos, hotels, and motels should be wheelchair accessible. Buildings such as the World Trade Center should have emergency elevators for the disabled with their own electrical generators that can be manually operated in times of emergency.

So although I say I'm slowing down, I'm always open to the next opportunity God brings my way. I'm sure that I'll always be active. I, like you, have an assignment to complete in this life God has given me. I'm a husband, a father, camp founder, a motivational speaker, and an advocate for the disabled and for kids with special needs, among many other things.

These are the roles God has given me to fulfill during the years I'm on earth, and it's in doing what He has given me to do that I find fulfillment. My other choice would be to complain about what I'm missing, to make myself and everyone around me miserable as I count those things that have been denied me, rather than the blessings I've been given.

Like any other man, I have my ups and downs, my good days and my not-so-good days. But through it all, I've found the secret to contentment, and it's all revealed in the name I chose for our camp—*Attitude.*

Life *is* an attitude. And no matter what we've been given or denied in life, we can choose what our attitude will be. From that choice, we will reap a harvest of happiness or of misery. It's up to each of us, no matter whether our disability is visible or invisible, to decide which will be ours.

I hope you choose wisely.

I hope you choose to *never give up.*

40

From Pain to Peace

~

My motto throughout this book has been that your attitude of never giving up will keep you catapulting forward in life so that you can accomplish your dreams, aspirations and hopefully exactly what God chooses for you.

My path of being thrown in a wheelchair and losing my body...me, the jock, the athlete, was only a part of the journey that brought many lessons for me. My day-to-day care is hard. Someone has to do all the daily things most people take for granted...from going to the bathroom first thing in the morning to brushing my teeth to having my first cup of coffee. The good part of course is that I know all the things I can't do but am also blessed with knowing all the things I can do.

For the people around me, it is more difficult. This difficulty has taken a toll on many of my relationships, and, as hard as it is to admit, on both of my marriages. The second time was even harder for me than the first. Ann was much younger than I when we married, and though we thought we had the strength to handle all the 'extras' that come with the life of a quadriplegic, we didn't. The truth is our lives could no longer contain the years of unresolved anger, bitterness, and resentment that I allowed to go on. We couldn't seem to find a way to resolve our issues.

Just as any other couple, we tried. We went on vacations. I buried myself in my work, the Lord's work. Ann thought a child would help. We used counseling even made new goals, but it was a condition of the heart and, like untreated cancer, our relationship turned terminal. Both

239

of us had a strong Christian faith that looked down on divorce, but we were not able to avoid it. The closing of 2002 was also the closing of our marriage.

Through it all, I have learned one thing: forgiveness is the way to peace. Peace with God and peace with others. I am truly glad that God has forgiven us, and that Ann and I have forgiven each other. We also took the honorable road with our daughter, sharing joint custody and responsibilities. Ann has since remarried, and Roni, with her loving spirit, is doing wonderfully well. I would like to express my gratitude to Ann for providing the excellent care and support necessary to help me fulfill some of my dreams over the years. My memories will remain positive.

41

Kelli

~

Note: Thanks to Robyn Eastman who gave this chapter a heartbeat.

The end of our marriage was a crushing blow for me because this was my second divorce. Was this God's plan for me…to never have someone to spend my nights and days with? Though I sat in a wheelchair, I didn't feel like a different person inside…I was the same Ron who had grown up gearing to a career as a professional football player. I was the same Ron who went with the guys to the nearby hang out and watched the girls go by. Was there going to be a line of women who would come in and out of my life and when they finally realized that living with me is taking care of me in so many moments of their day…they would give up thinking me just 'too high maintenance'? When we were kids, we didn't go out with girls who were 'high maintenance,' it was easier to date the cheerleader types who adored you because you were a jock. They would give anything to be out with you and as jocks, we took advantage of that.

After my second divorce, I was finally able to reexamine some of the very 'male' parts of me…my male attitudes. I had a great attitude about my speaking tours, the growth of Camp Attitude and the other projects of my life, but my personal relationships still had work to be done. Though I couldn't play football or surf or do the 'guy' things I used to do…I still had an all too familiar attitude about women. I was still a 'jock'. Looks and body shape were all important and I forgot sometimes to look deeper. Showing off was important to me and what others thought about me was way too important. I measured my "okayness" by

241

the perfection of the woman beside me and that perfection was measured far more in looks and appearances than in depth. That didn't mean that Julie and Ann were not deep, it just meant that I wasn't able to see all that they were and support them in the ways they needed to be supported. As each of them left my life, it was easy to see what they had done wrong... but how could I do anything wrong when I was just sitting in this chair?

There was one woman though, who came into my life and helped me with these 'attitudes'. She helped me to see that I was looking for the outside of things and not the inside. I had walls that were invisible to me, but all too visible to those who came into my inner circle. Marriage was important because it was the 'Christian' thing to do. You get married, have kids and go to church. It was so important to me to be married without understanding the real ramifications of what that is, means or does. All I heard was 'in sickness and in health' and that would cement us for life...that would take care of all the challenges for my lifestyle and abilities. Dealing with relationships was a challenge no one really spoke about. Though there are a million books about disabled relationships I didn't realize that some applied to me too. Bob and Donna King had been a great inspiration to me the way they loved their disabled children unconditionally, but could I find true unconditional love for me in a marriage relationship...it wasn't about my physical challenges, it was about my inner challenges that so many men don't want to see.

I prayed constantly for guidance but seemed to be making wrong choices. What I didn't understand at the time is that God leads us always though it doesn't feel like it or look like it at the time. Sometimes our religion creates blinders so that we can't see the bigger picture. At times we have to remember that religion and our spirituality can be two different things. Our spirituality...our faith and belief in the walk we take with God doesn't always 'look' like the picture we grow up with. Jesus partied with the tax collectors and the people that everyone turned their backs on and through this experience; many people turned their back on me. It was a 'walk' that I had to do alone for a while...though at the time, I didn't realize that there was someone there all along.

It all started about 10 years ago. An old acquaintance of Ann's came up to us in church one morning and reintroduced herself and her husband. We invited them over for dinner. As a people person, I loved having people over (and of course, I didn't have to 'do anything' involving the preparation of it.)

As we talked, Ann seemed to find someone she could grumble to about her extra duties of having to travel with me. To me, it was my…our ministry and I was embarrassed that she complained about it, especially to these new prospective friends.

Kelli and her husband looked through pictures and during that meeting, Kelli asked what I wanted the world to remember me by. Instead of answering her directly, I told her I wanted that Michael Bolton song played at my funeral—"When I'm Back on My Feet Again." She stared blankly at me, and only later did I find out how much that statement touched her. She had previously lost two children, and was moved by what I had said.

A week later, Kelli returned to my house, I thought unannounced. When I asked her how I could help her, she informed me that she was my new bookkeeper and was surprised that I didn't know anything about it. "Ann hired me to keep track of your checkbook, and help with handling the money you bring in from trips, so you better be watching your P's and Q's, because I'm keeping track of you." she said with a smile.

I quipped, "I thought I was the boss!" Though I sounded like I was kidding, I was hurt and angry at having Ann hire someone without discussing it with me first.

"You better get used to it," Kelli retorted, "Women are taking over the world!"

She was speaking light heartedly, but the truth of it stabbed at my male ego.

Kelli worked from home, doing an outstanding job, picking up new programs quickly, taking the time to take classes to educate herself and become more efficient. In 1997, I published my first book. It wasn't long after my book hit the market that I received a call from Kelli saying she needed to talk with me right away.

My first thoughts by the tone of her voice, was that my only true employee was about to quit. As we sat in the backyard next to the picnic table, she began to pour her heart out in a way I had never experienced before. She told me that my story was so moving, and that she really had no idea what I had experienced before she read a copy of my book.

Not only did she feel my pain, it made her reflect on her own loss she suffered a few years prior when she lost her first-born. She was so excited as she waited for her first child to be born. They prepared for the baby, never realizing that anything bad could happen. After 9 months, three weeks before her due date, something went terribly wrong. A trip to the emergency room confirmed her worst fears. There was no heartbeat. The child she had nurtured and loved, before it ever came into the world, was gone. Every dream she had for this child was gone, life had been flushed out and emptiness consumed her soul.

Reading in the book how my Mom watched over me while I lay lifeless in the hospital, brought back many of these feelings for Kelli, as she relived how it felt to give birth to a lifeless child, who laid without moving on her chest shortly after giving birth. My experiences touched her experiences…it made her uncover emotions that she had not really dealt with at the time. The helplessness and hopelessness of losing a child had emotionally paralyzed her. By reading my story, it brought these emotions to the surface so that she could finally feel them and put them to rest.

The tears streamed down her face as she poured out her heart. I realized that she had not been able to grieve and in the simple act of telling my story…my sharing helped her to unleash the incredible potential, love and tenderness that had been bound by the chains of unexpressed grief. This sharing…communicating and experiencing our personal losses together, allowed me to connect to another human being in a way different than I had known before. By being open to all of who we were in truthfulness without walls, we became best friends.

The following year, as I mentioned earlier, I had a dream to build a camp. Kelli and I continued to work together. I remember telling everybody about my dream about a wheelchair accessible camp. The majority of people that I loved and respected told me I was crazy, but when I told Kelli (expecting to hear the same…particularly because she was the bookkeeper), I figured the first words out of her mouth would be, "Where are you going to come up with the cash…buddy?"

Instead she looked at me and said it was an incredibly awesome dream. A camp for disabled kids is a great idea, you have such a big heart. I'll help you do it, but my time is limited with my two small children at home. I can give you a few extra hours in the evenings after the girls go to bed. You can call me on the phone, and dictate to me all your ideas. Soon there after, Camp Attitude was born, I was the President, and Kelli was the Secretary.

I had no idea the camp would flourish, nor did I comprehend the magnitude of the work and how quickly it would grow. I was putting in 16 hours a day, laboring over fundraising events, architectural designs, heading up work crews, ordering material, and jumping through the red tape trying to obtain the building permits.

As a typical, workaholic man, the time away from my wife added to an already struggling marriage. To the world we had a fairy tale relationship, but the truth was Ann and I were never able to communicate well. Anger and resentment had built to the point of moments of explosion.

One Sunday morning, after Daniel got me ready for the day, I noticed a newspaper lying on the couch opened to the real estate section. Someone had circled a number of homes for sale. When I confronted Ann, she informed me that she was done with our marriage and was moving out. It's so typical of the 'male attitude'…I wasn't conscious of the depth of our problems.

Ann told me that she called Kelli and her husband and they would be taking me to my speaking engagement that day, and she and Roni would be gone by the time I got home. I felt sick, but went on to the church to give my 'motivational speech'. I felt as though I was just reciting words that meant nothing. Though it was well received, Kelli knew instantly that something was desperately wrong and took me to coffee after the talk.

We had developed a great relationship, but to reveal my inadequacies and failure in relationship was not what I wanted to do with anyone. Thank goodness, she convinced me that I needed to talk to somebody about it. I knew I could trust her, and after much persuasion, I sat bawling telling Kelli everything that had gone on in my marriage during the past 5 years. She was shocked because she had assumed, like most people, that we had a good marriage. After talking for hours, I decided to go back and confront the issue with Ann.

Ann decided not to leave at this point, but that experience only escalated our problems. We struggled on over the next couple of years, and per Ann's request, Kelli started traveling with me, since she was no longer interested in doing so. During this time, mine and Kelli's relationship became stronger. Our ability to communicate and the fact that we were traveling together, placed us in a position where we discussed our personal struggles with each other, rather than our spouses.

Kelli's marriage had also been rocky for a number of years, and although we both knew it was wrong, the friendship we had developed over the years grew until we eventually realized we were in love with each other. At that point, our strong Christian morals and ethics kicked in and we knew we had to stop seeing each other. Kelli had become the one friend I could spill my heart to and yet, my Biblical upbringing demanded that I stop our relationship.

Kelli resigned and was removed as Secretary of the Board. Though we were apart, the love of our relationship only fanned the knowledge that her own marriage was dysfunctional and debilitating for her, so she divorced after counseling wouldn't heal her own marriage.

Though Ann and I also went through counseling, we were also unable to repair our marriage and divorced. Ann and I were able to leave each other on decent terms and created a good atmosphere for Roni, sharing joint custody.

For a year, I went into a depression, though my 'male attitudes' didn't allow me to see it that way. I threw myself into my work and tried to ignore my emotions. It was lonely like I had never known before this. The experience brought me face-to-face with God.

Though I felt guilt, regret and estrangement from many who I loved, I realized how much God loved me and how in spite of it all, I could still be used. Within these 'messages' from above, I knew it was time for me to find a new level of Truth and honesty within myself. I needed to be whole in ways I never understood. I needed to cut the 'male ego' crutches that allowed me to ignore my heart and rebuild myself as a whole person. It was time to learn to walk in a new way!

In AA, they have a step in their program where one has to make amends to those you've hurt, forgiving yourself and others. Almost a year to the date after Kelli and I parted ways, I decided I needed to talk to her. I still loved her but had cut her so out of my life as I went through the last vestiges of my marriage and my divorce that I had been a terrible friend. She had been there for me for years and I turned my back on a person I really loved.

As the phone rang, my heart throbbed, wondering if she was with someone else, moved on without me. I wondered if she was so mad or bitter towards me that perhaps I had lost the best friend I had ever had. When I heard her voice on the other end, it brought all the emotions back, like a burst of sunlight over a dark cloud. To my surprise, she too was on the mend, to my joy, was not with anyone else.

In the conversation, she told me that there wasn't a day that had gone by that she didn't think about me as well, but she did have a lot of other feelings and we needed to meet.

For the first time, we had a 'real' date. The day was electrifying; it was like our souls were reunited. Everything that we had was still there, only stronger. We were truly in love. The breath of love gave life to both of us, and from that moment on, we were inseparable.

As people within our circle of family, friends and acquaintances found out that we were seeing each other, we were judged. No one knew the true facts of everything that had happened and our Christian brothers and sisters judged us and put us down. To us, it felt like everyone we loved was opposed to our relationship. Kelli was judged as a brazen marriage wrecker and I was judged as leading her down the wayward path. Neither of us wanted to bring out all the underlying issues that had brought on our divorces and began to question our relationship's value. People began saying that as a motivational speaker, I had to be a role model and my being with Kelli did not make me a good role model in their eyes.

Kelli and I looked at scripture and found though there were specific verses about marriage and divorce, there were always exceptions to the rules. The example of Christ, is that "we must forgive one another, and if we cannot forgive others, God cannot forgive us." And it went on to say that God doesn't even listen to our prayers if we have unforgiveness in our hearts. Through my study, I soon realized that I had been forgiven, and I needed to move forward in what I felt in my heart was true, in spite of the unforgiving attitudes of others. Christ's example was one of unconditional love. This does not mean we condone evil thought or actions, but we restore relationships as soon as possible. I miss the friends I had hurt and who chose to abandon me during this hard time, and I hope that someday, all of those relationships will be restored.

The truth was I was 100 percent madly and completely in love with Kelli. Though I thought she was beautiful on the outside, the inside of her was so dazzling I could hardly believe the gift God had bestowed on me. The meaning of true relationship began to unfold and my old 'male' attitudes began to change.

My creativity was reborn. I was a hopeless romantic and it was time for me to lay a bed of roses down the path I wanted Kelli to take with me.

I asked Kelli to set aside a whole day to spend with me, but wouldn't tell her where I was taking her. She showed up at the office, dressed in a sundress that would turn any man's head. She looked beautiful, no unbelievably gorgeous. I had my accomplice (my mother) help me with a few of the finer details. Mom went to the store and got me fruit, cheese and crackers, all the essentials for a romantic picnic, which were hidden in the back of the van. I had secretly picked out CDs that had love songs on them that had meant something to the two of us, and had them hidden in the van as well. I went out to the garden, where my mom and I picked her a rose that I presented her, held between my teeth, when she walked in.

Like we were off to a prom, Mom took a picture of us with the rose, and we were off on our date. I gave Kelli directions to our first destination, which was a spot we used to go to park and talk. She seemed a bit confused at first, but after she parked, I asked her to put in one of the CDs. As our song blared out of the stereo, I began to tell her how much I loved her, and how much she meant to me.

Through tears, we shared with each other everything we were feeling in our hearts. We then got out of the van, and took another picture to commemorate the day, with the rose between us. After loading back up, I proceeded to give her directions to our next destination.

Over the course of the day, we drove to every spot that had ever had special meaning to us, and I had a love song picked out for each stop, that totally fit the experience at that place. Then at each destination point, after we reminisced about old times, and our thoughts and feelings for each other, we would take a picture with the rose. In the afternoon, I had Kelli drive us to the coast. There is a lighthouse there where we shared a lot of good memories together.

After she unloaded our things, I asked her to sit on my lap. As "After All" by Cher and Peter Cetera played, the moment was etched for us forever. The waves were crashing, the words from the song playing on the radio shouted out to our hearts and the cool ocean breeze blew through our hair. I twirled and danced with the love of my life in my wheelchair in perfect time with the song. I will never forget Kelli's smile as it was washed with the magical hues of a sunset we'll never forget.

As we feasted on our goodies, she bubbled over with amazement, understanding the planning and work I had put into making this our special day. We finished the evening at the coast with a candlelight dinner in a restaurant overlooking the ocean swells. Wanting Kelli to think the evening had come to a close, her phone rang with a message from me. I pre-programmed her cell phone to ring with my message of undying love and thanking her for spending such a magnificent, beautiful day with me.

After dinner, I asked her to drive to one more place before we went home. It was an empty field and seemingly not what you would think of as romantic, but it was where I first told Kelli that I loved her.

After we parked and unloaded (and of course listened to another music selection), I told Kelli there was something I needed to talk to her about. We went out in the middle of the field, and as every star in the universe looked down, along with a brilliant full moon, warm summer breezes blowing, she bent to kiss me.

My serious look stopped her before she reached my lips. "Kelli, I have something to say and I need you to hold my hands and look me in the eyes." I began to sing a song that I had specially prepared for this occasion. I sang it with all the love I had for her in my heart as it echoed throughout the expanse of the field. The song expressed my appreciation and love for her and as I got to the last line, she heard the words "Kelli you are the most wonderful thing that has happened to me in my life, and I want to take this special moment to ask you, will you be my wife?"

She stared at me silently with her big brown eyes, tears streaming down her face. My insides were trembling. After this entire day, the climax was at hand, and I was emotionally overwhelmed. Would she possibly say no?

I wondered if she heard me correctly because she was just staring at me blankly.

I again said, "Kelli I love you, will you be my wife?" Then she said the words I had longed to hear. "Yes Ron, yes I will marry you."

We laughed, hugged, kissed and danced under the moonlight in that empty field and then I told her that she had to look in my pee bag.

Yes, that's a bit unconventional but it's hard to find a 'hiding place' when someone else is taking care of all the 'things' around you! Don't worry, it was in the POCKET of the pouch.

Her eyes glistened as she opened the box, exposing a beautiful diamond ring. She placed it between my teeth, and as I slipped in on her finger with my mouth, it was like I could hear eternity sing. We took another picture of ourselves, tears and all, not with the rose this time, but holding up a beautiful diamond engagement ring on the finger of the woman I will spend the rest of my life with. And so the album of a new life began.

From that moment on, everything just fell into place. We sat our three daughters down to tell them our big news, and to our surprise, they too shared in our joy and excitement. My parents had planned to move to California, and asked us if we wanted to rent their house in Oregon. This was exciting because my house would not have accommodated three kids, a caregiver and Kelli and I, and of course, the hamster.

October 14, 2003 was by far the most awesome day I have ever experienced in my entire life, and to verbally express it, would be impossible. Kelli had never been to Hawaii, and so again, she would be in for another surprise. I had been working with a landowner in developing Camp Attitude Maui, who owns a beautiful plantation home on the ocean's shore, three miles from Lahaina. As a gift to us, he allowed us to use the entire facility to have our marriage ceremony performed at sunset.

When the airplane touched down in paradise, our excitement was intense. We were giddy like two kids playing in a toy store. That evening, Kelli walked barefoot toward me, silver laced dress flowing in the ocean breeze. She took my breath away, I had never seen her look more beautiful. With just a few Hawaiian friends, a swaying palm tree overhead, sounds of crashing waves and a native pastor, Kelli and I said our vows as the sun set behind the island of Lanai creating an array of brilliant color. We exchanged rings and Hawaiian leis and as the pastor blew into the seashell, Kelli sat on my chair and we rolled off into the sunset. Later that night, in the glow of our candlelit room, with the sounds of the ocean in the background, I made love for the first time to my best friend."

42

Never Say Never

~

Just when I thought I was done writing this book, guess what? A new chapter has opened.

It was eight months after our marriage. Kelli and I had been working overtime booking speeches, traveling, caring for our wonderful girls, and an array of other pressing issues. I had asked God to show us a specific direction He wanted us to follow, and not be distracted from that path.

A few days later, I rolled into my office and—to my dismay—Kelli walked in with her head down, and she was crying.

"What's the matter, sweetheart?"

"It's nothing, don't worry," she replied. "I can't talk about it right now. We will talk about it later when everyone has left, and you have no other distractions."

Her behavior was not normal, but due to her request, I decided to postpone the conversation until later. I had meetings outside the office, and was gone for several hours.

When I returned, Kelli met me with a smile. "Ron, I'm sorry for being upset earlier."

Before I asked what was bothering her that morning, I noticed a vase of flowers on my desk. Why was I receiving flowers when she was upset. I wheeled around to smell the flowers and I noticed a thermometer embedded within the arrangement. Confused and perplexed, I asked "What is this, and what does it mean?" Then after reading the card, it hit me like a hurricane. I could barely get the words out, "Are you pregnant?"

She smiled and said, "Yes, that's the reason for my tears earlier."

"Uh…how did you do that?"

"What do you mean? *You* did it." she responded.

"It's not possible…the doctors said…it's been 24 years I've been in my chair, and…and…I'm old."

"It's true" Kelli replied, "I'm pregnant."

I sat there, completely paralyzed from the top of my head down. "We've done nothing, well, besides, you know. This means that you have conceived naturally. You need to take another test, and I'm going to watch to make sure you don't cheat!"

Kelli had patience through two more tests with "Mr. Doubting Thomas." It wasn't until the ultrasound a couple of weeks later, when I actually heard the heartbeat racing at 167 beats a minute, that I was convinced. Baffled, bawling, and full of bewilderment, I said "We're going to have a baby!"

A boy? A girl? Just keep the faith!

It won't be long now!

D ear readers,
Over the years, you have asked me many of the same questions. For the sake of future books, I am not going into the details of answers for most frequently asked questions.

Also I am choosing to disclose information in the way that works for me. I am using answers only as my format.

May my examples of communication inspire you to be true to your own.

Love, Ron Heagy, Jr.

My name is Ron Heagy and I am not ugly. I have a good looking face that comes with a quadriplegic body. My spirit is just like yours, divine in essence and behooled by human weakness.

Here is my inventory for personal challenges.

1. Yes, I have been relationship challenged. Kelli is my third wife.

2. Yes, I also get what's important and what is urgent mixed up when it comes to those I love most, and those I am here to teach and serve.

3. No, I have never experienced sex like a "normal person." For me it's like yummy ice cream that never melts, always tastes good, and lasts forever—literally—(details forthcoming).

4. The hardest part of being physically disabled for me is having to keep my spirits up so people who choose to take care of me won't leave me. After all-who wants to lift, load, bathe, feed and care for a bad tempered mean spirited 6 foot 3 inch depressed quadriplegic man. NOBODY!

5. I hate disappointing my family, especially my parents, not meeting deadlines and people who pretend to be what they are not.

6. Yes, I have a mission. I want to be the best Dad I can be and husband to my wife Kelli, and carry out the purpose that God has granted for my life. I love Psalm 139.

7. I've had to let go of how much guilt I use to have because I didn't feel I deserved all the attention, time, and energy it requires to keep this body breathing.

8. Man, I just wanna be cool—for all the right reasons! I got my pride just like everybody else.

9. Yes, there have been moments when I've felt like giving up, and I wanted to just die, but I don't allow my mind to stay there. I focus on my purpose and potential. Others need me.

10. Regarding conflict: Sometimes my need to prove what I can accomplish with this broken body is greater than my willingness to receive my life lessons with patience and grace. Hey, I'm good looking, not perfect!

11. Sure, I have some things I'm ashamed of, but it's a short list and I'm saving it for my next book.

12. My biggest inspiration is a happy family and bringing smiles to the faces of children when they connect with their own purpose.

13. Basically, every relationship I've had, I've learned from. I've gleaned important truths about myself because of the people I've chosen to be in my life. True-I didn't always enjoy the process or appreciate the pain and heartache that came with the results, but I learned, and I'm rolling on.

14. Look, I'm driven, literally, but I know I accepted this physical condition for spiritual reasons. Everyone has trials, it just so happens you can see mine.

15. I am so grateful for my wheelchair—it has given me my freedom to move, and I hope to see many more people receive wheelchairs worldwide. Just in case you don't know, I operate my chair with my chin.

16. Some people ask, if you could choose to get out of your wheelchair, would you? Answer: My disability gave birth to my ability.

17. My favorite foods are Chinese, ice cream and I would choose fresh vegetables over any dessert.

18. I like fast cars and plenty of sunshine.

19. My favorite hobby is creating-whether it's developing property, building camps or creating pictures on a blank canvas.

20. To describe my paralysis: My entire body from my shoulders down, tingles as if asleep, like my skin is full of bugs. If you sleep incorrectly on your arm or leg, you will wake up with this feeling. Imagine being dipped up to your neck in a pool of wet cement, with your arms and legs stretched out, and the concrete hardened. You think you can move, you try, but you can't, you're stuck. Movement is trapped. It can drive you crazy if you let it.

21. When people ask me what it is I would like to leave behind, I tell them to help people understand to live, laugh, love and leave a legacy. To figure out their purpose, tap into their potential and maintain the right perspective-the right attitude of Never Giving Up!

My life is to affirm for you that being crippled is only a state of mind.

Perspective is EVERYTHING! You, my friend, are somebody; go make a difference.

I would like to thank Michelle Geddes for assisting me in developing these questions.

"*Why I do what I do.*"

~

My answer is the Lord, my wonderful family, friends and letters like the following. This is what keeps my wheelchair rolling and a smile on my face. God bless you and may this book encourage you to get the right attitude and go do your purpose. Do your dream and change somebody's life.

Ron,

Thank you so much for coming in and speaking to our school. In the past, I have thought about killing myself. I took a razor to my skin once and thought that I should take it to my neck.

After hearing your speech, I have changed my thoughts on life. Befor hearing your speech I thought that life was a waste of time. Now I view life differently and think it is the best thing that ever happened to me.

Thanks for all of your good advice and GOD BLESS YOU!

17-year-old student

P.S. if you could mail me a letter that would be great.

An assignment for the reader

1. Please describe your attitude.

2. What is your purpose in life?

3. For the next 21 days, before you go to bed, write down five things you are grateful for.

4. Ask five people you know this question, "What do you think MY purpose is?"

5. Wake up every morning for those 21 days saying "Lord, I'm breathing—it's going to be a great day!"

6. Share your smile with at least five people everyday.

It is my passion to carry out my purpose of empowering people to overcome challenges and unusual obstacles. I know that in spite of all my failures, God is using my life in a powerful way. The one area I have been humbled in is my tendency to operate independently. Therefore, I ask you to stand beside me as a partner. Would you consider spreading the word about my speaking, purchasing additional books, art and products, or making a tax deductible donation to my non-profit organization "Never Give Up USA"?

I would truly appreciate hearing from you. My contact information is provided below....lets roll on!

Ron Heagy Jr.
P.O. Box 972
Albany, Oregon 97321
(541) 924-3985
E-mail: ron@rollonron.com

Or visit his website at:
http://www.rollonron.com